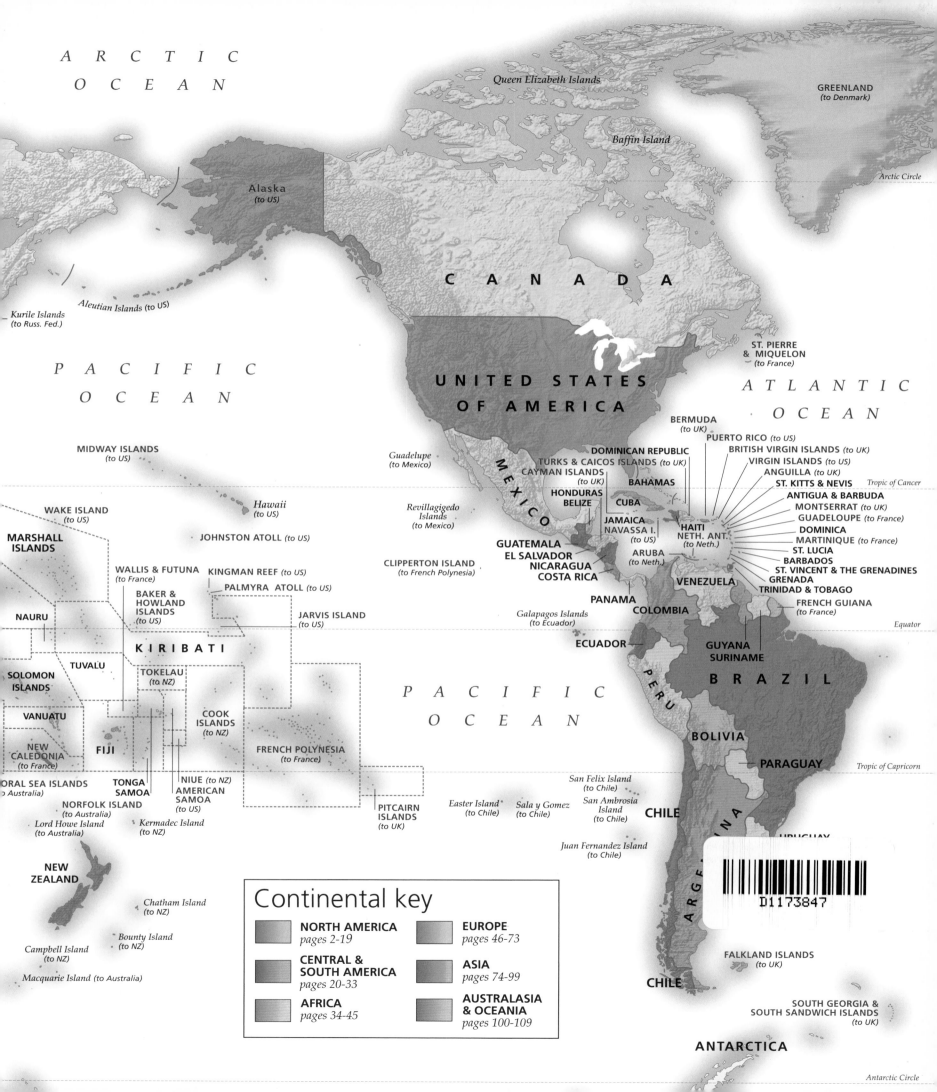

ARCTIC
OCEAN

Queen Elizabeth Islands

GREENLAND
(to Denmark)

Baffin Island

Arctic Circle

Alaska
(to US)

*Kurile Islands
(to Russ. Fed.)*

Aleutian Islands (to US)

C A N A D A

PACIFIC
OCEAN

ATLANTIC
OCEAN

UNITED STATES
OF AMERICA

ST. PIERRE
& MIQUELON
(to France)

MIDWAY ISLANDS
(to US)

*Guadelupe
(to Mexico)*

BERMUDA
(to UK)

PUERTO RICO *(to US)*

DOMINICAN REPUBLIC

BRITISH VIRGIN ISLANDS *(to UK)*

VIRGIN ISLANDS *(to US)*

TURKS & CAICOS ISLANDS *(to UK)*

ANGUILLA *(to UK)*

CAYMAN ISLANDS
(to UK)

BAHAMAS

ST. KITTS & NEVIS *Tropic of Cancer*

*Hawaii
(to US)*

WAKE ISLAND
(to US)

HONDURAS
BELIZE

CUBA

ANTIGUA & BARBUDA

*Revillagigedo
Islands
(to Mexico)*

MONTSERRAT *(to UK)*

GUADELOUPE *(to France)*

MARSHALL
ISLANDS

JOHNSTON ATOLL *(to US)*

JAMAICA
NAVASSA I.
(to US)

HAITI
NETH. ANT.
(to Neth.)

DOMINICA

MARTINIQUE *(to France)*

GUATEMALA

WALLIS & FUTUNA
(to France)

KINGMAN REEF *(to US)*

CLIPPERTON ISLAND
(to French Polynesia)

EL SALVADOR
NICARAGUA
COSTA RICA

ARUBA
(to Neth.)

ST. LUCIA

BARBADOS

ST. VINCENT & THE GRENADINES

GRENADA

NAURU

BAKER &
HOWLAND
ISLANDS
(to US)

PALMYRA ATOLL *(to US)*

PANAMA

VENEZUELA

TRINIDAD & TOBAGO

FRENCH GUIANA
(to France)

JARVIS ISLAND
(to US)

COLOMBIA

Equator

*Galapagos Islands
(to Ecuador)*

GUYANA
SURINAME

K I R I B A T I

ECUADOR

TUVALU

SOLOMON
ISLANDS

TOKELAU
(to NZ)

P E R U

B R A Z I L

COOK
ISLANDS
(to NZ)

PACIFIC

OCEAN

VANUATU

NEW
CALEDONIA
(to France)

FIJI

FRENCH POLYNESIA
(to France)

BOLIVIA

PARAGUAY *Tropic of Capricorn*

RAL SEA ISLANDS
o Australia)

TONGA
SAMOA

NIUE *(to NZ)*

AMERICAN
SAMOA
(to US)

*San Felix Island
(to Chile)*

NORFOLK ISLAND
(to Australia)

*Lord Howe Island
(to Australia)*

*Kermadec Island
(to NZ)*

PITCAIRN
ISLANDS
(to UK)

Easter Island
(to Chile)

*Sala y Gomez
(to Chile)*

*San Ambrosia
Island
(to Chile)*

CHILE

A R G E N T I N A

*Juan Fernandez Island
(to Chile)*

NEW
ZEALAND

*Chatham Island
(to NZ)*

URUGUAY

D1173847

*Campbell Island
(to NZ)*

*Bounty Island
(to NZ)*

Continental key

NORTH AMERICA *pages 2-19*	**EUROPE** *pages 46-73*
CENTRAL & SOUTH AMERICA *pages 20-33*	**ASIA** *pages 74-99*
AFRICA *pages 34-45*	**AUSTRALASIA & OCEANIA** *pages 100-109*

Macquarie Island (to Australia)

FALKLAND ISLANDS
(to UK)

CHILE

SOUTH GEORGIA &
SOUTH SANDWICH ISLANDS
(to UK)

ANTARCTICA

Antarctic Circle

CHILDREN'S WORLD ATLAS

Consultant
Dr. David Green

Written by
Simon Adams • Mary Atkinson • Sarah Phillips

DK Publishing

LONDON, NEW YORK, MUNICH,
MELBOURNE, and DELHI

Project editors Lucy Hurst, Sadie Smith,
Shaila Awan, Amber Tokeley
Art editors Joe Conneally, Sheila Collins,
Rebecca Johns, Simon Oon, Andrew Nash
Senior editor Fran Jones
Senior art editor Floyd Sayers
Managing editor Andrew Macintyre
Managing art editor Jane Thomas
US editors Christine Heilman, Margaret Parrish
Picture research Carolyn Clerkin, Brenda Clynch
DK Pictures Sarah Mills
Production Jenny Jacoby
DTP designer Siu Yin Ho

Cartography Department
Senior Cartographic Editor Simon Mumford
Cartographer Ed Merritt
Digital Cartography Encompass Graphics Limited
Satellite images Rob Stokes
3D Globes Planetary Visions Ltd., London

This *Children's World Atlas* has been conceived by Dorling Kindersley Limited

First American Edition, 2003

Published in the United States by
DK Publishing, Inc.
375 Hudson Street
New York, New York 10014

03 04 05 06 07 08 10 9 8 7 6 5 4 3 2

Copyright © 2003 Dorling Kindersley Limited

A Cataloging-in-Publication record for this book
is available from the Library of Congress.

ISBN 0-7894-9276-8

Color reproduction by Colourscan, Singapore
Printed and bound in Italy by L.E.G.O.

See our complete product line at
www.dk.com

Contents

NORTH AMERICA   2

CENTRAL AND SOUTH AMERICA   20

Introducing Earth

TO US, THE EARTH SEEMS HUGE. Vast oceans stretch farther than the eye can see and separate the giant landmasses that are home to billions of people, animals, and plants. However, Earth is just one of the nine planets that orbit the Sun—a huge, burning-hot star in the center of our Solar System. The Solar System, and all the stars in the night sky are part of our galaxy—the Milky Way, which contains as many as 200 billion stars. Beyond our galaxy are millions more galaxies. They all add together to make up the Universe.

Pluto

Neptune

Uranus

Saturn

Jupiter

Earth

Mars

Venus

Moon

Mercury

Sun

THE SOLAR SYSTEM

Planet Earth is part of a system of planets and their moons, as well as numerous asteroids and comets, which orbit around a huge star we call the Sun. The Sun itself consists of gas. Nuclear reactions inside its core produce the heat and light that make life on Earth possible. The Earth is the third of four small terrestrial (Earth-like) planets that orbit close to the Sun. Farther out in our Solar System are four huge gas planets, while distant Pluto, the smallest planet, is made of rock and ice.

A PLANET'S "year" is the time it takes to orbit the Sun. Earth's year is 365.25 days, but distant Pluto takes as long as 90,588 days to complete its orbit.

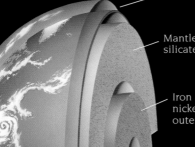

Crust

Mantle of silicate

Iron and nickel outer core

Inner core

THE EARTH

Earth's distance from the Sun allows just the right amount of heat and light to support life. It is warm enough for water to exist in liquid form—in fact, two-thirds of the Earth's surface is covered with water. As well as water, the planet consists of seven landmasses, or continents, which include Antarctica.

THE EARTH'S STRUCTURE

The Earth is not a solid ball. It is made up of different layers, much like an onion. The outer layer, or crust, is a thin sheet of rock that forms the continents and the ocean floor. Beneath it is the mantle, a layer of hot and, in places, molten (liquid) rock about 1,900 miles (3,000 km) thick. At the center of the Earth is a core of hot metal, which is liquid on the outside and solid on the inside.

OUR MOON

Unlike some other planets in the Solar System, the Earth has only one moon. The Moon is our nearest neighbor in space and circles the Earth once every 29.53 days. It is about a quarter of the size of Earth and is made of rock. Despite having no light of its own, it is clearly visible from Earth because it reflects sunlight.

MOVING EARTH

The continents that make up the Earth's surface are always on the move. Eight large and several smaller plates, which form the landmasses of the Earth (called tectonic plates), float on top of the mantle. Because the Earth's interior is extremely hot, magma wells up to the cooler surface and forces these plates to move and crack. This happens very slowly, but even so, it releases huge forces that can create new land, form mountains, and cause earthquakes.

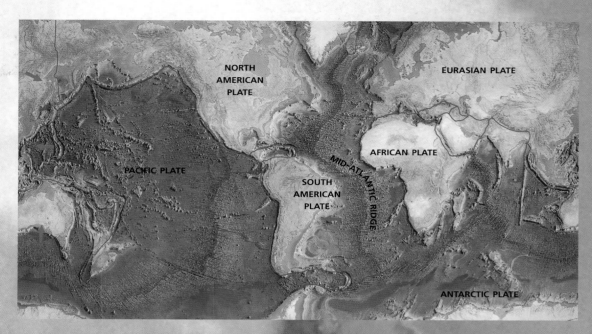

THE HIMALAYAS is a range of mountains that contains the world's highest peak, Mount Everest.

MOUNTAIN BUILDING

Mountains form in three main ways. In the case of the Himalayas, Alps, and Rockies, two tectonic plates collided, causing the Earth's crust to buckle, crumple, and be forced upward to create high mountains and deep valleys. But mountains can also be the result of a volcanic eruption, or caused by the edges of two plates fracturing into cracks called faults, pushing a chunk of land upward to create a block mountain.

VOLCANOES

When two continental plates collide, one of them can be subducted, or pushed down, under the other into the Earth's hot mantle. The rocks of the subsiding plate melt, and may be forced up through the cracks to erupt onto the Earth's surface as a volcano. In addition, volcanoes may form when plates pull apart. Molten rock from the Earth's mantle rises up to fill the gap as the plates spread. Volcanoes can be separated into three different categories: active (continuously erupting), dormant (sleeping), or extinct.

THE HAWAIIAN volcano Kilauea is constantly erupting. Its name means "spewing" in Hawaiian.

Moving plates

The Earth's continental plates move in three ways: pulling apart, moving together, or sliding past one another. Where two plates pull apart, magma (molten rock) from the Earth's mantle wells up and fills the gap. If this happens on the ocean floor, it creates an underwater spreading ridge. If two plates collide, either they fuse to form a mountain range or one subsides under the other, causing volcanoes to appear. Where two plates slide past each other, a transform fault appears, and earthquakes can occur. Often a long crack or fault line appears on the Earth's surface.

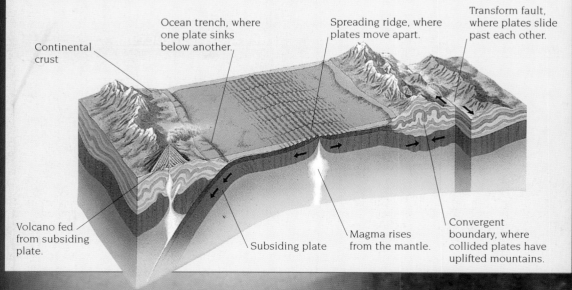

Continental crust

Ocean trench, where one plate sinks below another.

Spreading ridge, where plates move apart.

Transform fault, where plates slide past each other.

Volcano fed from subsiding plate.

Subsiding plate

Magma rises from the mantle.

Convergent boundary, where collided plates have uplifted mountains.

Climate and Vegetation

ON EARTH, A REGION'S WEATHER CAN CHANGE from day to day and even from hour to hour. But its climate—the average pattern of weather and temperature over a long period of time—remains fairly constant. Climate is affected by latitude (how far north or south of the Equator a region is), height above sea level, prevailing winds, and the circulation of ocean currents. An area's climate, as well as its landscape, affects the type of plant life, or vegetation, found there. Climate and vegetation also affect the lives of the animals, birds, and people that make the area their home.

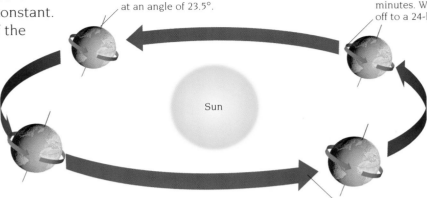

Earth's axis is tilted at an angle of 23.5°.

Earth spins on its axis once every 23 hours, 56 minutes. We round this off to a 24-hour day.

Sun

Earth circles, or orbits, the Sun once every 365.25 days, a length of time known as a year.

THE FOUR SEASONS

As the Earth orbits the Sun, its tilted axis gradually tilts each hemisphere toward the Sun and then away from it. This causes the seasons. For example, summer occurs when a hemisphere tips toward the Sun and gets more sunlight, more heat, and longer days. Most regions of the world have four seasons, but some areas near the Equator are always hot and have only wet and dry seasons.

SPRING

SUMMER

FALL

WINTER

EARTH'S ORBIT

The Earth does not sit upright on its axis but tilts at an angle of 23.5°. It maintains this same tilt as it travels around the Sun on its 590 million-mile (950 million-km) journey, a journey that lasts for one year. The Earth also spins on its axis, turning once every 24 hours to give us night and day.

ASIA

EUROPE

NORTH AMERICA

ATLANTIC OCEAN

TROPIC OF CANCER

OCEAN

AFRICA

PACIFIC OCEAN

EQUATOR PACIFIC OCEAN

CENTRAL & SOUTH AMERICA

TROPIC OF CAPRICORN

INDIAN OCEAN

AUSTRALASIA & OCEANIA

ANNUAL RAINFALL

More than 79 in (2,000 mm)

20–79 in (500–2,000 mm)

Less than 20 in (500 mm)

RAINFALL

This map of the world shows the amount of rain that falls in a year. The light brown areas receive so little rain that they tend to be either hot desert or cold polar regions. They are difficult places in which to live, and have little vegetation. The blue areas receive a moderate amount of rainfall each year. The purple areas are mainly areas of rain forest, where high rainfall allows vegetation to flourish.

PEOPLE AND CLIMATE

Some climates are easier to live in than others, but people can still adapt to a variety of different environments. These Moroccan girls (left) live in the Sahara desert. They are members of a nomadic tribe that travels from place to place in search of food and water. Other tribes have made their homes in humid rain forests, and still others inhabit the icy polar regions.

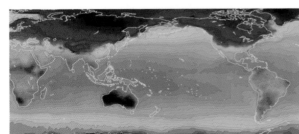

SATELLITE MAP of the world's average surface temperature in January.

WORLD TEMPERATURES

This map compares temperatures during January. The values range from −36°F (−38°C) in the purple regions, through blue, green, yellow, and red, to black, which is 104°F (40°C). As expected, temperatures are hotter near the Equator and cooler near the poles. Australia is tilted closer to the Sun during January, giving it a scorching summer.

VEGETATION ZONES

Several factors influence the vegetation (plant life) and animal life of a particular region—the climate, latitude, and physical landscape. After studying the different types of plant life, scientists have divided the Earth into nine main vegetation zones, or biomes. Over millions of years, plants and animals, as well as people, have adapted to life in these different zones, often developing special features that enable them to survive.

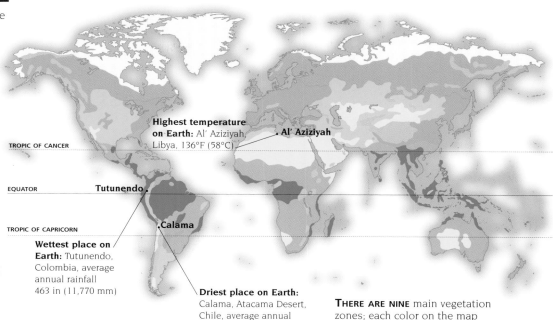

TROPIC OF CANCER

Highest temperature on Earth: Al' Aziziyah, Libya, 136°F (58°C)

. Al' Aziziyah

EQUATOR   **Tutunendo** .

TROPIC OF CAPRICORN

.**Calama**

Wettest place on Earth: Tutunendo, Colombia, average annual rainfall 463 in (11,770 mm)

Driest place on Earth: Calama, Atacama Desert, Chile, average annual rainfall 0 in (0 mm)

THERE ARE NINE main vegetation zones; each color on the map corresponds to the boxes below.

☐ POLAR AND TUNDRA

The freezing areas around the North and South Poles are covered with ice. South of the North Pole lies the tundra, where lower layers of soil stay frozen. Only hardy mosses, lichens, and shrubs can survive.

☐ TAIGA

The word taiga is Russian for "cold forest." It refers to the regions of northern Canada, Scandinavia, and Russia. These areas are home to forests of evergreens such as fir, spruce, and pine, all of which are able to withstand the long, cold, snow-filled winters.

☐ MOUNTAIN REGIONS

In mountain ranges, the higher the altitude, the colder it gets. Though vegetation can survive on the lower parts of the mountains, there is a point, called the tree line, above which it is too cold for trees to grow. Snow can be found on high peaks year-round.

☐ TEMPERATE FOREST

Temperate climates—not too hot or too cold—occur in northern Europe, eastern North America, and eastern Asia. These areas were once covered by forests of deciduous trees, which lose their leaves in winter. Though many have been cut down, large woodland areas still survive.

☐ MEDITERRANEAN

This vegetation zone refers not just to areas around the Mediterranean Sea in Europe, but also to places such as California. With hot, dry summers and cool winters, plants such as olive and citrus trees are able to grow.

☐ DRY GRASSLAND

Hot, dry summers and very cold winters, as well as sparse rainfall, give rise to areas too dry for trees to grow. These vast, dry grasslands are often found in the center of continents, such as the prairies of North America. They are sometimes plowed and used to grow wheat or raise cattle.

☐ TROPICAL RAIN FOREST

The regions of tropical rain forest lie either side of the Equator, where the climate is hot and wet year-round. Up to 50,000 different species of trees, as well as millions of species of plants, animals, birds, and insects—50 percent of all animal and plant life—flourish in these humid conditions.

☐ HOT DESERT

The hottest places on Earth are deserts, though at night temperatures may plummet to below freezing. These dry regions get no rain for years at a time, so very little vegetation is found here. Cacti, evolved to cope without water for long periods, are usually the only plants that can survive.

☐ TROPICAL GRASSLAND

Between tropical rain forests and hot deserts lie tropical grasslands, such as the Pampas of South America and the African savanna. Tall grasses, low trees, and shrubs grow in these hot climates, which have only two seasons: wet and dry.

Population

EVERY SECOND, AROUND THE WORLD, four people are born and two people die. This means that over a year, the world's population increases by about 70 million people. In some of the richest countries of the world, population growth is slow. Elsewhere—especially in the poorer countries of Asia, Africa, and South America—the population is growing rapidly. Cities in such regions are growing fastest, and several now have populations of over 10 million people. When it comes to providing employment, housing, education and health care, such rapid growth rates can strain resources to the limit.

IN BURKINO FASO, less than 30 percent of the population has access to a clean water supply, such as the water pump shown here.

THREATENED RESOURCES

As the world's population continues to rise, more people are chasing fewer natural resources. Only a small proportion of the Earth's land is suitable for growing food, while in some areas fresh water for drinking, cooking, and irrigating crops is scarce. Fossil fuels, such as oil and natural gas, will soon be in short supply, unless people begin to conserve energy or develop alternatives, such as solar power.

LIFE EXPECTANCY

A person's life expectancy is a measure of how long they are likely to live. This can vary dramatically from country to country, and depends on many factors, including health care, nutrition, and access to fresh water. At present, the world's average life expectancy is 63 years.

Moscow
8.6 million

London
7 million
EUROPE

ASIA

Paris
9.3 million

NORTH
AMERICA

Tehran
6.8 million

Lahore
5 million

Beijing
10.9 million

Tianjin
8.8 million

Seoul
10.2 million

Istanbul
6.4 million

New York
7.4 million

Cairo
6.8 million

Karachi
9.3 million

Dhaka
6.1 million

Tokyo
7.8 million

Shanghai
13.5 million

Mexico City
16.7 million

AFRICA

Delhi
8.4 million

Hong Kong
6.8 million

Bogotá
6 million

Bombay
(Mumbai)
12.6 million

Calcutta
11 million

Bangkok
5.6 million

KEY:

Lima
6.5 million

SOUTH
AMERICA

Madras
(Chennai)
5.4 million

Jakarta
8.3 million

AUSTRALASIA
& OCEANIA

◼ Over 5 million people
○ 1–5 million people
· 50,000–1 million people

Rio de Janeiro
10.2 million

Santiago
5.1 million

São Paulo
16.6 million

Buenos Aires
11.7 million

FAMILY PLANNING

To help slow population growth, many countries now provide people with better health education and information, allowing them to plan the size of their families. Some governments even actively promote smaller families, as shown in this Chinese poster (above). But in many poorer parts of the world, a large family is often still necessary, so that the workload can be shared.

DISTRIBUTION OF PEOPLE

This map (above) shows the current populations of the major cities of the world. At the start of the 20th century, only one in ten people lived in a city. But over time, people have been forced into the cities to find work, as factors such as poverty and loss of land have pushed them out of the countryside. Today, half the world's population lives in cities.

POPULATION GROWTH

In the past, the world's population grew slowly, but from about 1800, the pace began to quicken. Better diet, clean water, and improved health care helped to reduce the death rate. In advanced countries, children began to survive longer, so people started to have smaller families. However, because many people in the poorer countries still have large families, the rate of population growth has exploded.

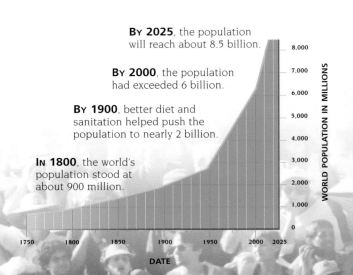

BY 2025, the population will reach about 8.5 billion.

BY 2000, the population had exceeded 6 billion.

BY 1900, better diet and sanitation helped push the population to nearly 2 billion.

IN 1800, the world's population stood at about 900 million.

WORLD POPULATION IN MILLIONS

8,000
7,000
6,000
5,000
4,000
3,000
2,000
1,000
0

1750   1800   1850   1900   1950   2000   2025

DATE

Mapping the World

ABOUT THE ATLAS

This atlas is divided into six continental sections—North America, Central and South America, Africa, Europe, Asia, and Australasia and Oceania. Each country, or group of countries, then has its own map that shows cities, towns, and main geographical features, such as rivers, lakes, and mountain ranges. Photographs and text provide detailed information about life in that country—its people, traditions, politics, and economy. Each continental section has a different color border to help you locate that section. There is also a gazetteer and an index to help you access information.

FOREIGN NAMES

Features on the maps are generally labeled in the language of that country. For example, it would be:
  Lake on English-speaking countries
  Lago on Spanish-speaking countries
  Lac on French-speaking countries
However, if a feature is wellknown, or mentioned in the main text on the page, it will appear there in English so that readers can find it easily.

MAP LOCATOR

This map shows, in red, the location of each country, part of a country, or group of countries in relation to the continent in which it belongs. There is a locator for each map in the book.

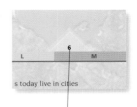

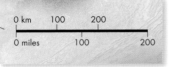

PAGE CONTINUATION

The numbers that appear in a triangle at the top and side borders tell the reader the page of the neighboring country, or region. For example, on USA: Midwest, the area that lies directly north of the Great Lakes is Eastern Canada—page 6 in the book.

LONGITUDE AND LATITUDE

Lines of longitude are vertical lines that run through the Poles. Lines of latitude are horizontal lines that run parallel to the Equator. These imaginary lines help locate places on a map.

SCALE

Each map features a scale that shows how distances on the map relate to miles and kilometers. The scale guide can be used to see how big a country is. Not all maps in the book are drawn to the same scale.

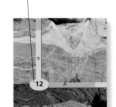

USING THE GRID REFERENCES

The letters and numbers around the outside of the page form a grid to help you find places on the map. For example, to find Wichita, look up its name in the gazetteer (pp 112–133), and you'll find the reference 12 G8. The first number is the page; the letter and number refer to the square made by following up or down from G and across from 8 to form G8.

KEY TO MAP SYMBOLS

BORDERS

▬▬▬▬	International border: Border between countries which is mutually recognized.
▬▬▬▬	State border: Border used in some large countries to show internal divisions.
▬▬ ▬▬	Disputed border: Border used in practice, but not mutually agreed between two countries.
• • • •	Claimed border: Border which is not mutually recognized – where territory belonging to one country is claimed by another.
✕▬✕▬✕	Ceasefire line
▪▪▪▪▬	Undefined boundary

PHYSICAL FEATURES

△	Mountain
▽	Depression
⏃	Volcano
⤬	Pass/Tunnel

DRAINAGE FEATURES

────	Major river
────	Minor river
-------	Seasonal river
──┼──	Dam
────	Canal
⏽	Waterfall
⌁⌁⌁	Seasonal lake

MISCELLANEOUS FEATURES

◇	Site of interest
⌇⌇⌇	Ancient wall

COMMUNICATIONS

═══	Highway
────	Major road
────	Minor road
────	Railway
✈	Airport

TOWNS & CITIES

◉	More than 500,000
◉	100,000 – 500,000
○	50,000 – 100,000
○	Less than 50,000
●	National capital
◉	Internal administrative capital
○	Polar research station

LATITUDE & LONGITUDE

────	Lines of Latitude/ Longitude
────	Equator
-------	Tropics
25°	Degrees of Latitude/ Longitude

NAMES

REGIONS

FRANCE	Country
JERSEY (to UK)	Dependent territory
KANSAS	Administrative region
Dordogne	Cultural region

TOWNS & CITIES

PARIS	National capital
SAN JUAN	Dependent territory capital city

NAMES continued

Seattle **Limón** Comayagua San José	Other towns & cities

PHYSICAL

Andes *Ardennes*	Landscape features
Balearic Islands	Island group
Majorca	Island
Lake Baikal	Lake/River /Canal
PACIFIC OCEAN *Gulf of Mexico* *Bay of Campeche*	Sea features
Chile Rise	Undersea feature

OTHER FEATURES

Tropic of Cancer	Graticule text

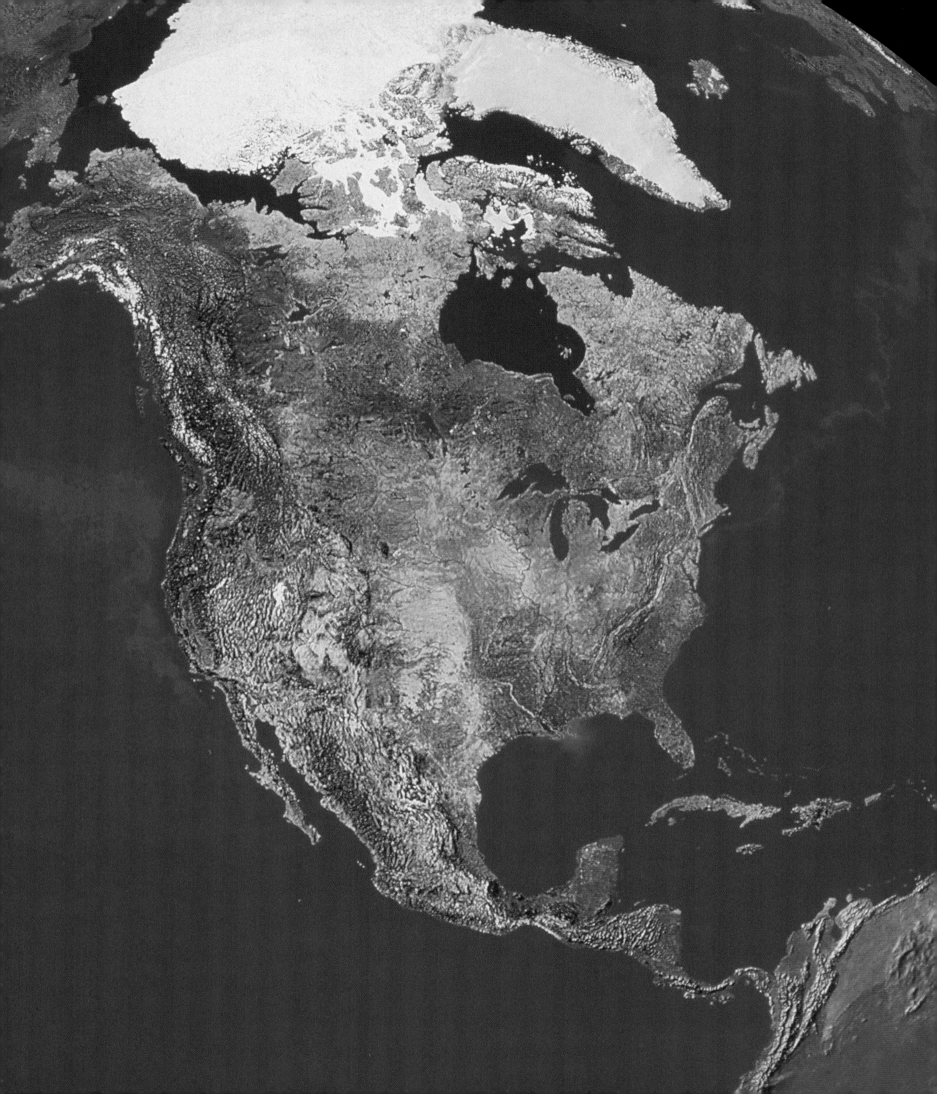

NORTH AMERICA

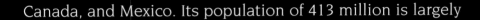

NORTH AMERICA INCLUDES the United States of America,

Canada, and Mexico. Its population of 413 million is largely

based on immigrants, who arrived here from the 1500s onward. North

 America's varied landscape ranges from frozen tundra in

the north to hot desert and lush rain forest in the south.

Mexico is Spanish-speaking and, despite vast oil and gas reserves, is relatively

poor. In contrast, the US and Canada enjoy high standards of living and most

people speak English—except for the French-speakers in

Québec. They also have other features in common—they are

 roughly the same size and share the longest undefended

land border in the world. However, the US has a far larger

population and is the wealthiest nation on Earth. American technology, such

as computer software, has a global influence—as do its movies and music.

Western Canada and Alaska

CANADA IS A HUGE COUNTRY and its western half stretches from the flat prairies in the east to the towering Rocky Mountains in the west, and from the relatively mild south to the permanently frozen area north of the Arctic Circle. Harsh conditions over much of the region mean that most of the population is concentrated in cities in the south, such as Vancouver, Calgary, and Winnipeg. The prairies—once a vast expanse of grassland— are now used mainly for growing wheat on huge mechanized farms. Oil and natural gas are found there as well. These natural resources are also important in Alaska, a part of the United States. The majority of Alaska's population moved there to work in these lucrative industries.

FORESTRY

Large parts of western Canada are covered in forests and lumbering is a major part of the local economy. The trees are used to make buildings, furniture, and paper. In the past, whole areas of trees were cleared, but now sustainable methods such as selective cutting and replanting are practised.

FELLED trees are transported down a river near Vancouver.

TOTEM POLES

The native peoples of British Columbia use totem poles to record their clan history. Each carved and painted totem describes a real or mythical event and often features animals that the clan has a connection with, such as the eagle (left).

DOGSLED RACING

The state sport of Alaska is dogsled racing. Here, competitors take part in the annual Iditarod Trail Sled Dog Race, a grueling run across the rugged landscape for drivers and their teams of dogs.

VANCOUVER

This city's vibrant cultural mix is typical of Canada's diversity. Many Chinese, as well as other ethnic groups, live here and reflect Vancouver's historic role as a destination for migrants. Its bustling economy, mild climate, and cultural links make it an attractive place to live.

Map labels

Chukchi Sea
ARCTIC OCEAN
Prince Patrick Island
Mould Bay
Beaufort Sea
Banks Island
Wevok
Point Lay
Barrow
Kivalina
Prudhoe Bay
Colville River
Umiat
Kaktovik
Sachs Harbour
Near Islands
Rat Islands
Gambell
Wales
Deering
Bering Strait
Saint Lawrence Island
Norton Sound
Brooks Range
Tuktoyaktuk
Amundsen Gulf
Holma
Bering Sea
Alakanuk
Grayling
Yukon River
Kokrines
Fort Yukon
Aklavik
Inuvik
Paulatuk
Pribilof Islands
Nunivak Island
Kwigillingok
Fairbanks
Fort McPherson
ALASKA (to US)
Andreanof Islands
Aleutian Islands
Atka
Platinum
Kuskokwim Mts
Alaska Range
McKinley Park
Mount McKinley 20,320ft (6194m)
Iliamna Lake
Susitna
Anchorage
Fort Good Hope
Kugluktuk
Great Bear Lake
Echo B
Umnak Island
Unalaska Island
Unimak Island
Dutch Harbor
Bristol Bay
Hope
Gulkana
Valdez
Chitina
YUKON TERRITORY
Mackenzie
NORTHWES TERRITORIE
Belkofski
Alaska Peninsula
Shumagin Islands
Kodiak
Kodiak Island
Cordova
Katalla
Mount Logan 19,550ft (5959m)
Whitehorse
Tungsten
Fort Simpson
Edzo
Yellowknife
Great S Lak
PACIFIC OCEAN
Gulf of Alaska
Yakutat
Rocky Mountains
Fort Providence
Fort Liard
Haines
Gustavus
Atlin
Juneau
Kake
BRITISH COLUMBIA
Fort Nelson
Fort Sm
Fort Vermil
Alexander Archipelago
Port Alexander
Ketchikan
Ware
Fort St. John
McMu
ALBERTA
Grande Prairie
Athabasca
Prince Rupert
Queen Charlotte Islands
Kitimat
Ocean Falls
Queen Charlotte Sound
Prince George
Edmonton
Mount Robson
Port Hardy
Campbell River
Vancouver Island
Nanaimo
Vancouver
Kamloops
Red Deer
Calgar
Kelowna
Lethbridge
Cranbrook
Victoria
Milk Riv
Mount Waddington
UNITE

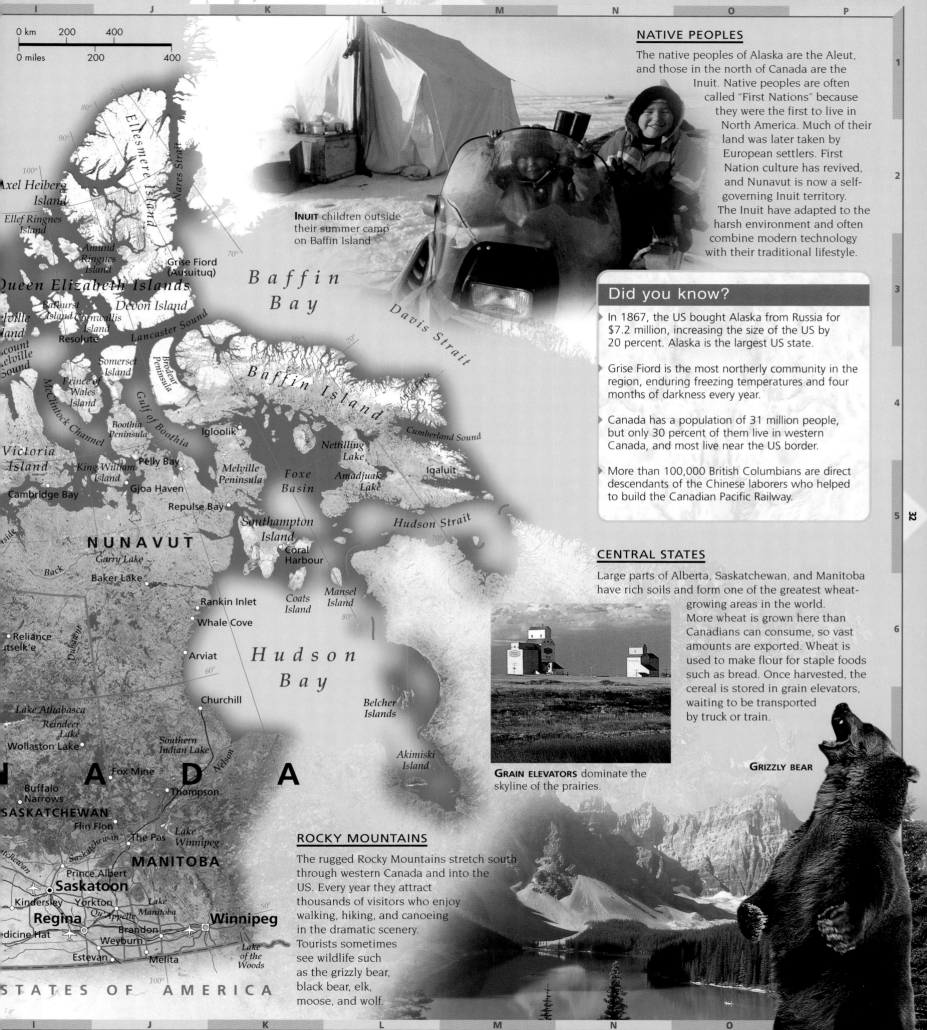

0 km   200   400
0 miles   200   400

NATIVE PEOPLES

The native peoples of Alaska are the Aleut, and those in the north of Canada are the Inuit. Native peoples are often called "First Nations" because they were the first to live in North America. Much of their land was later taken by European settlers. First Nation culture has revived, and Nunavut is now a self-governing Inuit territory. The Inuit have adapted to the harsh environment and often combine modern technology with their traditional lifestyle.

INUIT children outside their summer camp on Baffin Island

Did you know?

▶ In 1867, the US bought Alaska from Russia for $7.2 million, increasing the size of the US by 20 percent. Alaska is the largest US state.

▶ Grise Fiord is the most northerly community in the region, enduring freezing temperatures and four months of darkness every year.

▶ Canada has a population of 31 million people, but only 30 percent of them live in western Canada, and most live near the US border.

▶ More than 100,000 British Columbians are direct descendants of the Chinese laborers who helped to build the Canadian Pacific Railway.

CENTRAL STATES

Large parts of Alberta, Saskatchewan, and Manitoba have rich soils and form one of the greatest wheat-growing areas in the world. More wheat is grown here than Canadians can consume, so vast amounts are exported. Wheat is used to make flour for staple foods such as bread. Once harvested, the cereal is stored in grain elevators, waiting to be transported by truck or train.

GRAIN ELEVATORS dominate the skyline of the prairies.

GRIZZLY BEAR

ROCKY MOUNTAINS

The rugged Rocky Mountains stretch south through western Canada and into the US. Every year they attract thousands of visitors who enjoy walking, hiking, and canoeing in the dramatic scenery. Tourists sometimes see wildlife such as the grizzly bear, black bear, elk, moose, and wolf.

Map labels

Ellesmere Island
Axel Heiberg Island
Ellef Ringnes Island
Amund Ringnes Island
Grise Fiord (Ausuittuq)
Nares Strait
Queen Elizabeth Islands
Bathurst Island
Cornwallis Island
Devon Island
Lancaster Sound
Resolute
...count ...elville ...ound
Prince of Wales Island
Somerset Island
Brodeur Peninsula
Gulf of Boothia
Boothia Peninsula
McClintock Channel
Victoria Island
King William Island
Pelly Bay
Melville Peninsula
Gjoa Haven
Cambridge Bay
Repulse Bay
Igloolik
Nettilling Lake
Amadjuak Lake
Foxe Basin
Iqaluit
Cumberland Sound
Baffin Bay
Baffin Island
Davis Strait
NUNAVUT
Garry Lake
Back
Baker Lake
Southampton Island
Coral Harbour
Hudson Strait
Rankin Inlet
Coats Island
Mansel Island
Whale Cove
Reliance
...tselk'e
Dubawnt
Arviat
Hudson Bay
Belcher Islands
Lake Athabasca
Reindeer Lake
Wollaston Lake
Churchill
Akimiski Island
...side
Southern Indian Lake
Nelson
Buffalo Narrows
Fox Mine
Thompson
...ADA
SASKATCHEWAN
Flin Flon
The Pas
Lake Winnipeg
MANITOBA
Prince Albert
Saskatoon
Kindersley
Yorkton
Lake Manitoba
Regina
Qu'Appelle
Brandon
...dicine Hat
Weyburn
Winnipeg
Estevan
Melita
Lake of the Woods
STATES OF AMERICA

Eastern Canada

THE MOST INDUSTRIALIZED AND HEAVILY populated parts of Canada are in the east. Ottawa, the capital, is located here, along with other important cities, such as Toronto, Montreal, and Québec. Some of the earliest settlers were French and many people speak French as their first language. The Great Lakes—the largest system of lakes in the world—and the St. Lawrence Seaway link the interior to the coast. The most easterly parts of Canada, the Atlantic Provinces, have rugged coastlines and dramatic scenery. However, soils are thin and so commercial agriculture is limited to a few areas. Fishing used to be the main activity, but fish stocks have been so depleted that few people are now employed in the industry. Despite a thriving tourist industry, the Atlantic Provinces struggle to keep their population, as many people migrate to the bustling cities further west.

MAPLE SAP is collected from cuts in the tree trunk.

MAPLE SYRUP

The colorful maple trees of Québec and Ontario are tapped for maple syrup, a major export, and a popular topping on pancakes for Canadians. The maple leaf is the national symbol of Canada and features on the nation's flag.

Did you know?

▶ In Québec, 82 percent of people speak French as their first language.

▶ The province of Ontario got its name from native Iroquois. Translated, it means "glittering waters" and was inspired by the many lakes in the region.

▶ Canada produces 75 percent of the world's maple syrup. Native peoples were the first to discover and extract the syrup. They passed their techniques on to early European settlers.

▶ Canadians have a high life expectancy—the average person lives to be nearly 80.

TORONTO

Toronto is Canada's most important economic center. Located on Lake Ontario, close to the US border, it is not only an industrial and commercial center but also home to a wide diversity of ethnic and cultural groups. The Canadian National (CN) tower, which dominates the Toronto skyline, is the world's tallest freestanding structure, and locals and tourists can get an impressive view of the city and Lake Ontario from the top.

CN TOWER

HOCKEY

Sports and leisure are important to Canadians. A popular sport is hockey, which thousands of people enthusiastically play or watch. Teams of skaters use long, curved sticks to try to get a hard rubber disk, called a puck, into the opposing team's goal. Both the men's and women's national hockey teams won gold medals at the 2002 Olympics.

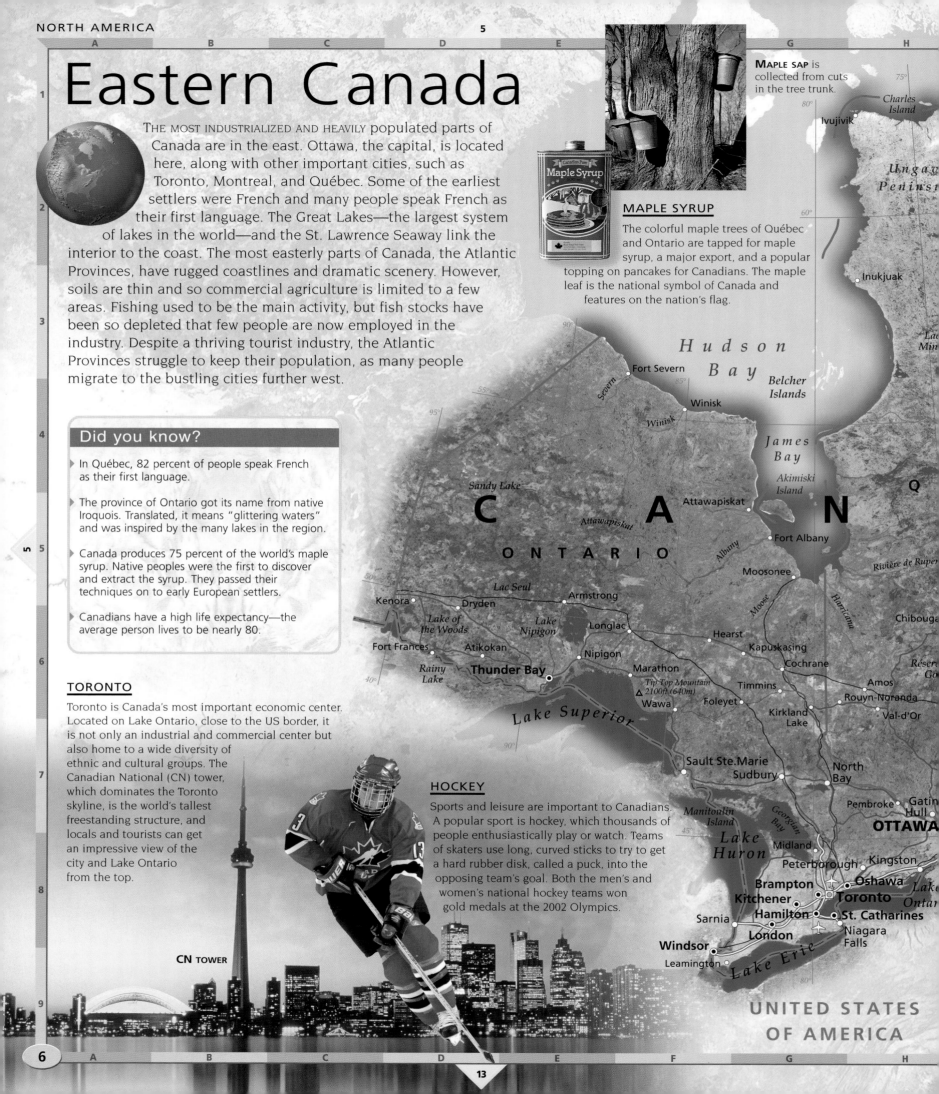

Maple Syrup

Charles Island

Ivujivik

Ungava Peninsula

Inukjuak

Hudson Bay

Fort Severn

Severn

Winisk

Winisk

Belcher Islands

James Bay

Akimiski Island

Sandy Lake

C A N

Attawapiskat

Attawapiskat

Fort Albany

O N T A R I O

Albany

Moosonee

Rivière de Ruper

Moose

Lac Seul

Armstrong

Kenora

Dryden

Hearst

Kapuskasing

Longlac

Lake Nipigon

Lake of the Woods

Cochrane

Amos

Fort Frances

Atikokan

Nipigon

Marathon

Timmins

Rouyn-Noranda

Val-d'Or

Rainy Lake

Thunder Bay

Tip Top Mountain △ 2100ft (640m)

Wawa

Foleyet

Kirkland Lake

Chibouga

Rése

Go

Lake Superior

Sault Ste.Marie

Sudbury

North Bay

Pembroke

Gatin

Hull

OTTAWA

Manitoulin Island

Georgian Bay

Lake Huron

Midland

Kingston

Peterborough

Brampton

Oshawa

Kitchener

Toronto

Sarnia

Hamilton

St. Catharines

London

Niagara Falls

Windsor

Leamington

Lake Erie

Lake Ontar

UNITED STATES OF AMERICA

13

Atlantic Provinces

Nova Scotia, New Brunswick, Prince Edward Island, and Newfoundland and Labrador attract tourists for their landscape, wildlife, and quaint seaside villages. Icebergs are a regular sight off the coast of Newfoundland and Labrador as they drift south from the Arctic.

FISHERIES

The Grand Banks, off the coast of Newfoundland, are shallow waters that once contained huge stocks of fish. Stocks have declined, however, due to overfishing, and now catches are severely restricted. This has resulted in hardship for those who relied on fishing for their livelihood.

FRENCH signs in Québec city

FRENCH CANADA

Québec Province is the main French-speaking part of Canada. With a different language and cultural traditions from other parts of the country, there have been calls in the past for Québec to become independent from the rest of Canada.

ST. LAWRENCE SEAWAY

Stretching far inland, the St. Lawrence Seaway provides a link from the Great Lakes to the Atlantic. A series of huge locks descends from Lake Ontario to sea level, allowing ocean-going ships to transport their cargo as far inland as Lake Superior. Large amounts of iron ore, for example, are transported inland from Labrador to Ontario for processing. Corn, soy, and other agricultural products move in the opposite direction, from the prairies east to the markets of the world.

Map labels

Baffin Island
Hudson Strait
Resolution Island
Akpatok Island
Button Islands
Ungava Bay
Kuujjuaq
Rivière à la Baleine
Rivière à la Baleine
Nain
Hopedale
Makkovik
Cape Harrison
Cartwright
Labrador Sea
Lac nville
Schefferville
Smallwood Reservoir
Lake Melville
Churchill
NEWFOUNDLAND & LABRADOR
St.Anthony
Réservoir de Caniapiscau
B E C
A D A
Laurentian Mountains
Réservoir Manicouagan
Lac Mistassini
Havre-St-Pierre
Île d'Anticosti
Gander
Grand Falls
St.John's
Newfoundland
Corner Brook
Sept-Îles
Lac St-Jean
Baie-Comeau
Gaspé
Gulf of St. Lawrence
Péninsule de Gaspé
Îles de la Madeleine
Cabot Strait
Channel-Port aux Basques
Cape Race
Chicoutimi
Matane
Rimouski
Bathurst
ST PIERRE & MIQUELON (to France)
Jonquière
Rivière-du-Loup
Edmundston
PRINCE EDWARD ISLAND
Glace Bay
Sydney
Cape Breton Island
La Tuque
Charlesbourg
NEW BRUNSWICK
Charlottetown
Moncton
Amherst
New Glasgow
Québec
St-Georges
Oromocto
Truro
NOVA SCOTIA
Trois-Rivières
Fredericton
Saint John
Dartmouth
Sable Island
Laval
Drummondville
Bay of Fundy
Halifax
Montréal
Sherbrooke
Liverpool
Yarmouth
ATLANTIC OCEAN
St.Lawrence

Scale

0 km 100 200
0 miles 100 200

USA: Northeast

THE NORTHEASTERN UNITED STATES is a heavily populated area that is steeped in history. This is traditionally the main immigration point into the States, with the Statue of Liberty lighting the way for those arriving into New York by boat. People from all over the world have settled in this region to live and work, creating a "melting pot" of cultures and ethnic groups. Important historical events, such as the signing of the Declaration of Independence and the Constitution, took place in Philadelphia. These documents set the foundations for American life today. It is also here that the capital and center of government was established. Today, while industry and agriculture are still important, finance and commerce are the driving forces of the economy.

THRIVING CITY

New York is the largest city in the United States. It grew because it has a good harbor and sits at the mouth of the Hudson River. Immigrants from overseas flooded into the city in the 19th and 20th centuries, boosting its population and economy. Today, it is the main financial center, not just of the US, but of the world.

Lake Ontario

Hudson River

Appalachian Mountains

New York City

Did you know?

▸ There are more than 100 universities and colleges in Boston.

▸ Every minute, about 40 million gallons (180 million liters) of water plunges over Niagara Falls, located on the border between the US and Canada.

▸ The White House in Washington, D.C., has been home to every president except George Washington, whom the city is named after.

▸ The stock exchange on Wall Street, New York City, is the world's largest. The street's name came from a wall built by Dutch settlers to keep the British out.

PITTSBURGH

Once a major steel-manufacturing center with a polluted environment, Pittsburgh is now a thriving financial center with a large number of corporate headquarters. Bridges span the three rivers that run through the city, connecting the core downtown area (above) to the suburbs.

CENTER OF GOVERNMENT

All three branches of the federal government, the executive, legislative, and judicial, reside in Washington, D.C. The United States Congress (the legislative branch) meets here in the Capitol building. Many of the city's residents work for the government.

THE SEAT of government is here at the Capitol building.

CANADA

ONTARIO

St. Lawrence

Ogdensburg

Adirondack Mountains

Watertown

Boonville

A p

Mohawk Rive

Lake Ontario

Oswego

Niagara Falls

Lockport

Rochester

Newark

Syracuse

Utica

Niagara Falls

Buffalo

Avon

NEW YORK

Oneonta

Hamburg

Dansville

Ithaca

Catski Mounta

Dunkirk

Binghamton

Erie

Jamestown

Elmira

Sayre

Allegheny Plateau

Mansfield

Warren

Scranton

Wilkes Barre

Middleto

Meadville

Wilcox

Milford

PENNSYLVANIA

Lock Haven

Stroudsberg

Mercer

Allegheny River

Du Bois

Milton

Allentown

OHIO

Butler

State College

Reading

Trento

Indiana

Appalachian Mountains

Aliquippa

Pittsburgh

Altoona

Harrisburg

Philadelphia

Washington

Bedford

Carlisle

Lancaster

Wilmington

Cherry Hill

Uniontown

York

Hagerstown

Aberdeen

Vineland

Cumberland

Towson

WEST VIRGINIA

Oakland

Baltimore

Dover

Columbia

DELAWA

Annapolis

WASHINGTON, D.C

VIRGINIA

Cambridge

Ocean City

MARYLAND

Salisbur

Chesapeake Bay

CRANBERRIES

The northeast US is a major cranberry-growing region. Cranberries grow in flooded bogs, and once harvested, often with high-tech equipment (above), they can be eaten in pies and sauces.

MAINE

Although Maine is a large state, it is relatively sparsely populated. Early settlers were attracted to its coastline, and fishing communities gradually sprang up. To this day, fishing remains an important activity, while colorful foliage attracts tourists in the fall.

MAINE is famous for its clam chowder and lobsters.

THANKSGIVING

The first Thanksgiving was held in 1621 as a gesture of friendship between the Pilgrims and American Indians after the Pilgrims' first successful harvest. Americans honor that tradition every November by gathering with family and friends to give thanks for life's blessings and to share a meal.

HIGHER EDUCATION

A large number of universities are located in this region, including two of the most famous: Harvard (above) and Yale. As well as studying, students enjoy a full campus life, including taking part in sports. Links between industry and education are strong, so many high-tech companies have been established here.

TOURISTS can take an elevator to the top of the Statue of Liberty.

NEW YORK CITY

The center of US commerce and business is New York City. People living here have a fast-paced lifestyle, and many travel by train or ferry from the suburbs to work in the towering high-rise offices of Manhattan. People traveling by boat across the harbor pass the Statue of Liberty, a huge monument that represents freedom and opportunity to Americans.

Map labels

QUEBEC

VERMONT
Newport
Burlington
Lake Champlain
Montpelier
Rutland
Berlin
Chelsea

NEW HAMPSHIRE
Lebanon
Laconia
Concord
Hillsboro
Rochester

MAINE
Madawaska
Presque Isle
Mars Hill
Houlton
Mount Katahdin 5267ft (1605m)
Moosehead Lake
Jackman
Milo
Lincoln
Calais
Machias
Bangor
Millbridge
Searsport
Bar Harbor
Mount Desert Island
Waterville
Augusta
Lewiston
Camden
Bath
Portland
Biddeford
Portsmouth

NEW BRUNSWICK

Bay of Fundy

Gulf of Maine

Penobscot River

Appalachian Mountains
Green Mountains
Connecticut River
Mount Washington 6288ft (1917m)

Falls
Manchester
Nashua
Lawrence
Lowell

MASSACHUSETTS
Albany
Schenectady
Troy
Pittsfield
Greenfield
Worcester
Boston
Provincetown
Cape Cod
Springfield
Orleans
Pawtucket
Windsor
Providence
New Bedford
Martha's Vineyard
Nantucket
Nantucket Island

CONNECTICUT
Bristol
Hartford
Warwick
Waterbury
New Haven
Bridgeport
Stamford

RHODE ISLAND

Groton

Yonkers
Paterson
New York
Long Island
Newark
Middletown

NEW JERSEY

ATLANTIC OCEAN

Atlantic City

0 km   50   100   150
0 miles   50   100   150

40°
45°
70°

USA: South

THE SOUTHERN STATES have a varied landscape and an interesting mix of people, both culturally and economically. Some areas of the region are poor, especially the Appalachian Mountain communities, while other parts, such as the Florida coast, are wealthy and attract many people from other states and countries. The cultural mix includes people of Latin American origin, African Americans, Cajuns (French Canadians), and European Americans, giving rise to diverse music styles, dialects, pastimes, and food. While coal mining in the Appalachian Mountains has declined in recent years, agriculture is still important, as are tourism and industry. Tourism is particularly important in Florida and in New Orleans, which is near the mouth of the mighty Mississippi River.

COTTON CROPS

Cotton was once the mainstay crop of the south and was grown by African-American slaves. Today, cotton is still important for the economy of the region and is grown in large fields and harvested with huge machinery. Cotton has many uses, primarily as the raw material for textiles.

COTTON POD, OR BOLL

Did you know?

▶ The Mississippi is the largest river in North America, and the third largest in the world. It stretches 2,340 miles (3,770 km) from Lake Itasca in Minnesota to its mouth near New Orleans.

▶ Memphis, Tennessee, is named for the ancient Egyptian capital situated south of the Nile Delta.

▶ Half the nation's peanuts are grown in Georgia. Most of them are made into peanut butter.

MUSIC ORIGINS

The southern US is famous for its music, much of which reflects the cultural mix of the region. New Orleans and other parts of Louisiana are the birthplaces of jazz and Cajun music, while bluegrass and country have origins in Nashville and Memphis. These music styles started here, but quickly spread throughout the country and developed even further in the cities.

JAZZ musician on Bourbon Street in New Orleans.

A CHEF holds a skillet of jambalaya, a Cajun dish.

CAJUN CULTURE

The Cajuns in this region are French-speaking people who were expelled from Canada in the 18th century. They mixed with other cultures in Louisiana, but their French influence can be seen in the music, food, and place names, such as Lafayette.

FLORIDA EVERGLADES

The increasing population of Florida means that the Everglades, swampy plains inhabited by alligators and other wildlife, are under threat as land is needed for houses and farms. However, the Everglades National Park protects part of this important ecosystem.

Map labels

0 km 50 100 150 200
0 miles 50 100 150 200

INDIANA
Cincinnati
Newp
Louisville
Evansville
Frankf
Lexington
Henderson
Owensboro
Richmo
Elizabethtown
Paducah
KENTUCK
Somerset
Hopkinsville
Bowling
Green
Kentucky
Lake
Clarksville
Cookeville
Cumberland Plat
MISSOURI
Rogers
Mountain
Home
Pocahontas
Union
City
Nashville
Bull Shoals
Lake
Fayetteville
Walnut Ridge
Blytheville
Dyersburg
Franklin
Murfreesboro
Mar
Boston Mountains
Jonesboro
Wa
Lak
Fort Smith
ARKANSAS
Jackson
TENNESSEE
OKLAHOMA
Russellville
Searcy
West
Memphis
Lawrenceburg
Columbia
Chattanooga
Cleve
Da
North
Little Rock
Forrest City
Memphis
Corinth
Tennessee River
Huntsville
Ouachita
Mountains
Little Rock
Holly
Springs
Florence
Scottsboro
Rome
Hot Springs
Benton
Clarksdale
Tupelo
Hamilton
Cullman
Mariet
Pine
Bluff
Grenada
Decatur
Gadsden
Atlan
Red River
Texarkana
Greenwood
Columbus
Anniston
Camden
El Dorado
Greenville
Tuscaloosa
Birmingham
Gr
Bastrop
MISSISSIPPI
Alexander City
Shreveport
Ruston
Monroe
Yazoo City
Canton
ALABAMA
Opelika
Colu
Bossier City
Tallulah
Clinton
Meridian
Demopolis
Prattville
Phenix City
LOUISIANA
Vicksburg
Jackson
Montgomery
Natchitoches
Natchez
Laurel
Troy
Alexandria
Brookhaven
Hattiesburg
Andalusia
Ozark
Alb
De Ridder
McComb
Brewton
Dothan
Opelousas
Bogalusa
Prichard
Crestview
Lake Seminole
Baton Rouge
Mobile
Fort Walton
Beach
Tallahas
Lake Charles
Lafayette
Gulfport
Biloxi
Pensacola
Panama
City
New Iberia
Metairie
New Orleans
Morgan City
Houma
Chandeleur
Islands
Cape San Blas
Venice
Apalac
Bay
Mississippi River
Delta
Gulf of Mexico

PENNSYLVANIA

OHIO

WEST VIRGINIA
Parkersburg
Clarksburg
Winchester
Spruce Knob 4862ft (1482m)
Portsmouth
Saint Albans
Huntington
Charleston
Beckley
Bluefield
Pikeville
Idlesboro
Bristol
Greeneville
Knoxville
Asheville

WASHINGTON, D.C.
Arlington
Dale City
Harrisonburg
Staunton
Fredericksburg
MARYLAND
Charlottesville
Chesapeake Bay

VIRGINIA
Richmond
Lynchburg
Petersburg
Cape Charles
Roanoke
Newport News
Norfolk
Portsmouth
Virginia Beach
Danville
Roanoke River
Elizabeth City
James River
Potomac River

Pulaski
Kingsport
Greensboro
Durham
Rocky Mount
Greenville
Winston Salem
High Point
Raleigh
Cary
Mount Mitchell 6684ft (2037m)
NORTH CAROLINA
Goldsboro
New Bern
Pamlico Sound
Cape Hatteras 35°
Gastonia
Charlotte
Fayetteville
Havelock
Spartanburg
Rock Hill
Laurinburg
Greenville
Union
Jacksonville
Onslow Bay
SOUTH CAROLINA
Greenwood
Wilmington
Florence
Cape Fear
Athens
Columbia
Myrtle Beach
Long Bay
Clark Hill Lake
Lake Marion
Aiken
Orangeburg
Georgetown
Augusta
Savannah River
North Charleston
GEORGIA
Milledgeville
Charleston
Macon
Statesboro
Hilton Head Island
Dublin
Vidalia
Cordele
Savannah
Tifton
Hinesville
Altamaha River
Waycross
Brunswick
Valdosta
Thomasville
Okefenokee Swamp
Jacksonville
Lake City
Saint Augustine
Gainesville
Lake George
Ocala
Daytona Beach
De Land
Deltona
Spring Hill
Orlando
Cape Canaveral
Clearwater
Lakeland
Melbourne
Largo
Tampa
Lake Kissimmee
Saint Petersburg
Fort Pierce
Tampa Bay
FLORIDA
Hutchinson Island
Sarasota
Port Charlotte
Lake Okeechobee
West Palm Beach
Charlotte Harbor
Boca Raton
Fort Myers
Pompano Beach
Naples
Big Cypress Swamp
Fort Lauderdale
Miami Beach
The Everglades
Miami
Cape Sable
Key Largo
Florida Bay
Key West
Florida Keys
Straits of Florida

ATLANTIC OCEAN

KENTUCKY DERBY

Every year on the first Saturday in May, the Kentucky Derby takes place in Louisville. This horse race, and the festivities based around it, mark the beginning of spring for people in the area. The best horses and jockeys, as well as massive crowds of spectators from around the country, travel here for the event .

TOURISM

Tourism is an important industry in the south, especially for Florida. As well as warm weather and appealing scenery, tourists are attracted to the theme parks around Orlando. Jobs and income are generated by tourism, with many people working in retail outlets, restaurants, hotels, and theme parks.

KUMBA roller coaster at Busch Gardens is the fastest in Florida.

MARTIN LUTHER KING, JR.

Martin Luther King, Jr. (left) was born in Atlanta in 1929. In the 1960s, he led many peaceful protests to end the laws that discriminated against black Americans. King was assassinated in 1969 and has since been seen as a symbol of the struggle for racial equality. Many African Americans live in the southern US where, before the Civil War (1861–65), their ancestors were forced to work on cotton plantations and farms.

MARTIN LUTHER KING, JR. speaking at the final rally of the March Against Fear, Mississippi, 1966

FLORIDA'S SUNSHINE COAST

Florida's sunny weather and sandy beaches have traditionally attracted many retired people, many of whom live in apartments along the coast in resorts such as Miami Beach (right). Florida also attracts young people, particularly to the vibrant city of Miami, where many immigrants from Central America, Cuba, and other Caribbean islands live, and Spanish is spoken by half the population. The Florida Keys, an island chain in the south of the peninsula, is also popular with tourists, and contains one of the largest living coral formations in North America.

USA: Midwest

THE AMERICAN MIDWEST is dominated by the Great Plains, once the home of cattle ranches, cowboys, and tribes of American Indian people. However, the discovery of gold in South Dakota brought a rush of settlers to the area. This, combined with a decline in buffalo numbers, led to the eventual displacement of the American Indians from the Plains. The area is prone to dramatic weather—with tornadoes, freezing blizzards, and blazing-hot summers. To the west, vast areas of farmland generate more wheat and corn than anywhere else in the world. East of the Mississippi the landscape varies, and although farming is still important, this is the industrial center of the country. Big cities such as Chicago, Detroit, and Cleveland form the major manufacturing centers.

BUFFALO ON THE PLAINS

Up to 100 million buffalo once grazed on the Great Plains. They provided local American Indians with food for the family, and skin for clothes and teepees. But overhunting and the destruction of their habitat by early European settlers drastically reduced the number of animals. Buffalo are now a protected species that live in reserves. This herd is from a reserve in South Dakota.

THE DAKOTA people used buffalo bones to make shields and tools. The animal's bladder made a bag for carrying water.

MOUNT RUSHMORE NATIONAL MEMORIAL

Mount Rushmore was created as a tribute to the American presidency. Four of the United States' greatest presidents—Lincoln, Roosevelt, Jefferson, and Washington—were carved into the granite cliff between 1927 and 1941. Teams of workers hung from saddles anchored to the mountain to complete the work, often enduring harsh winds or blazing sun. Today, it is a popular tourist attraction.

Each carved face is about 60 ft (18 m) high.

TORNADO ALLEY

Dramatic tornadoes, or "twisters," regularly tear through the states of Kansas and Missouri, along a path known as Tornado Alley. Tornadoes occur when warm and cold air masses meet. As the warm air rises, it cools, and under the right conditions, it can suck in more and more air until a whirling twister develops. The more air that is drawn in, the greater the power of the tornado.

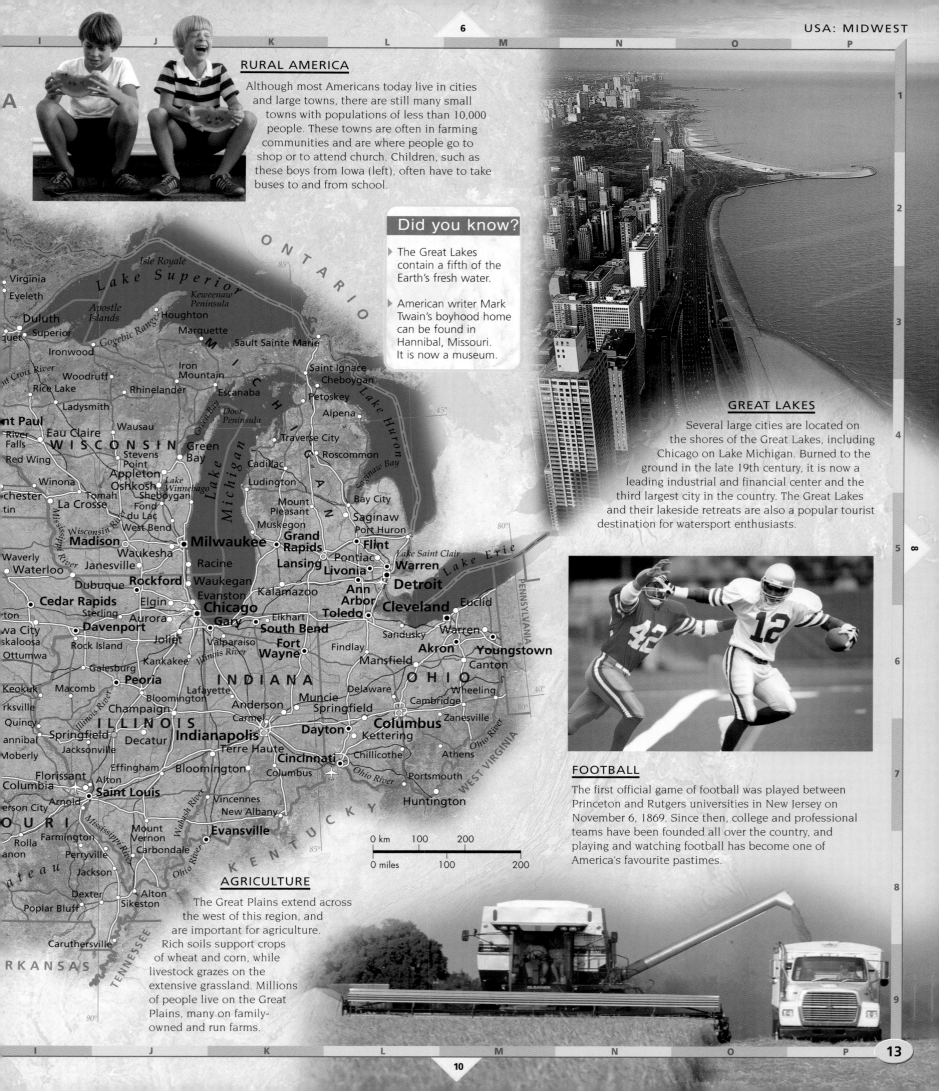

RURAL AMERICA

Although most Americans today live in cities and large towns, there are still many small towns with populations of less than 10,000 people. These towns are often in farming communities and are where people go to shop or to attend church. Children, such as these boys from Iowa (left), often have to take buses to and from school.

Did you know?

▶ The Great Lakes contain a fifth of the Earth's fresh water.

▶ American writer Mark Twain's boyhood home can be found in Hannibal, Missouri. It is now a museum.

GREAT LAKES

Several large cities are located on the shores of the Great Lakes, including Chicago on Lake Michigan. Burned to the ground in the late 19th century, it is now a leading industrial and financial center and the third largest city in the country. The Great Lakes and their lakeside retreats are also a popular tourist destination for watersport enthusiasts.

FOOTBALL

The first official game of football was played between Princeton and Rutgers universities in New Jersey on November 6, 1869. Since then, college and professional teams have been founded all over the country, and playing and watching football has become one of America's favourite pastimes.

AGRICULTURE

The Great Plains extend across the west of this region, and are important for agriculture. Rich soils support crops of wheat and corn, while livestock grazes on the extensive grassland. Millions of people live on the Great Plains, many on family-owned and run farms.

Map labels:

ONTARIO
Isle Royale
Lake Superior
Apostle Islands
Keweenaw Peninsula
Gogebic Range
MICHIGAN
Virginia
Eveleth
Duluth
Superior
quet
Ironwood
Woodruff
Rice Lake
Ladysmith
nt Croix River
Houghton
Marquette
Sault Sainte Marie
Iron Mountain
Rhinelander
Escanaba
Saint Ignace
Cheboygan
Petoskey
Alpena
Lake Huron
Saginaw Bay
nt Paul
River Falls
Red Wing
Eau Claire
WISCONSIN
Wausau
Stevens Point
Green Bay
Door Peninsula
Great Bay
Traverse City
Roscommon
Cadillac
Ludington
Mount Pleasant
Muskegon
Bay City
Saginaw
Port Huron
Winona
chester
tin
La Crosse
Tomah
Appleton
Oshkosh
Fond du Lac
West Bend
Lake Winnebago
Sheboygan
Wisconsin River
Mississippi River
Madison
Waukesha
MICHIGAN
Lake Michigan
Milwaukee
Grand Rapids
Flint
Lake Saint Clair
Waverly
Waterloo
Janesville
Racine
Lansing
Livonia
Warren
Detroit
Dubuque
Rockford
Waukegan
Evanston
Kalamazoo
Ann Arbor
Cleveland
Euclid
Lake Erie
PENNSYLVANIA
Cedar Rapids
Elgin
Sterling
Aurora
Chicago
Gary
Elkhart
Toledo
Warren
Akron
Youngstown
ton
Davenport
Rock Island
Joliet
Valparaiso
South Bend
Fort Wayne
Findlay
Sandusky
Mansfield
Canton
wa City
skaloosa
Ottumwa
Galesburg
Kankakee
Illinois River
INDIANA
OHIO
Wheeling
Keokuk
Macomb
Peoria
Lafayette
Muncie
Delaware
Springfield
Cambridge
rksville
Quincy
Champaign
Bloomington
Anderson
Columbus
Zanesville
annibal
ILLINOIS
Carmel
Springfield
Indianapolis
Dayton
Kettering
Moberly
Jacksonville
Decatur
Terre Haute
Cincinnati
Chillicothe
Athens
Ohio River
WEST VIRGINIA
Florissant
Alton
Effingham
Bloomington
Columbus
Portsmouth
Columbia
Saint Louis
Vincennes
New Albany
Huntington
erson City
Arnold
KENTUCKY
OURI
Rolla
Farmington
Mount Vernon
Carbondale
Evansville
anon
Perryville
Wabash River
Mississippi River
Ohio River
Jackson
Dexter
Alton
Sikeston
Poplar Bluff
Caruthersville
TENNESSEE
RKANSAS
ateau

0 km   100   200
0 miles   100   200

USA: West

THE ROCKY MOUNTAINS separate the coastal region from the drier inland states. Large and fast-growing cities, such as San Francisco, Los Angeles, and San Diego, hug the Pacific Coast, and have attracted many migrants because of good job opportunities. Inland, blazing desert and towering mountains provide some of the most dramatic landscapes in the country. National parks, such as Yellowstone in northwestern Wyoming and Montana and Yosemite in central California, protect some of these wilderness areas. Further east, the foothills of the Rockies give way to vast plains grazed by large herds of cattle.

NORTHERN FORESTS

The coastal areas of Oregon and Washington contain large forests. These produce economically important lumber, but much land is also left in its natural state and is popular with hikers. Most people here live in large cities like Seattle, and in the fertile inland valleys.

CALIFORNIA AGRICULTURE

California is warm, fertile, and, with irrigation, ideal for agriculture. Grapes are an important crop north of San Francisco in the Napa Valley. Further south, citrus crops, such as oranges, also flourish. Premium farming land is under threat, however, as the population expands.

Did you know?

▶ The American Indian name for Death Valley is *Tomesha*, which means "land where the ground is on fire."

▶ The majority of the world's geysers and hot springs are in Yellowstone National Park.

LOS ANGELES

This sprawling city—the second largest in the US—is home to migrants from all over the world, as well as from other states in the country. Sandwiched between the coast and the mountains, the city has massive air pollution problems. This mostly arises from the exhaust fumes from the high number of cars used by commuters on the city's highways.

Map labels

0 km 100 200 300
0 miles 100 200 300

N E V A D A

ALBERTA SASKATCHEWAN

110° 105°

reka
hitefish
Kalispell
Flathead Lake
issoula Helena
Anaconda Boulder
Butte
Pioneer Mountains
Bozeman
Dillon

Shelby Havre Milk River Malta
△ Baldy Mountain 6916ft (2108m) Fort Peck Lake
Missouri River Sidney
Great Falls
M O N T A N A Glendive
Lewistown
Yellowstone River Miles City
Billings
Livingston Laurel Powder River
Bighorn River Little Missouri River

N O R T H D A K O T A

S O U T H D A K O T A

45°

IDAHO
Rexburg
Idaho Falls
Blackfoot
Pocatello
American Falls Reservoir
in Falls Burley

Snake River Plain

Yellowstone National Park
Cody Powell
Cloud Peak 13,167ft (4013m)
Worland
Sheridan
Gillette

W Y O M I N G

Riverton Douglas
Lander
Casper
Laramie Mountains
Wheatland
Torrington

N E B R A S K A

Brigham City Logan
Great Salt Lake
Ogden Evanston
Magna
Salt Lake City
Sandy City
Tooele Orem
Utah Lake Provo
Great Salt Lake Desert

Green River
Rawlins
Rock Springs
Laramie
Cheyenne

40°

Bountiful

Price
Vernal
Grand Junction
Steamboat Springs
Craig
Loveland
Longmont
Boulder
Lakewood
Vail
Denver Aurora
Englewood
Fort Collins
Greeley
Brighton
Sterling
Fort Morgan

U T A H
Richfield
Mount Ellen △ 11,522ft (3512m)
Moab
Montrose
Aspen
Mount Elbert 14,433ft (4399m)
Gunnison
Pikes Peak 14,110ft (4301m)
Colorado Springs
Pueblo

C O L O R A D O

Uncompahgre Peak 14,309ft (4361m)
San Juan Mountains
Canon City
Lamar
La Junta

Sangre de Cristo Mountains

K A N S A S

evier Lake
Cedar City
Saint George
Lake Powell
Colorado River
Durango
Rio Grande
Alamosa
Trinidad

OKLAHOMA

A R I Z O N A N E W M E X I C O

110° 105°

Missouri River
Absaroka Range

CATTLE RANCHES

Many people who live in Montana, Wyoming, Utah, and Colorado work in the booming farming and mining industries. Much of the land on these foothills and plains is grazed by cattle on huge ranches, originally established to provide food for the flourishing east coast. Modern cowboys may use horses, trucks, or even helicopters to watch over the cattle.

DEATH VALLEY

The driest place in the US is Death Valley, which once held the world's highest recorded temperature at 134°F (57°C). Although seemingly inhospitable, its canyons, rock formations, and sudden spring blooms make it popular with tourists.

COLORADO

The Rocky Mountains cut through this region. The stunning terrain and the light, dry snow that falls here support the skiing industry in Colorado. Resorts such as Aspen are popular with Americans as well as with overseas visitors.

YELLOWSTONE

The first national park in the world, Yellowstone was established in 1827 in Wyoming and Montana to protect the abundant wildlife and hydrothermal activity. The United States now has more than 350 national parks that attract millions of visitors every year.

TOURISTS watch Old Faithful geyser in Yellowstone National Park.

SILICON VALLEY

THE ELEMENT silicon is used in many computer products

The area between Palo Alto and San Jose has been nicknamed "Silicon Valley" because of the many companies engaged in high-technology research and manufacturing here. It is now the center of the world's computer industry.

Earthquakes

San Francisco, California, suffers frequent earthquakes due to its location on the San Andreas faultline. Modern skyscrapers are designed to withstand tremors, but many houses, especially those on typically steep streets (right), are still at risk.

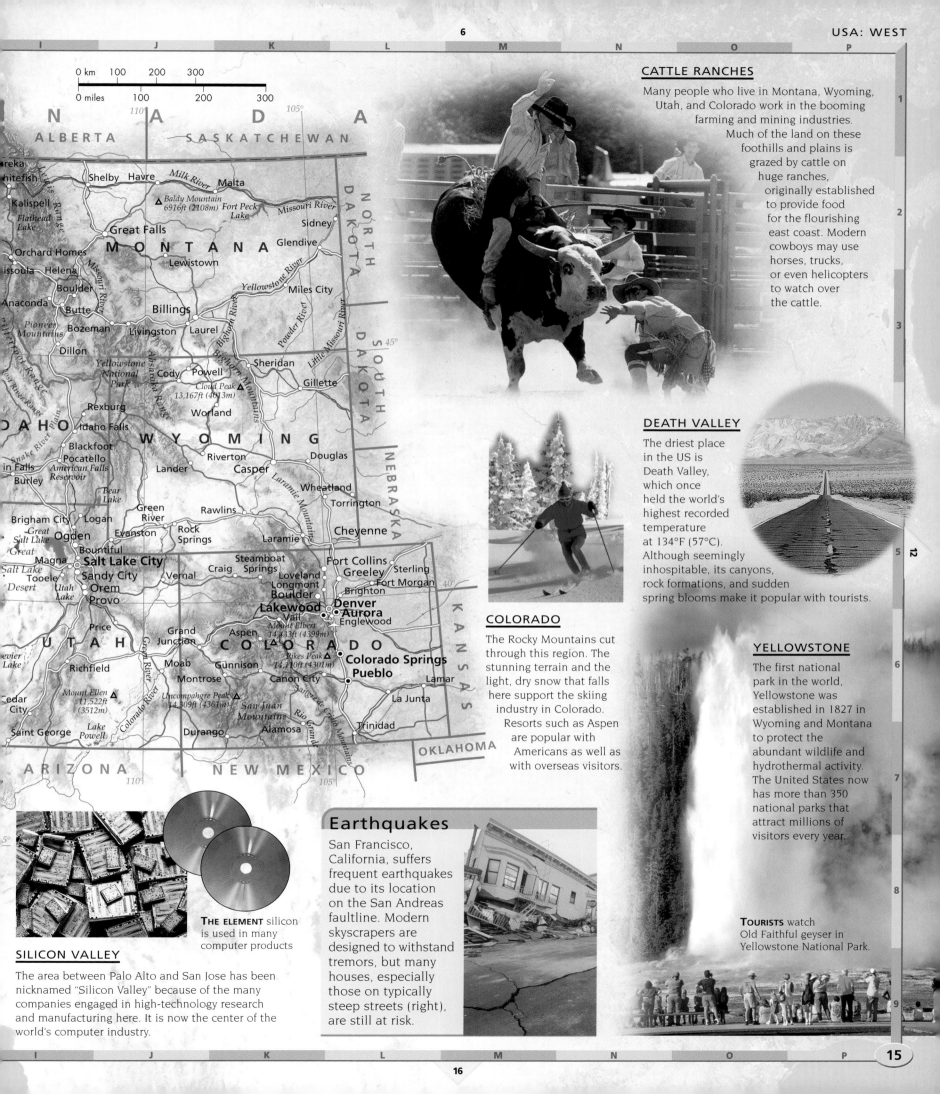

USA: Southwest

THE SOUTHWEST IS AN AREA of great contrasts. Much of Oklahoma and Texas consists of flat, rolling grasslands and huge farms, while both Arizona and New Mexico are hot, arid, and mountainous, with vast canyons and river valleys carving their way through the land. Since the discovery of oil in 1901, Texas has become the country's top oil producer after Alaska, with Houston as the center of the billion-dollar industry. Tourism is also important to the southwest, as visitors flock to see the Grand Canyon, the Painted Desert, and other natural wonders. Buildings here reflect the mix of American Indians, Hispanic, European American, and modern American cultures.

HOT PLACE TO LIVE

The climate across much of the southwest is hot and dry, with summer temperatures often reaching 100°F (38°C). Although water can be scarce, many people have a swimming pool in their yard so they can cool off.

SUBURBS OF PHOENIX, ARIZONA

DESERT LIFE

The Saguaro cactus (left) can reach up to 50 ft (15 m) tall, grow as many as 40 branches, and live for 200 years. Cacti, yucca, and other plants have all adapted to the hot, dry desert conditions found in the southwest. So, too, have many animals, including the deadly rattlesnake.

SAGUARO CACTI in the Sonoran Desert

0 km 50　100　150　200
0 miles　50　100　150　200

THE GRAND CANYON

The Grand Canyon in northern Arizona is one of the natural wonders of the world. This incredibly deep gorge was slowly cut out of the rock by the Colorado River, beginning six million years ago. People can hike around its edge or venture down into the canyon to camp overnight.

AMERICAN-INDIAN CULTURES

American Indians, including Navajo, Hopi, and Apache, used to live across the southwest but are now concentrated in reservations set up by the US government. The largest of these is in Arizona and New Mexico, and is home to the Navajo people. The Navajo farm the land and produce crafts, like the woven blanket wrapped around these Navajo children (below).

KACHINA dolls are made by the Hopi.

Map labels

NEVADA · CALIFORNIA · UTAH · Colorado · ARIZONA · NEW MEXICO · MEXICO · COL

Lake Powell · San Juan River · Page · Shiprock · Aztec · Bloomfield · Farmington · Wheeler Peak 13,159ft (4011m)
Lake Mead · Grand Canyon · Coconino Plateau · Tuba City · Chuska Mountains · Los Alamos · Espanola
Humphreys Peak 12,635ft (3851m) · Painted Desert · Gallup · Rocky · Santa Fe
Kingman · Hualapai Peak 8419ft (2566m) · Sedona · Flagstaff · Sanders · Corrales · Albuquerque
Lake Havasu City · Prescott · Holbrook · Grants · Mountains
Wickenburg · Show Low · Belen · Willard
Colorado River · Signal Peak 4879ft (1487m) · Glendale · Scottsdale · Globe · Socorro
Phoenix · Mesa · San Carlos
Gila River · Casa Grande · Clifton · Black Range · Rio Grande · Elephant Butte Reservoir · Sacramento Mountains
Yuma · Eloy · Safford · Alamogordo
Somerton · Sonoran Desert · Ajo · Las Cruces · Organ Peak 8871ft (2704m)
Tucson · Willcox · Deming
Sierra Vista · Benson · El Paso
Nogales · Bisbee · Douglas · Fabens

115° · 110° · 35° · 30°

14

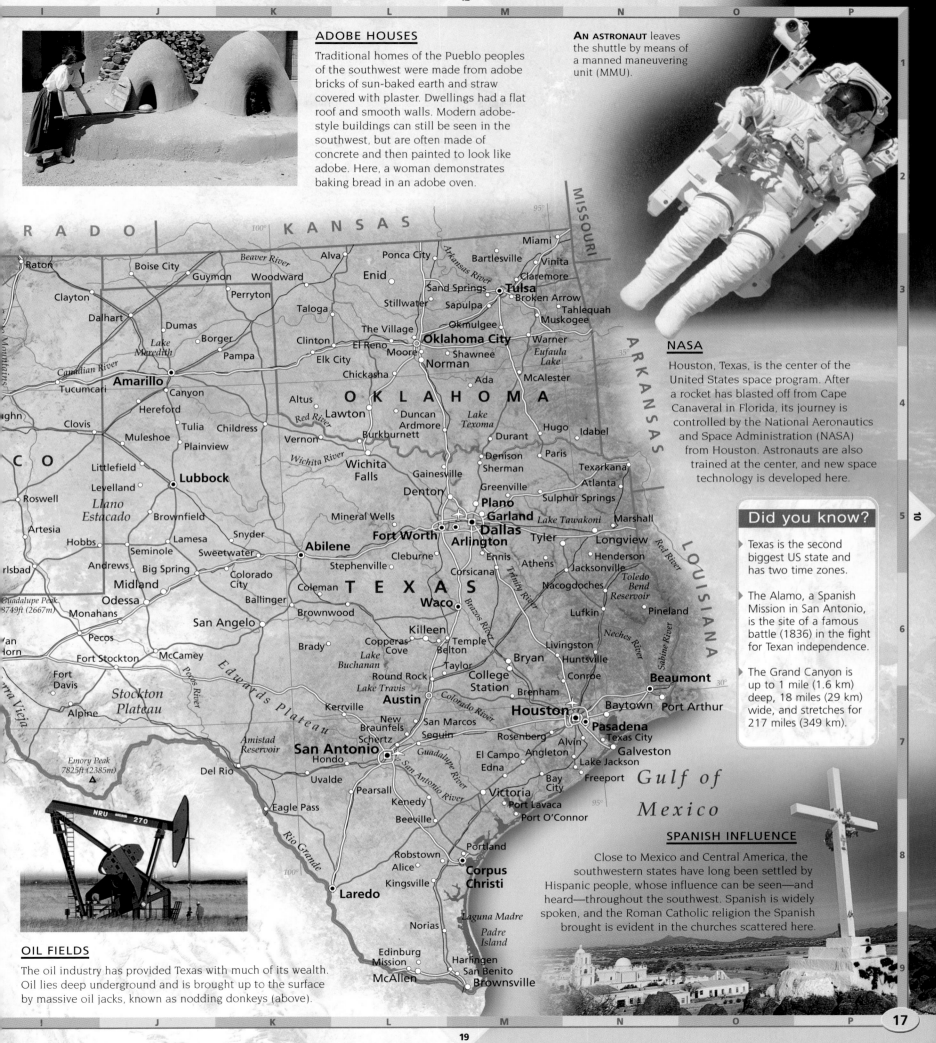

ADOBE HOUSES

Traditional homes of the Pueblo peoples of the southwest were made from adobe bricks of sun-baked earth and straw covered with plaster. Dwellings had a flat roof and smooth walls. Modern adobe-style buildings can still be seen in the southwest, but are often made of concrete and then painted to look like adobe. Here, a woman demonstrates baking bread in an adobe oven.

AN ASTRONAUT leaves the shuttle by means of a manned maneuvering unit (MMU).

NASA

Houston, Texas, is the center of the United States space program. After a rocket has blasted off from Cape Canaveral in Florida, its journey is controlled by the National Aeronautics and Space Administration (NASA) from Houston. Astronauts are also trained at the center, and new space technology is developed here.

Did you know?

▶ Texas is the second biggest US state and has two time zones.

▶ The Alamo, a Spanish Mission in San Antonio, is the site of a famous battle (1836) in the fight for Texan independence.

▶ The Grand Canyon is up to 1 mile (1.6 km) deep, 18 miles (29 km) wide, and stretches for 217 miles (349 km).

SPANISH INFLUENCE

Close to Mexico and Central America, the southwestern states have long been settled by Hispanic people, whose influence can be seen—and heard—throughout the southwest. Spanish is widely spoken, and the Roman Catholic religion the Spanish brought is evident in the churches scattered here.

OIL FIELDS

The oil industry has provided Texas with much of its wealth. Oil lies deep underground and is brought up to the surface by massive oil jacks, known as nodding donkeys (above).

Mexico

ONCE HOME TO THE great Aztec and Mayan civilizations, then the focus of Spanish conquistadors who came in search of wealth, the culture and architecture of Mexico today reflects its colorful past. The majority of Mexicans are *mestizo* (mixed race), of Spanish and native Indian descent. Mexico City, site of the ancient Aztec capital, is today one of the largest cities in the world, with a population of over 16 million. Despite oil and natural gas reserves, and a plentiful supply of labor, large numbers of Mexicans are still poor, especially in the rural areas and the urban slums.

ALONG THE BORDER

In 1994, Mexico signed the North American Free Trade Agreement (NAFTA), which effectively bound its economy to that of the US. A large industrial area has developed along the Mexican border with the US, and many American companies have relocated south of the border to benefit from the lower labor costs.

DAY OF THE DEAD

One of the biggest festivals in Mexico is the Day of the Dead. It is believed that once a year, the souls of the dead can come back and visit their loved ones. In celebration of this, special food is prepared to welcome the souls, and offerings of flowers, candles, and incense are made at the gravesides.

LIFE IN THE CITY

Mexico City is the political, economic, and cultural hub of the country, and is home to millions. Its site, in a basin surrounded by a mountain, means that expansion is difficult. Air pollution from factories and cars cannot escape, so on most days a thick layer of smog builds up over the city. Attempts to deal with the pollution, including banning cars in some parts, have had limited success.

THE VOLCANO
Popocatépetl is the highest peak around the city.

MEXICO CITY is contained within a ring of mountains.

WORKING ON THE LAND

Agriculture employs seven million people— about one-quarter of Mexico's work force. However, only 12 percent of the land is suitable for farming because the land is so mountainous and dry. The peasant communities of the south rely on farming for their food, while communities in the north are more industrialized. Here, the agave plant is being harvested near the town of Tequila.

Map labels

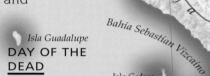

UNITED STATES OF

Mexicali
San Luis
Tijuana
Rosarito
Ensenada
Colorado River
Sierra San Pedro Mártir
Desierto de Altar
Ciudad Juárez
Rio Grande
Río Bravo del Norte
Nogales
Agua Prieta
Samalayuca
Cananea
Caborca
Magdalena
Río Bavispe
Nuevo Casas Grandes
El Sueco
Ojinag
Cumpas
San Pedro de la Cueva
El Sáuz
Río Conchos
Isla Ángel de la Guarda
Hermosillo
Río Yaqui
Chihuahua
Delicias
Cuauhtémoc
Isla Tiburón
Ciudad Camargo
Empalme
Baja California
Isla Guadalupe
Bahía Sebastián Vizcaíno
Isla Cedros
Guerrero Negro
Guaymas
Esperanza
San Francisco del Oro
Jiménez
Hidalgo del Parral
Santa Barbara
Ciudad Obregón
Navojoa
Huatabampo
Sierra Madre Occidental
Gómez Pala
San Ignacio
San Blas
Los Mochis
Gulf of California
Sierra de la Giganta
Loreto
Guasave
Guamúchil
M E
Bahía de La Paz
Navolato
Culiacán
Durango
Isla Magdalena
Isla Santa Margarita
El Dorado
La Paz
Tropic of Cancer
Santa Genoveva 7894ft (2406m)
Miraflores
Mazatlán
Escuinapa
PACIFIC OCEAN
Acaponeta
Islas Marías
Tepic
Puerto Vallarta
Manzan

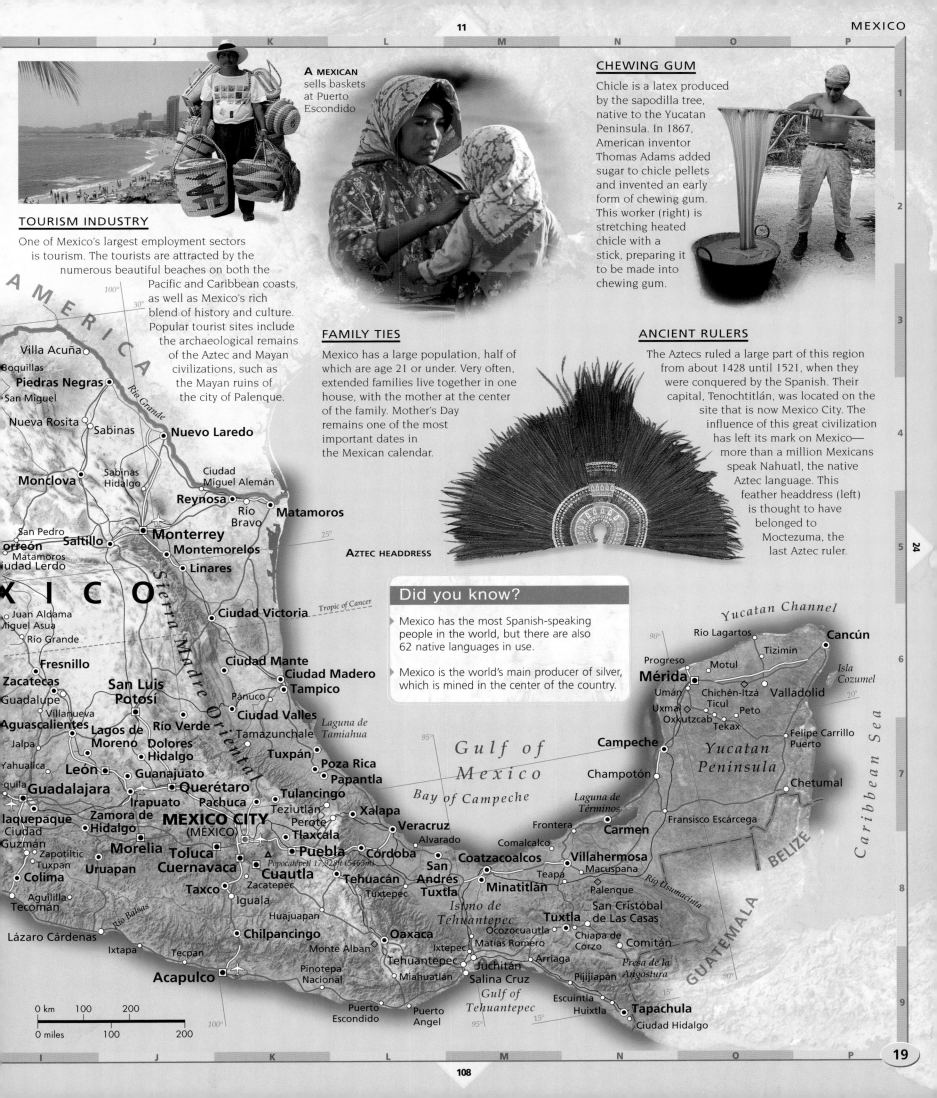

A MEXICAN sells baskets at Puerto Escondido

TOURISM INDUSTRY

One of Mexico's largest employment sectors is tourism. The tourists are attracted by the numerous beautiful beaches on both the Pacific and Caribbean coasts, as well as Mexico's rich blend of history and culture. Popular tourist sites include the archaeological remains of the Aztec and Mayan civilizations, such as the Mayan ruins of the city of Palenque.

CHEWING GUM

Chicle is a latex produced by the sapodilla tree, native to the Yucatan Peninsula. In 1867, American inventor Thomas Adams added sugar to chicle pellets and invented an early form of chewing gum. This worker (right) is stretching heated chicle with a stick, preparing it to be made into chewing gum.

FAMILY TIES

Mexico has a large population, half of which are age 21 or under. Very often, extended families live together in one house, with the mother at the center of the family. Mother's Day remains one of the most important dates in the Mexican calendar.

ANCIENT RULERS

The Aztecs ruled a large part of this region from about 1428 until 1521, when they were conquered by the Spanish. Their capital, Tenochtitlán, was located on the site that is now Mexico City. The influence of this great civilization has left its mark on Mexico—more than a million Mexicans speak Nahuatl, the native Aztec language. This feather headdress (left) is thought to have belonged to Moctezuma, the last Aztec ruler.

AZTEC HEADDRESS

Did you know?

▶ Mexico has the most Spanish-speaking people in the world, but there are also 62 native languages in use.

▶ Mexico is the world's main producer of silver, which is mined in the center of the country.

Map labels

AMERICA

Villa Acuña
Boquillas
Piedras Negras
San Miguel
Nueva Rosita
Sabinas
Nuevo Laredo
Monclova
Sabinas Hidalgo
Ciudad Miguel Alemán
Reynosa
Río Bravo
Matamoros
San Pedro
orreón
Saltillo
Monterrey
Matamoros
Ciudad Lerdo
Montemorelos
Linares
MEXICO
Sierra Madre Oriental
Juan Aldama
Miguel Asúa
Río Grande
Ciudad Victoria
Tropic of Cancer
Fresnillo
Zacatecas
Guadalupe
Villanueva
Aguascalientes
Lagos de Moreno
Jalpa
Río Verde
Dolores Hidalgo
Ciudad Mante
Ciudad Madero
Tampico
Pánuco
Ciudad Valles
Tamazunchale
Laguna de Tamiahua
Yahualica
León
Guanajuato
Tuxpán
aquila
Guadalajara
Querétaro
Poza Rica
Papantla
Irapuato
Pachuca
Tulancingo
Teziutlán
Xalapa
Laguna de Términos
laquepaque
Zamora de Hidalgo
MEXICO CITY (MÉXICO)
Perote
Veracruz
Frontera
Carmen
Fransisco Escárcega
Ciudad Guzmán
Morelia
Tlaxcala
Alvarado
Comalcalco
Villahermosa
Toluca
Cuernavaca
Puebla
Córdoba
Coatzacoalcos
Macuspana
Zapotiltic
Tuxpan
Cuautla
Popocatépetl 17,929 ft (5465 m)
Tehuacán
San Andrés Tuxtla
Teapa
Minatitlán
Palenque
Uruapan
Taxco
Zacatepec
Tuxtepec
Istmo de Tehuantepec
Colima
Aguililla
Tecomán
Iguala
San Cristóbal de Las Casas
Lázaro Cárdenas
Huajuapan
Chilpancingo
Oaxaca
Ocozocuautla
Chiapa de Corzo
Comitán
Ixtapa
Monte Alban
Ixtepec
Matías Romero
Tuxtla
Tecpan
Tehuantepec
Arriaga
Presa de la Angostura
Pinotepa Nacional
Miahuatlán
Juchitán
Pijijiapán
Acapulco
Salina Cruz
Escuintla
Gulf of Tehuantepec
Puerto Escondido
Puerto Angel
Huixtla
Tapachula
Ciudad Hidalgo

Río Grande
Río Bravo
Sierra Madre Oriental
Gulf of Mexico
Bay of Campeche
Laguna de Tamiahua
Río Balsas
Río Usumacinta
Yucatan Channel
Rio Lagartos
Tizimín
Cancún
Progreso
Motul
Isla Cozumel
Mérida
Chichén-Itzá
Valladolid
Umán
Ticul
Peto
Uxmal
Oxkutzcab
Tekax
Campeche
Yucatan Peninsula
Champotón
Chetumal
Felipe Carrillo Puerto
Caribbean Sea
BELIZE
GUATEMALA

0 km 100 200

0 miles 100 200

CENTRAL & SOUTH AMERICA

FROM THE VOLCANOES of Central America to the towering

Andes Mountains and vast grassy plains of South America,

this region offers a vast range of landscapes. South America is triangle-

shaped, tapering down from the warm Caribbean Sea

to the icy tip of Cape Horn. In the north lies the Amazon

rain forest, the largest tropical rain forest in the world. Some 420 million

people live in Central and South America, in 32 countries that vary in size

from small islands to the vast expanse of Brazil. The

languages, history, and cultures of this continent have

been shaped by colonization. The main influence has

been Spanish, which is still widely spoken. Portugal has

left its stamp on Brazil, while English, French, and Dutch influences remain

evident in several countries on the mainland and in the Caribbean.

Central America

VOLCANOES, EARTHQUAKES, and hurricanes threaten the livelihoods of people in the seven countries of Central America. People have also struggled with poverty and civil war. In more recent years, however, peace and economic recovery have offered hope, and education is now free in all countries. Remains of the ancient Mayan civilization that flourished until the 16th century when the Spanish invaded, can be seen throughout the region. Large numbers of the native population died after the invasion, mostly from disease. Today, Spanish is the main language of the region.

FAUNA AND FLORA

Ecotourism, which encourages visitors but aims to protect and preserve the environment, is increasingly important in the region. In Belize, tourists can dive in the clear, warm waters off the world's second-largest barrier reef, and there are wildlife treks to many forest areas. Animals include jaguars, howler monkeys, and butterflies.

TEMPLE PYRAMIDS

Between AD 250 and 900, the Maya designed ceremonial centers filled with temples, courts, and plazas. Without metal, they shaped tools from the solid lava of volcanoes to carve the limestone buildings. The largest site is at Tikal (left), in Guatemala, where temple remains lie in a huge area of tropical rain forest.

Pyramid has nine sloping terraces.

Steps lead up to the temple at the top.

Volcanic region

Central America is an unstable area because it lies along the meeting point of two of the Earth's tectonic plates. There are at least 14 active volcnoes here, including Volcán de Pacáya (left). Although this makes it a dangerous place to live, the volcanic soil is very fertile and good for crops.

DECORATED CHURCHES

The Spanish colonizers of the 1500s, and the missionaries who came with them, converted the native population and established Roman Catholicism throughout Central America. They also built many fabulously decorated churches. The one shown here, El Merced, is built in a low, "squat" style to resist the ever-present threat of earthquakes. The majority of people still follow the Roman Catholic faith.

Map labels

MEXICO

Corozal
Caledonia
Orange Walk
Indian Church
San Pedro
Altun Ha
Hill Bank
Belize City
Carmelita
Santa Elena
Tikal
San Ignacio
Flores
BELMOPAN
San Benito
BELIZE
Dangriga
La Libertad
Maya Mountains
Monkey River Town
Dolores
Sayaxché
San Antonio
San Luis
Punta Gorda
Gulf of Honduras
Islas de la Bahía
Roatán
Barillas
Chisec
Puerto Barrios
Puerto Cortés
Tela
La Ceiba
Irio
Trujillo
Limón
Jacaltenango
GUATEMALA
San Pedro Sula
Morales
El Progreso
Tocoa
Savá
Chajul
Nebaj
Cobán
Lago de Izabal
Los Amates
Yoro
La Unión
San Esteban
Gualaco
Huehuetenango
Rabinal
Salamá
Río Montagua
Gualán
HONDURAS
Catacam.
Santa Cruz del Quiché
Zacapa
Copán
Santa Rosa de Copán
Siguatepeque
Guaimaca
Juticalpa
Campamento
San Marcos
Quezaltenango
Chiquimula
Comayagua
Bo
GUATEMALA CITY
Volcán de Pacaya 8376ft (2553m)
Jutiapa
La Esperanza
TEGUCIGALPA
Danlí
Escuintla
Metapán
Chalatenango
Jalapa
San José
Santa Ana
Ahuachapán
SAN SALVADOR
San Vicente
San Miguel
Ocotal
Somoto
Condega
Sonsonate
EL SALVADOR
Usulután
Choluteca
Somotillo
Estelí
Jinoteg
Matag
Sébaco
Muy
Chinandega
Ciudad Darío
NICA
Corinto
Lago de Managua
Bo
León
Tipitap
MANAGUA
Masay
Grar
Jinotepe
Nandaime
Belén
Rivas
La Cru
PACIFIC OCEAN
Golfo de Papagayo
Li
Filade
N
Peníns de Nic

109

FOOD MARKETS

Coffee, bananas, and sugar cane are all key exports from here to the food markets of the world. Most are cultivated on large plantations. However, food for the local population, such as potatoes, avocados, rice, and corn, is grown on small farms and sold at local markets.

MARKETS, such as this one in Guatemala City, sell fresh fruit and vegetables.

NATIVE PEOPLES

These Cuna Indians of Panama wear traditional embroidered clothes. Native Indians and mestizos (people of mixed heritage) form a small minority in the region, although the ethnic mix varies from country to country. In Guatemala, more than half the people are direct descendants of the Maya Indians.

BANANA INDUSTRY

The hot, wet climate of Honduras is perfect for cultivating fruit, such as bananas. These are often grown on huge plantations, which employ local people who may work long hours for very little pay. Once cut down, the bananas are washed, inspected, and packed into boxes to be sent abroad. Bananas are a major export for Honduras.

As bananas grow, they begin to point upward.

COFFEE BEANS

Costa Rica was the first country in Central America to grow coffee and, today, produces more than 160,000 tons each year. Coffee is harvested from the fruit of the coffee bush. Once picked, the beans are left to dry in the sun. This worker is raking the beans as they dry.

PANAMA CANAL

Forming a vital link between the Atlantic and Pacific Oceans, the Panama Canal is one of the world's busiest waterways. After sharing the canal with the US, Panama took full control in 1999. Over the years, trade has made Panama City a major financial center.

Brus Laguna
Laguna de Caratasca
Río Patuca
Puerto Lempira
Río Coco
Cayos Miskitos
Waspam
Tuapi
Yablis
Puerto Cabezas
Bonanza
Siuna
Prinzapolka
La Sirena
Barra de Río Grande
Laguna de Perlas
Mosquito Coast
GUA
El Rama
Bluefields
go de icaragua
Punta Gorda
San Carlos
San Juan del Norte
Upala
Río San Juan
Bagaces
Cañas
Puerto Viejo
COSTA RICA
Quesada
Siquirres
10°
Alajuela
Heredia
SAN JOSÉ
Limón
Puntarenas
Cartago
Cerro Chirripó Grande 12,530ft (3819m)
olfo de Nicoya
Guabito
Almirante
Quepos
Buenos Aires
Cortés
Palmar Sur
Cordillera de Talamanca
Laguna de Chiriquí
Volcán Barú 11,401ft (3475m)
Boquete
Cordillera Central
La Concepción
David
Península de Osa
Golfo Dulce
Bahía de Coronado
85°
Golfo de Chiriquí
Guarumal
Santiago
Ocú
Península de Azuero
Isla Coiba
Isla Cébaco
80°
80°

Caribbean Sea
Panama Canal
Mosquito Gulf
Lago Gatún
Istmo de Panamá
Portobelo
El Porvenir
Colón
Cristóbal
Cordillera de San Blas
Ailigandí
Balboa
San Miguelito
PANAMA CITY
Chimán
Lago Bayano
Puerto Obaldía
Capira
La Palma
PANAMA
Pénonomé
Aguadulce
Archipiélago de las Perlas
Isla del Rey
Serranía del Darién
El Real
Garachiné
Yaviza
Chitré
Las Tablas
Gulf of Panama
Jaqué
Gulf of Darien
COLOMBIA

km 50 100 150 200
miles 50 100 150 200

The Caribbean

UNITED STATES OF AMERICA

THIS REGION CONSISTS of thousands of islands stretching from Cuba in the west to Trinidad and Tobago in the east. European colonists wanted control of the islands in the 1500s, but the diseases they brought wiped out most of the local Carib and Arawak peoples. African slaves, imported to work on plantations, replaced local peoples, and today most of the population are descended from those Africans. English, Spanish, and French are spoken in different countries, depending on which European power claimed the territory. Tourism and agriculture are major sources of employment.

CUBA

Cuba is the largest island and the only communist country in the region. It has a rich mix of people and customs. The Cuban government invested its money in improving social services, so the people benefit from a good health service and a high literacy rate. Children who complete pre-university education are awarded the *Bachillerato*.

CUBA specializes in making top-quality cigars.

JAMAICA

The Rastafarian religion began in Kingston, Jamaica, in the 1930s. Followers worship Haile Selassie, the former Emperor of Ethiopia (Ras Tafari), and believe that God will lead black people back to Ethiopia, the Promised Land. Jamaica is also home to reggae music, a rhythmic blend of African, European, and South American styles that can be heard across the island. The lyrics often tell of hardship and political struggle.

THE RASTAFARIAN religion forbids the cutting of hair.

Did you know?

▶ The Bahamas consists of hundreds of coral islands, but only about 40 of them are inhabited.

▶ The most densely populated country is Barbados.

▶ Steel bands, which use old oil drums as instruments, originated in Trinidad and Tobago.

▶ Rastafarians often wear red, green, and yellow because these are the colors of the Ethiopian flag.

CARIBBEAN CROPS

The semtropical climate here creates ideal conditions for many crops, especially sugar. The growing and processing of sugar is an important industry in Cuba, Jamaica, and many of the Lesser Antilles, providing jobs and income for the region. Fermented cane sugar is used to make rum and is a major export.

Map labels

Grand Bahama Island
Freeport
Marsh Harbour
Great Abaco
Bimini Islands
Berry Islands
Northeast Providence Channel
Nicholls Town
NASSAU
Eleuthera Island
New Providence
Rock Sound
Andros Town
Exuma Sound
Cat Island
Andros Island
Exuma Cays
San Salva
B A H A M A S
Anguilla Cays
George Town
Great Exuma Island
Rum Cay
Long Island
Archipiélago de Camagüey
Clarence Town
Croo
Islan
HAVANA (LA HABANA)
Guanabacoa
Artemisa
Cárdenas
Sagua la Grande
Crooked Island Passage
Pinar del Río
Matanzas
Santa Clara
Acklins Island
Consolación del Sur
Cienfuegos
Placetas
Mayaguana Passag
Nueva Gerona
Morón
Sancti Spíritus
Ciego de Ávila
C U B A
Ragged Island Range
Isla de la Juventud
Cayo Largo
Camagüey
Nuevitas
Archipiélago de los Canarreos
Bahía de Cochinos
Las Tunas
Holguín
Lake R
Matthew Town
Archipiélago de los Jardines de la Reina
Manzanillo
Bayamo
Guantánamo
Little Cayman
Cayman Brac
Palma Soriano
Santiago de Cuba
GEORGE TOWN
Grand Cayman
G r e a t e r
Guantánamo Bay (to US)
Windward
Île de la Go
CAYMAN ISLANDS (to UK)
Montego Bay
NAVASSA ISLAND (to US)
Jérémie
Spanish Town
Jamaica Channel
Cayes
JAMAICA
KINGSTON
C a r i b b e a n   S e a
Straits of Florida
Yucatan Channel
Tropic of Cancer

0 km 50 100 150 200
0 miles 50 100 150 200

Sugar cane
Breadfruit
Sweet potato
Papaya
Okra

Hurricanes

The Caribbean islands can be devastated by hurricanes between May and October each year. These powerful and damaging storms occur when a normal storm builds up energy as it moves across the Atlantic Ocean. Eventually, violent winds and torrential rain are released on the islands.

FAMILY LIFE

Family is very important here, and is usually the center of everyday life. Some Caribbean people migrate to other countries, such as the UK, but return when they retire—often bringing considerable money back with them.

TROPICAL ISLES

White sands and warm seas attract vast numbers of visitors to these islands. Tourism is important to the economies of many countries including the Bahamas and the Dominican Republic. Many people work in tourism-related jobs, such as in hotels.

HAITI

Haiti was the first Caribbean country to become independent. However, political unrest, combined with poor soils, have made Haiti one of the poorest countries in the world. Health care and sanitation levels are poor and, as a result, life expectancy is low.

HAITIAN MAN
selling flowers

A TIME TO CELEBRATE

The celebration of Divali (Hindu), Eid-ul-Fitr (Muslim), and Christmas (Christian) reflect the varied religions of people in Trinidad and Tobago. The woman above is dressed for Carnival in Port of Spain to mark the beginning of the Christian season of Lent.

Tropic of Cancer

Mayaguana

Caicos Passage

TURKS & CAICOS ISLANDS
(to UK)

COCKBURN TOWN

Little Inagua
Great Inagua

DOMINICAN REPUBLIC

Monte Cristi

Cap-Haïtien

Puerto Plata
Santiago

Gonaïves

HAITI
Cordillera Central

San Francisco de Macorís

La Vega

La Romana

Isla Saona

PORT-AU-PRINCE

SANTO DOMINGO

Mona Passage

Isla Mona

Isla Beata

Antilles

SAN JUAN

Caguas

Ponce

Mayagüez

PUERTO RICO
(to US)

St Croix

VIRGIN ISLANDS
(to US)

BRITISH VIRGIN ISLANDS
(to UK)

ROAD TOWN

CHARLOTTE AMALIE

ANGUILLA
(to UK)

THE VALLEY

Sint Maarten
(to Netherlands)

BASSETERRE

SAINT KITTS & NEVIS

MONTSERRAT
(to UK)

PLYMOUTH

ANTIGUA & BARBUDA

Barbuda

ST. JOHN'S
Antigua

GUADELOUPE
(to France)

Grande Terre

Pointe-à-Pitre

BASSE-TERRE
Basse-Terre

Marie-Galante

DOMINICA

ROSEAU

Martinique Passage

MARTINIQUE
(to France)

FORT-DE-FRANCE

St. Lucia Channel

ST. LUCIA

CASTRIES

Vieux Fort

Saint Vincent Passage

Saint Vincent

SAINT VINCENT & THE GRENADINES

KINGSTOWN

The Grenadines

BARBADOS

BRIDGETOWN

GRENADA

ST. GEORGE'S

ARUBA
(to Netherlands)

Lesser Antilles

NETHERLANDS ANTILLES
(to Netherlands)

ORANJESTAD

Curaçao

Bonaire

WILLEMSTAD

COLOMBIA

VENEZUELA

Tobago

TRINIDAD & TOBAGO

PORT-OF-SPAIN

Trinidad

Gulf of Paria

San Fernando

Leeward Islands

Lesser Antilles

Windward Islands

ATLANTIC OCEAN

Northwest South America

HIGH MOUNTAINS AND PLATEAUS, dense tropical rainforest, and coastal swamps are found in this region. In the 16th century, promises of untold riches attracted the Spanish to the countries here. They found the vast empire of the Incas, which stretched from what is now Peru into Northern Colombia. To the north and east, other colonizers arrived—Dutch, English, and French. Today, although the countries are independent (with the exception of French Guiana), Spanish remains the main language. The population is mainly a mix of native peoples and Europeans, except along the Caribbean coast, where descendants of former African slaves live.

ANDES MOUNTAINS

The Andes, the world's longest mountain chain, extends 4,505 miles (7,250 km) down the western edge of South America. Barley, wheat, and potatoes grow well in highland areas, and are cultivated on the terraced hillsides.

FRENCH GUIANA

French Guiana is the only remaining colony in South America, and is governed by France. Tropical forests cover more than four-fifths of its land. In 1968, the European Space Agency established a launch site on the coast at Kourou, which is still used today.

CARACAS

Venezuela's population is growing rapidly, and more than 87 percent of the people now live in cities. The oil industry brings in considerable wealth, but many people are still poor. Although Caracas (left), Venezuela's capital city, is an important financial center, it has many shantytowns.

Map labels

ATLANTIC OCEAN

CAYENNE
FRENCH GUIANA (to France)
PARAMARIBO
SURINAME
GEORGETOWN
GUYANA
CARACAS
VENEZUELA
COLOMBIA
BOGOTÁ
ECUADOR
QUITO
PACIFIC OCEAN
Caribbean Sea
PANAMA
BRAZILIAN HIGHLANDS
Guiana Highlands

ANGEL FALLS

Each year thousands of tourists visit the spectacular Angel Falls on the River Churún in eastern Venezuela. They were spotted by an American pilot, Jimmy Angel, in 1935, and later named after him. The water drops for 3,212 ft (979 m), making Angel Falls the highest uninterrupted waterfall in the world.

THE INCAS

The Incas first lived in the mountainous area near Cusco in Peru. By the time of the Spanish invasion, the Inca Empire extended north into southern Colombia and south through Bolivia and into Argentina and Chile. The Quechua Indians were the most powerful group in the empire, and theirs was the official language. The Quechua and Aymará peoples now live on the high plains in the Andes.

QUECHUA woman from Peru

LIFE ON THE HIGH PLAINS

The Altiplano is a cold plateau at high altitude between two ranges of the Andes Mountains in southwest Bolivia and southern Peru. The native peoples who live here graze sheep and llamas on the windy plains. They have generally retained their own language and customs.

MACHU PICCHU

The conquering Spaniards never found the remains of this important Inca city—it remained a secret until Hiram Bingham, an American archaeologist and explorer, discovered its ruins hidden in the forest in 1911. Situated on a high ridge northwest of Cusco, this magnificent ruined city covers 5 sq miles (13 sq km), and has small houses, temples, and stairways built around a central square.

MINERALS

Many countries in this area have extensive reserves of gold, silver, copper, and gems. Colombia produces more than half the world's emeralds. The Incas made good use of these resources and created many beautiful golden objects, such as this llama (below).

LAKE TITICACA

At 12,503 ft (3,812 m), Lake Titicaca is the highest navigable lake in the world. It is also South America's largest lake. The Uru people live here in houses built on huge, floating reed islands. They grow potatoes, hunt birds, and catch fish, using boats made from tightly bundled reeds (right).

Map labels:

Piura
Ferreñafe
Chiclayo
Chachapoyas · Tarapoto
Cajamarca
San Pedro de Lloc
Trujillo
Chimbote
Huaraz
Huarmey
Chiquián
Huánuco
Huacho
Callao
LIMA
Pisco
Ica
Nazca
Lomas
Camaná
Moquegua
Arequipa
Tacna
Puno
Juliaca
Ayaviri
Ayacucho
Cusco
Machu Picchu
Quillabamba
Puerto Maldonado
Cobija
Riberalta
Fortaleza
Reyes
Trinidad
Magdalena
Montero
Santa Cruz
San Matías
San José
Puerto Suárez
Buena Vista
Aiquile
SUCRE
Montero
Monteagudo
Tarija
Villazón
Tupiza
Villa Martín
Villa Uyuni
Sabaya
Uncía
Potosí
Oruro
Cochabamba
LA PAZ
Copacabana
Pucallpa
Aguaytía
Cerro de Pasco
Huancayo

PERU
BOLIVIA
BRAZIL
PARAGUAY
ARGENTINA
CHILE

Andes
Cordillera Occidental
Cordillera Oriental
Altiplano

Río Ucayali
Río Huallaga
Río Madre de Dios
Río Beni
Río Mamoré
Río Guaporé
Río San Miguel
Río Abuná

Lago Titicaca
Lago Poopó

PACIFIC OCEAN

Nevado Pupuja 19,088 ft (5818m)
Nevado Sajama 21,391 ft (6520m)
Nevado Ampato 20,702 ft (6310m)

Tropic of Capricorn

0 km 100 200 300 400
0 miles 100 200 300 400

Brazil

THE VIBRANT CULTURE OF BRAZIL—with its fusion of music and dance— reflects the rich mix of its ethnic groups. The country also boasts immense natural resources with well-developed mining and manufacturing industries. Brazil grows all its own food, and exports large quantities of coffee, sugar cane, soybeans, oranges, and cotton. However, the wealth is not evenly distributed, with some people living in luxury while most struggle with poverty. São Paulo is home to almost 10 million people, but poverty and lack of housing mean that many live in shantytowns without running water or sanitation. Brazil was colonized in the 16th century by the Portuguese, who established their language and their Roman Catholic faith. It remains a deeply Catholic country with a strong emphasis on family life.

COFFEE

Brazil produces about one-quarter of the world's coffee, which is grown on large plantations in the states of Parana and São Paulo. However, since world coffee prices go up and down so much, Brazilians are now growing other crops for export, as well.

VENEZUELA

COLOMBIA

Guiana Highland

Uraricoera

Boa Vista

Caracaraí

Roraima

Equator

Pico da Neblina
9888ft (3014m)

70°

Rio Negro

Rio Japurá

Represa
Balbina

Rio Içá

Manaus

Amazon

Tefé

Rio Juruá

Coari

Rio Javari

Rio Madeira

Amazon Basin

Humaitá

Japiim

Feijó

B **R**

Rio Purus

Acre

Rio Abunã

Porto Velho

70°

10°

BOLIVIA

Rondônia

Chapada dos Parecis

Guaporé

Vilhen

60°

20°

AMAZON RAIN FOREST

Covering more than one-third of Brazil, the rain forest is home to a huge variety of animal and plant life. At one time, more than 5 million native Indians also lived here, but now only about 200,000 remain. Over the years, vast areas of forest have been cut down to provide timber for export, to make way for farmland, or to mine minerals such as gold, silver, and iron. The Kaxinawa Indians, left, still cultivate root vegetables as a food crop.

THE BRAZILIAN MORPHO BUTTERFLY has brilliant blue wings and lives in rain forests from Brazil to Venezuela.

BRASÍLIA

Brasília became Brazil's new capital (after Rio de Janeiro) in 1960 as part of a plan to develop the interior. Situated on land that was once rain forest, the city is laid out in the shape of an airplane. Government buildings are in the "cockpit," residential areas are in the "wings."

PEOPLE OF BRAZIL

Brazilians come from a variety of different ethnic groups, including descendants of the original native Indians, the Portuguese colonizers, African slaves brought over to work in the sugar plantations, and European migrants.

SOCCER ENTHUSIASTS

Brazilians are passionate about soccer, which is played everywhere from beaches to shantytowns. There is fervent support for the national team, which has won the World Cup more times than any other country, most recently in 2002.

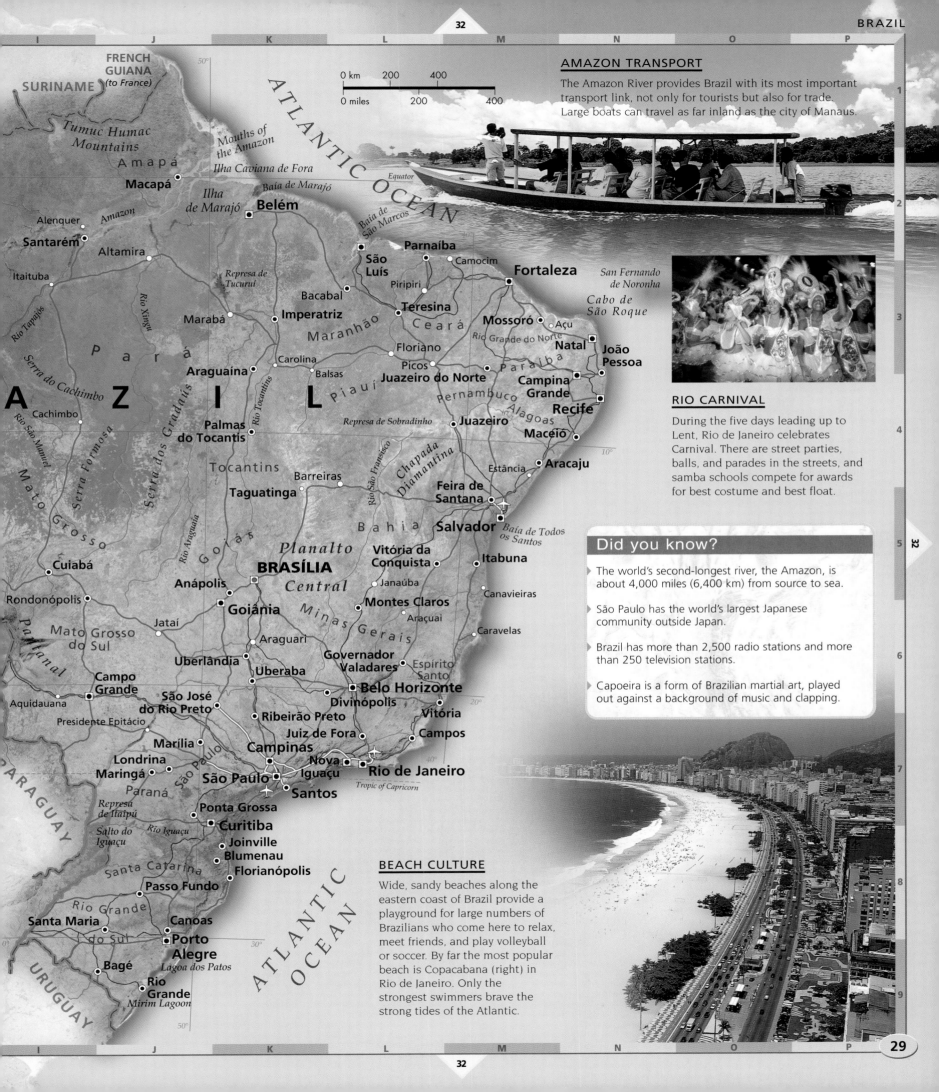

AMAZON TRANSPORT

The Amazon River provides Brazil with its most important transport link, not only for tourists but also for trade. Large boats can travel as far inland as the city of Manaus.

RIO CARNIVAL

During the five days leading up to Lent, Rio de Janeiro celebrates Carnival. There are street parties, balls, and parades in the streets, and samba schools compete for awards for best costume and best float.

Did you know?

- The world's second-longest river, the Amazon, is about 4,000 miles (6,400 km) from source to sea.

- São Paulo has the world's largest Japanese community outside Japan.

- Brazil has more than 2,500 radio stations and more than 250 television stations.

- Capoeira is a form of Brazilian martial art, played out against a background of music and clapping.

BEACH CULTURE

Wide, sandy beaches along the eastern coast of Brazil provide a playground for large numbers of Brazilians who come here to relax, meet friends, and play volleyball or soccer. By far the most popular beach is Copacabana (right) in Rio de Janeiro. Only the strongest swimmers brave the strong tides of the Atlantic.

Map labels:

FRENCH GUIANA
SURINAME
Tumuc Humac Mountains
Amapá
Macapá
Ilha de Marajó
Belém
Mouths of the Amazon
Ilha Caviana de Fora
Baía de Marajó
Baía de São Marcos
ATLANTIC OCEAN
Equator
Alenquer
Santarém
Altamira
Itaituba
Amazon
Rio Tapajós
Rio Xingu
Represa de Tucuruí
Marabá
Imperatriz
Bacabal
São Luís
Parnaíba
Camocim
Fortaleza
San Fernando de Noronha
Cabo de São Roque
Piripiri
Teresina
Ceará
Mossoró
Açu
Natal
João Pessoa
Araguaína
Carolina
Floriano
Balsas
Picos
Juazeiro do Norte
Rio Grande do Norte
Paraíba
Campina Grande
Recife
Pernambuco
PARÁ
Serra do Cachimbo
Cachimbo
Rio São Manuel
Serra Formosa
Serra dos Gradaís
BRAZIL
Palmas do Tocantis
Rio Tocantins
Represa de Sobradinho
Juazeiro
Alagoas
Maceió
Mato Grosso
Tocantins
Barreiras
Rio São Francisco
Chapada Diamantina
Estância
Aracaju
Taguatinga
Feira de Santana
Bahia
Salvador
Baía de Todos os Santos
Goiás
Planalto
BRASÍLIA
Central
Vitória da Conquista
Itabuna
Cuiabá
Anápolis
Janaúba
Canavieiras
Rondonópolis
Goiânia
Minas Gerais
Montes Claros
Araçuaí
Jataí
Mato Grosso do Sul
Araguari
Caravelas
Pantanal
Uberlândia
Uberaba
Governador Valadares
Espírito Santo
Aquidauana
Campo Grande
São José do Rio Preto
Belo Horizonte
Divinópolis
Vitória
Presidente Epitácio
Ribeirão Preto
Juiz de Fora
Campos
Marília
Campinas
Nova Iguaçu
Rio de Janeiro
Londrina
Maringá
São Paulo
Santos
Tropic of Capricorn
Paraná
Represa de Itaipú
Ponta Grossa
Salto do Iguaçu
Rio Iguaçu
Curitiba
Joinville
Blumenau
Santa Catarina
Florianópolis
Passo Fundo
Rio Grande do Sul
Santa Maria
Canoas
Porto Alegre
Bagé
Lagoa dos Patos
ATLANTIC OCEAN
URUGUAY
Rio Grande
Mirim Lagoon
PARAGUAY

0 km 200 400
0 miles 200 400

Southern South America

TOWERING MOUNTAINS, vast grassy plains, and hot deserts create a very diverse geographical landscape. The four countries in this region—Chile, Paraguay, Uruguay, and Argentina—were once Spanish colonies but gained their independence in the early 1800s. Each country has an elected government, but their economies remain fragile. Most of the population speak Spanish and are mestizo—of mixed Spanish and native Indian descent—except for Argentina, where 97 percent are descended from Europeans.

Atacama Desert

Sandwiched between the high Andes and the sea, the Atacama Desert in northern Chile is one of the hottest and driest areas in the world. Rain hardly ever falls here. This harsh landscape, however, is rich in copper deposits.

CHILEAN EDUCATION

Chile has the highest literacy rate (ability to read and write) in all of South America. Between the ages of 6 and 13, schooling is both free and compulsory.

MONTEVIDEO'S rich history shows in the mix of Colonial Spanish, Italian, and art deco styles of architecture.

URUGUAY'S CAPITAL

The capital of Uruguay, Montevideo, is home to nearly half the country's population. It is also the main port and economic center. This lively capital lies on the east bank of the Río de la Plata, and is a popular vacation resort because of its white sand beaches.

ITAIPÚ DAM

The enormous Itaipú dam on the Paraná River in Paraguay is one of the world's largest hydroelectric projects. It can generate all the electricity Paraguay needs, as well as large amounts for export.

Map labels

BRAZIL

BOLIVIA

PARAGUAY

Capitán Pablo Lagerenza
General Eugenio A. Garay
Mariscal Estigarribia
Fuerte Olimpo
Concepción
Pedro Juan Caballero
Coronel Oviedo
Ciudad del Este
Eldorado
Encarnación
Posadas
Rosario
Villarrica
Caazapá
Yuty
Pilar
San Juan Bautista
ASUNCIÓN
Formosa
Las Lomitas
Corrientes
Santo Tomé
Artigas
Rivera
Tacuarembó
URUGUAY
Salto
Paysandú
Mercedes
Melo
Chuy
BUENOS AIRES
La Plata
Florida
Trinidad
Dolores
Gualeguaychú
Zárate
Paraná
Rosario
Santa Fe
Concordia
Monte Caseros
Goya
Reconquista
Vera
Rafaela
Rio Salado
Añatuya
Metan
San Miguel de Tucumán
Santiago del Estero
Frías
Villa María
Río Cuarto
Córdoba
Villa Mercedes
San Luis
Villa Dolores
Jesús María
Deán Funes
La Rioja
San Fernando del Valle de Catamarca
San Salvador de Jujuy
Salta
La Quiaca
Cafayate
Nevado de Chañi 20,341ft (6200m)
Cerro Galán 21,654ft (6600m)
San Ramón de la Nueva Orán
BRAZIL
Mar Chiquita
Laguna
Pergamino
Junín
Rufino
Realicó
Mendoza
Godoy Cruz
SANTIAGO
Rancagua
San Rafael
San Juan
Cerro Aconcagua 22,831ft (6960m)
Cerro Ojos del Salado 22,572ft (6880m)
Valparaíso
Viña del Mar
San Antonio
La Ligua
Salamanca
Illapel
Ovalle
La Serena
Coquimbo
Vallenar
Copiapó
Caldera
Chañaral
Taltal
Antofagasta
Mejillones
Tocopilla
Calama
Chuquicamata
Monte Patria
Domeyko
La Galera
Pichilemu
Curicó
CHILE
ANDES
Cordillera Occidental
Atacama Desert
PERU
Arica
Iquique
Lagunas
Río Bermejo
Pilcomayo
Paraguay
Paraná
Uruguay
Río Negro
Mirim Lagoon
Tropic of Capricorn

DANCING THE TANGO

Popular around the world today, the tango originated in the slums of Buenos Aires in the late 1800s. This passionate dance with its characteristic rhythm is accompanied by music on a type of concertina known as a *bandoneon*, together with piano and violin.

Did you know?

▶ The national drink in South America is *mate*. This healthy tea is made from a bitter herb, and drinking it with friends is a daily custom for most people.

▶ Across the region, four out of every five people live in cities.

▶ Chile has the largest concentration of astronomical observatories in the world because of its exceptionally clear skies.

BUENOS AIRES

More than one-third of Argentina's population lives in or around the capital, Buenos Aires. A thriving port on the Plate River estuary, it is the largest city in Argentina. The colourful La Boca district (above) with its painted walls is home to the descendants of Italian immigrants.

A GAUCHO herds cattle in the Pampas region.

PAMPAS

Vast, treeless plains called the Pampas—which means "flat" in Spanish—cover much of southern and western Argentina. The Pampas are used to grow cereals and raise cattle. Gauchos, Argentinian cowboys, work on large ranches, or *estancias*.

WINES FROM CHILE

About 90 percent of Chileans live in the central region, where the rich soil is ideal for a wide range of agriculture. Vines were brought to Chile by the Spaniards, and the country now has an important wine-making industry that exports wine all over the world.

0 km 200 400
0 miles 200 400

ANDES MOUNTAIN WEATHER

The Andes stretch the entire length of South America, and this has a major effect on the weather. As westerly air from the Pacific Ocean rises over the mountains, its moisture can fall as rain and snow. By the time it reaches the eastern side, the air is much drier and the landscape is more arid.

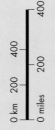

Map labels

ARGENTINA
CHILE

ATLANTIC OCEAN
PACIFIC OCEAN

Talcahuano, Chillán, Concepción, Los Ángeles, Lebu, Temuco, Loncoche, Valdivia, Osorno, Puerto Varas, Puerto Montt, Ancud, Castro, Isla de Chiloé

Santa Rosa, Olavarría, Azul, Tandil, Tres Arroyos, Balcarce, Coronel Dorrego, Necochea, **Mar del Plata**, Bahía Blanca, Punta Alta, Choele Choel, San Antonio Oeste, Viedma, Bahía Blanca, Rawson, Golfo San Matías, Península Valdés, Golfo Nuevo, Trelew

Neuquén, Zapala, Cipolletti, Río Colorado, Río Negro, San Carlos de Bariloche, Lago Nahuel Huapi, Maquinchao, Esquel, Paso de Indios, Río Chubit, Lago Musters, Sarmiento, Comodoro Rivadavia, Golfo San Jorge, Caleta Olivia, Puerto Deseado, Río Deseado

Coihaique, Puerto Aisén, Chile Chico, Cochrane, Lago Buenos Aires, Perito Moreno, Río Chico, Puerto San Julián, Bahía Grande

Río Gallegos, El Calafate, Río Santa Cruz, Puerto Natales, Punta Arenas, Porvenir, Tierra del Fuego, Ushuaia, Strait of Magellan, Isla de los Estados, Beagle Channel, Cape Horn (Cabo de Hornos)

Golfo Corcovado, Archipiélago de los Chonos, Golfo de Penas, Isla Wellington, Cerro San Valentín 13,314 ft (4058 m), Cerro Murallón 11,900 ft (3630 m), Cerro Paine 8,000 ft (2438 m)

Patagonia

Atlantic Ocean

THE WORLD'S SECOND-LARGEST OCEAN, the Atlantic covers one-fifth of the Earth's surface. It separates the Americas from Europe and Africa. The world's youngest ocean, the Atlantic started to form about 180 million years ago, as the continental plates began to separate. This movement continues today, as the oceanic plates that meet at the Mid-Atlantic Ridge continue to pull apart. The Atlantic is a major source of fish, but due to overfishing, stocks are now low. Many shipping routes cross the Atlantic, and pollution is an international problem as ships dump chemicals and waste. There are substantial reserves of oil and gas in the Gulf of Mexico, off the coast of West Africa, and in the North Atlantic.

GREENLAND

Fishing for halibut

The largest island in the world, Greenland is a self-governing part of Denmark. Most Greenlanders live on the southwest coast. Mainly Inuit, with some Danish-Norwegian influences, they make their living by seal hunting, fishing, and fur trapping.

TOURISM

The volcanic islands and black beaches of the eastern Atlantic, especially the Canaries (left), Madeira, and the Azores, are popular with tourists, who are attracted by the scenery and subtropical climate.

Warm currents

The Gulf Stream flows up the east coast of North America and across the Atlantic. It brings warm water and a mild climate to northern Europe, which would otherwise be cooler.

MID-ATLANTIC RIDGE

Tristan da Cunha island

At the center of the ridge is a valley at least 10 miles (16 km) wide.

UNDERWATER MOUNTAINS

The Mid-Atlantic Ridge is a great underwater mountain chain that runs the entire length of the Atlantic. It was formed by magma that oozed up from the seabed, cooled to create solid rock, and gradually built up to form a ridge. Some peaks are so high that they break the surface to form volcanic islands such as the country of Iceland.

ATLANTIC FISHING INDUSTRY

The Atlantic Ocean contains more than half the world's total stock of fish. Herring, anchovy, sardine, cod, flounder, and tuna are among the most important fish found here. However, overfishing, particularly of species such as cod and tuna, has caused a significant decline in numbers.

WHALES

Humpback whale breaching

Many whales live in the Atlantic, migrating from summer feeding grounds in the cold polar regions to warmer waters in the Caribbean for the winter. They give birth and mate again before returning north.

FALKLANDS

Set in the windy South Atlantic off the coast of Argentina, the Falkland Islands belong to the UK but are also claimed by Argentina. Fishing and sheep farming are important. The land is rocky, mountainous, boggy, and almost treeless.

NORTH AMERICA

BERMUD (to

Gulf of Mexico

Hatteras Plain

Greater Antilles

Puerto R Trench

Caribbean Sea

Guatemala Basin

Colombian Basin

Lesser Ant

Panama Basin

Galapagos Islands (to Ecuador)

SOUTH

Peru-Chile Trench

Peru Basin

A n d e s

PACIFIC OCEAN

Peru-Chile Trench

Chile

Chile Basin

Chile Rise

GREENLAND
(to Denmark)

Labrador
Sea

Denmark Strait

ICELAND

REYKJAVIK   FAEROE ISLANDS
(to Denmark)

Reykjanes   *Iceland*
Basin   *Basin*

Labrador   *Rockall Bank*   *North*
Basin   *Sea*   *Baltic Sea*

Charlie-Gibbs Fracture Zone   *British*
                                     Isles   EUROPE

Newfoundland   *Bay of*   *Alps*
Grand Banks of   *Biscay*
Newfoundland   *Mediterranean Sea*

Newfoundland
Basin   *Azores*
                   (to Portugal)

Bermuda   *East Azores Fracture Zone*   *Atlas Mountains*
Rise
Sohm   *Madeira*
Plain   (to Portugal)
                   Great Meteor   *Canary Islands*
                   Tablemount   (to Spain)   S a h a r a

Sargasso   *Madeira*
Sea   *Plain*

Kane Fracture Zone   *Cape Verde*   S a h e l
                        Basin
                                     Cape Verde
Demerara   *Plain*
Plain   ATLANTIC   PRAIA   AFRICA
                                   CAPE
                                   VERDE

Amazon   OCEAN   *Doldrums Fracture Zone*   *Sierra*
Fan   *Leone*   *Sierra*
                                                   Rise   *Leone*
                                                                 Basin

Ceará Plain   *Guinea*   *Gulf of*
                                                   Basin   *Guinea*
                                    M i d
AMERICA   *Fernando de*   *Ascension Fracture Zone*
                   Noronha   *Pernambuco*
                   (to Brazil)   *Plain*
                                                   ASCENSION ISLAND
                                                   (to St Helena)
                   Brazil
                   Basin   A t l a n t i c   *Angola*
                                                                                 Basin
                                                   ST HELENA
                                                   (to UK)

                   Vitória   *Ilha da*   *Zubov*
                   Seamount   *Trindade*   *Seamount*
                                    (to Brazil)
                                                                 Walvis Ridge
                                    R i d g e
                   Rio Grande   *Cape*
                   Rise   *Basin*
                                                                 Orange Fan   *Cape of*
                                                                                      Good Hope
                                                   TRISTAN DA CUNHA
Argentine   (to St Helena)
Basin   *Gough Island*
Gulf of San Matias   (to Tristan da Cunha)
                                    Gough Fracture Zone
Gulf of San Jorge
                   Zapiola Ridge
FALKLAND ISLANDS   BOUVET
(to UK)   *Scotia*   SOUTH SANDWICH ISLAND
                   Sea   ISLANDS   (to Norway)
Cape   SOUTH GEORGIA   (to UK)
Horn   (to UK)
        Drake Passage   SOUTHERN OCEAN

                   East Scotia
                   Basin

THE MINERAL-RICH
waters of Iceland's
Blue Lagoon are
said to be
beneficial to
people's health.

ICELAND

Iceland is situated in the North Atlantic on
the Mid-Atlantic Ridge. As a result, it has at
least 20 active volcanoes and suffers
frequent earthquakes. There are
numerous thermal springs with boiling
mud lakes and geysers. Water from hot
springs (above) is used to provide hot
water and heating for much of
Iceland's population, most of whom
live on the coast. The warm Gulf
Stream ensures that the country's
ports stay ice-free in winter.

Did you know?

▸ Iceland has fewer people per
square mile (kilometer) than
any other country in Europe.

▸ The Atlantic is the most
polluted ocean in the world.

ICEBERGS

Icebergs in the Atlantic Ocean are
formed as ice sheets and glaciers
reach the sea. Parts break off and start
to drift, driven by winds and currents.

AFRICA

THE SECOND-LARGEST CONTINENT after Asia, Africa has plenty of record-breakers.

The Sahara is the world's largest desert, the Nile its longest river, Lake

Victoria its second-largest freshwater lake, and the Congo

river basin its second largest tropical rain forest. The

people of Africa are culturally and religiously diverse—those north of the

 Sahara are mainly Muslim, while people in the south follow

a variety of religions, including Christianity. With a rapidly

growing population of 793 million, spread across 52 countries, Africa also

contains some of the world's poorest countries. Many

economies depend heavily on exporting one crop or

product, and if prices fall, the country becomes poorer. Most people live on

 the land and are vulnerable to drought, floods, and famine,

with limited access to clean drinking water. However,

growing number of people are moving to cities in search of a better life

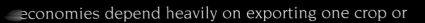

Northwest Africa

FOUR COUNTRIES, PLUS THE DISPUTED area of Western Sahara, make up this part of Africa. Algeria, Libya, and Tunisia have rich supplies of oil and natural gas that boost their economies. Morocco relies on tourism, phosphates used for chemicals and fertilizer, and agriculture. In the fertile valleys of the Atlas Mountains, farmers grow grapes, citrus fruit, dates, and olives. The area also attracts tourists to its colorful markets, historical sites, and sandy beaches. The Sahara Desert dominates the region, particularly in Algeria and Libya.

SUN AND SEA

Many tourists visit Tunisia and Morocco each year to enjoy the warm climate and sandy beaches. Tourism provides jobs for the local people and brings much-needed income.

ARAB INFLUENCE

Arab invasions during the 7th and 11th centuries have influenced the culture, religion (Islam), architecture, and language of northwest Africa. Today, Arabic is the main language, and more than 95 percent of the people are Muslim.

MOROCCAN MARKET

In a *souk*, or market, craftworkers sell handmade products to tourists. Goods are displayed in booths along the bustling streets.

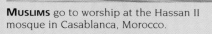

MUSLIMS go to worship at the Hassan II mosque in Casablanca, Morocco.

BERBERS

The Berber people were the original inhabitants of northwest Africa. Most now live in the Atlas Mountains or the desert. Although most Berbers converted to Islam when the Arabs arrived, they kept their own language and way of life. In 2001, Algeria recognized Berber as an official language.

ATLANTIC OCEAN

Strait of Gibraltar

GIBRALTAR (to UK)
Ceuta (to Spain)
Tangier
Ksar-el-Kebir
Tetouan
Chefchaouen
Melilla (to Spain)
Salé
Kénitra
RABAT
Casablanca
Fès
Mohammedia
El-Jadida
Oujda
Tlemcen
Jerada
Djelfa
Safi
Khouribga
Beni-Mellal
Essaouira
Marrakech
Atlas Mountains
MOROCCO
Er-Rachidia
Figuig
Béchar
Ouarzazate
Agadir
Tiznit

Tizi Ouzou
ALGIERS (ALGER)
Chlef
Blida
Oran
Mostaganem
Sidi Bel Abbès
Hauts Plateaux
Chott ech Chergui
Laghoua
Ghardaïa

Grand Erg Occidental
El Goléa

Tan-Tan
Hamada du Dra
ALGE
Plateau du Tademaït

LAÂYOUNE
El Mahbas
Tindouf
Adrar
I-n-Salah
Boujdour
Smara
Bou Craa
Reggane

Galtat-Zemmour
Erg Iguîdi
MAURITANIA

WESTERN SAHARA
(disputed territory under Moroccan occupation)

Ad Dakhla

Erg Chech
S a

Tropic of Cancer

Tanezrouft

Lagouira

A BERBER WOMAN works on the land in the Atlas Mountains.

MALI

DATE PALMS

Dates are an important crop for Algeria and Tunisia. Date palms are often grown at oases, where water lies close to the surface of the desert. Here the clusters of dates are shown ripening beneath polythene. Leaves from the trees can be used for thatch, and the trunk is cut for timber.

ANCIENT RUINS

Phoenicians, Romans, and Greeks from ancient times have all left their mark on this part of Africa. Today, tourists come to admire the historical sites along the coast. These ruins at Carthage, near Tunis, date from the 9th century BC, when the Romans controlled the whole north African coast.

RUINS OF A ROMAN BATH AT CARTHAGE

Did you know?

▶ The stones from dates can be roasted and ground to make a traditional date coffee.

▶ Since Spain gave up control of Western Sahara in 1976, Morocco has been fighting a guerrilla group of desert tribesmen for control of the area.

Map labels

Mediterranean Sea

Bizerte
Annaba
Carthage
étif
TUNIS
Constantine
Sousse
Kairouan
Batna
Kasserine
Mahdia
iskra
Chott Melghir
Gafsa
Sfax
Golfe de Gabès
Tozeur
Gabès
Île de Jerba
Chott el Jerid
Médenine
El Oued
Zuwārah
TRIPOLI (ṬARĀBULUS)
Al Bayḍā'
Darnah
Touggourt
TUNISIA
Az Zāwiyah
Al Khums
Al Marj
Ṭubruq
Ouargla
Nālūt
Yafran
Gharyān
Miṣrātah
Benghazi (Banghāzī)
Al Jabal al Akhḍar
Surt
Gulf of Sirte (Khalīj Surt)
Ajdābiyā
Wādī al Ḥamīm
Marsā al Burayqah
Al Jaghbūb
Grand Erg Oriental
Marādah
Jālū
Great Sand Sea
A
Waddān
Bordj Omar Driss
Tiguentourine
Birāk
Sabhā
Ramlat Rabyānah
L I B Y A
Awbārī
Libyan
Zawīlah
Tassili-n-Ajjer
Al 'Uwaynāt
Al Khufrah
Desert
Tropic of Cancer
h
Djanet
a
Idhán Murzuq
r
a
Ahaggar
Tahat 9573ft (2918m)
Pic Bette 7500ft (2286m)
Tamanrasset
NIGER
CHAD
SUDAN
EGYPT

SURVIVAL IN THE SAHARA

The Sahara Desert covers almost one-third of Africa and is an inhospitable place to live, with high daytime temperatures and freezing nights. The Tuareg are nomads for whom the desert is home. Traditionally, they keep camels for transport, and to provide meat, milk, and hides. Many Tuareg now live in the cities.

TUAREG NOMADS in the Sahara carry salt to trade in markets.

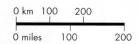

0 km 100 200
0 miles 100 200

LIBYAN OIL FIELD

LIBYAN OIL RESOURCES

The discovery of oil and gas in 1959 brought considerable wealth to Libya and currently makes up 99 percent of the country's exports. As a result, Libya's cities have grown as people have moved from rural areas to find work in the oil industry. Some of the money from oil is being spent on better health care and education for Libyans.

Northeast Africa

THIS REGION, KNOWN AS THE HORN of Africa, contains the oldest civilizations on the continent, and some of its poorest countries. The borders that divide the countries today were mostly created by colonial rulers in the last hundred years. Pastoral nomads with their herds of animals often cross these borders in search of pasture. Most people still live in the countryside and farm the land, but increasing numbers are moving to cities. Tourism and agriculture are important sources of income for Egypt and Kenya, two of the richest and fastest-growing countries in the region. Elsewhere, tribal rivalries and disputes over land and resources have sometimes erupted into full-scale war, which, together with drought and poverty, has blighted the lives of millions of people in this region.

NILE RIVER

The Nile is the world's longest river. It flows north from Burundi to run along the Tanzania–Rwanda border, then through Uganda, Sudan, and Egypt to the coast. Most of Egypt's population lives around the valley and delta of the Nile, which provides the region's water. The river also provides irrigation for local crops, such as cotton.

SUEZ CANAL

The Suez Canal is one of the world's longest and most important artificial waterways. It links the Mediterranean Sea with the Gulf of Suez and the Red Sea, providing a crucial shortcut from Europe to India and East Asia. The tolls from the canal are a great source of income for Egypt.

LOSING FARMLAND

As the population grows in Ethiopia, more and more people cut down forests for firewood, or to cultivate new areas for food crops. The soil, no longer held firm by the trees, is easily blown or washed away, and valuable farmland is lost.

PLOWING FIELDS IN ETHIOPIA

ABU SIMBEL

Tourists come to Egypt to see the pyramids at Giza and the temples along the Nile, such as these two built at Abu Simbel, south of Aswan. Tourism brings in money to preserve these historical sites.

Mediterranean Sea

Red Sea

Gulf of Aden

Nubian Desert

Sahara el Gharbiya (Western Desert)

Great Sand Sea

Gilf Kebir Plateau

E G Y P T

S U D A N

LIBYA

CHAD

Darfur

ERITREA

DJIBOUTI

Danakil Desert

Tropic of Cancer

Alexandria
El'Alamein
Port Said
Dumyât
Zagazig
El Giza
CAIRO
Ismâ'ilîya
Suez
Sinai
Beni Suef
El Minya
Mallawi
Asyût
Sohâg
Akhmîm
Qena
Luxor
Isna
Idfu
Aswân
Lake Nasser
Aswan Dam
El Khârga
Farâfra
Qasr
Bawiti
Siwa
Sidi Barrâni
Qattara Depression

Hurghada
Port Sudan
Suakin
Tokar
Massawa
Zula
ASMARA
Teseney
Gonder
Mekelê
Mây Ch'ew
Laîbela
Gedaref
Kassala
Khashm el Girba
Haîya
Atbara
Ed Damer
Shendi
Abu Hamed
Shereik
Akasha
Delgo
Argo
Merowe
Dongola
Ed Debba
Umm Ruwaba
El Obeid
Sodiri
El'Atrun
Wadi Halfa
Omdurman
KHARTOUM
Wad Medani
Sennar
Blue Nile
El Fasher
El Geneina
Kebkabiya
Nyala
Umm Buru

(administered by Sudan)
(administered by Egypt)

0 km 100 200 300 400
0 miles 100 200 300 400

INDIAN OCEAN

SOMALIA

ETHIOPIA

KENYA

UGANDA

TANZANIA

RWANDA

BURUNDI

DEM. REP. CONGO

CENTRAL AFRICAN REPUBLIC

ZAMBIA

MALAWI

MOZAMBIQUE

Did you know?

The Masai tribe lives on the borders of Kenya and Tanzania. Between the ages of 14 and 30, young Masai men live in the bush and learn how to become great warriors.

Water makes up almost one-fifth of the surface area of Uganda.

CHRISTIANITY

The Ethiopian Orthodox Union Church has been in existence since the 4th century AD. It is a branch of the Coptic Church, and mixes some Christian beliefs, such as Catholic saints, with some traditional African spiritual beliefs.

COPTIC CROSS

TEA IN KENYA

Kenya is an important world producer of tea, which is grown on plantations in the highland areas (such as this one below). High rainfall here ensures a good crop. Coffee is also a valuable export.

KENYAN workers carefully select tea leaves for picking.

CAIRO

The largest city in Africa is Cairo, the capital of Egypt. The city has a population of nearly seven million. Here, Arab, African, and European influences exist alongside more traditional Egyptian customs.

BUSY STREET bazaar in Cairo

SUDANESE DINKA

There are more than 500 different tribes in Sudan, who speak over 100 languages and dialects. Like many tribal people here, the Dinka are nomadic—their cattle graze on the plains east of the Nile. Cattle are central to their lives—young Dinka men officially become adults with an initiation ceremony in which they are given an ox of their own.

YOUNG DINKA MAN

GORILLAS

The Volcanoes National Park in Rwanda is one of the few places where you can still see a mountain gorilla (right) in the wild. These animals are threatened with extinction because of poachers and the destruction of their habitat. Tanzania and Kenya also have many important game reserves, which preserve the wildlife of the savanna.

West Africa

0 km 100 200 300 400

0 miles 100 200 300 400

DRAMATICALLY DIFFERENT CLIMATES and landscapes influence life in West Africa. In the hot, dry, northern areas of the Sahara and Sahel, it is extremely difficult to grow crops. To the south, the climate is warm and wet, and crops such as cocoa and coffee are grown on large plantations. The region also has many valuable minerals. Despite these rich resources, most countries are very poor. Since independence from colonial powers, there has been much political unrest, often sparked by poverty and tribal rivalries in the region. West Africa is also divided by religion, with Islam dominant in the north and Christianity in the south.

GAMBIA

In recent years, tourism has become increasingly important to the economy of Gambia. Visitors come to see wildlife along the Gambia River and to visit the Atlantic coast beaches. These safari tourists are admiring a giant termite mound.

PEOPLE OF GHANA

Family ties and a sense of community are important to the people of Ghana, and ceremonies throughout each year mark the events of childbirth, puberty, marriage, and death. About half of Ghanaians are Ashanti people whose ancestors developed one of the richest and most notable civilizations in Africa.

DIAMONDS AND GOLD

West Africa has many valuable minerals, including diamonds, uranium, copper, and gold. In Sierra Leone, where diamonds (left) provide crucial income, the mines were a focu of fighting in the civil war between rebel groups and the government

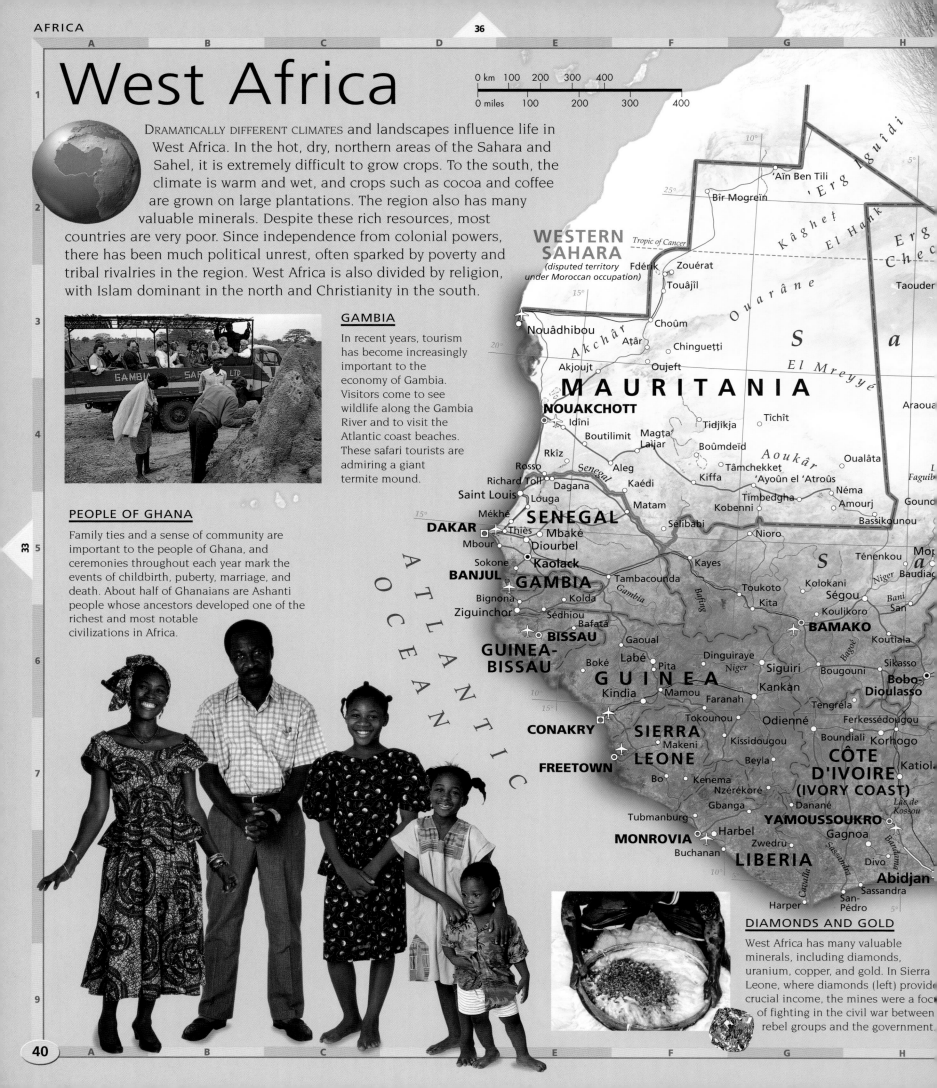

WESTERN SAHARA
(disputed territory under Moroccan occupation)

'Aïn Ben Tili
Bîr Mogreïn
Fdérik · Zouérat
Touâjîl
Taouder

'Erg Aguïdi
Kâghet
El Hank
Erg
Chec

MAURITANIA

S   a

Nouâdhibou
Choûm
Atâr
Chinguetti
Akjoujt
Oujeft
Ouarâne
El Mreyyé
Tîchît
Araoua

NOUAKCHOTT
Idîni
Boutilimit
Magta'Lajar
Tidjikja
Boûmdeïd
Aoukâr
Oualâta
Faguib

Rkîz
Rosso
Aleg
Tâmchekket
'Ayoûn el 'Atroûs
Néma
Gound

Richard Toll
Dagana
Senegal
Kaédi
Kiffa
Amourj

Saint Louis
Louga
Matam
Timbedgha
Kobenni
Bassikounou

Mékhé
SENEGAL
Sélibabi
Nioro
Ténénkou
Mo
a

DAKAR
Thiès · Mbaké
Kayes
S
Baudia

Mbour
Diourbel
Kolokani
Niger

Sokone
Kaolack
Koulikoro
Ségou
Bani
San

BANJUL
GAMBIA
Tambacounda
Toukoto
Kita

Bignona
Kolda
Gambia
BAMAKO

Ziguinchor
Sédhiou
Bafatá
Koutiala

BISSAU
Gaoual
Labé · Pita
Dinguiraye
Sikasso

GUINEA-BISSAU
Boké
Niger
Siguiri
Bougouni
Bobo-Dioulasso

GUINEA
Kindia · Mamou
Kankan

Kissidougou
Boundiali
Korhogo

CONAKRY
Tokounou
Odienné
Ferkessédougou

Makeni
SIERRA LEONE
Beyla
CÔTE D'IVOIRE (IVORY COAST)
Katiola

FREETOWN
Bo · Kenema
Nzérékoré
Danané
Luc de Kossou

Gbanga
YAMOUSSOUKRO
Gagnoa

Tubmanburg
MONROVIA
Harbel
Zwedru
Divo

Buchanan
LIBERIA
Abidjan

Harper
San-Pédro
Sassandra

ATLANTIC OCEAN

Tropic of Cancer

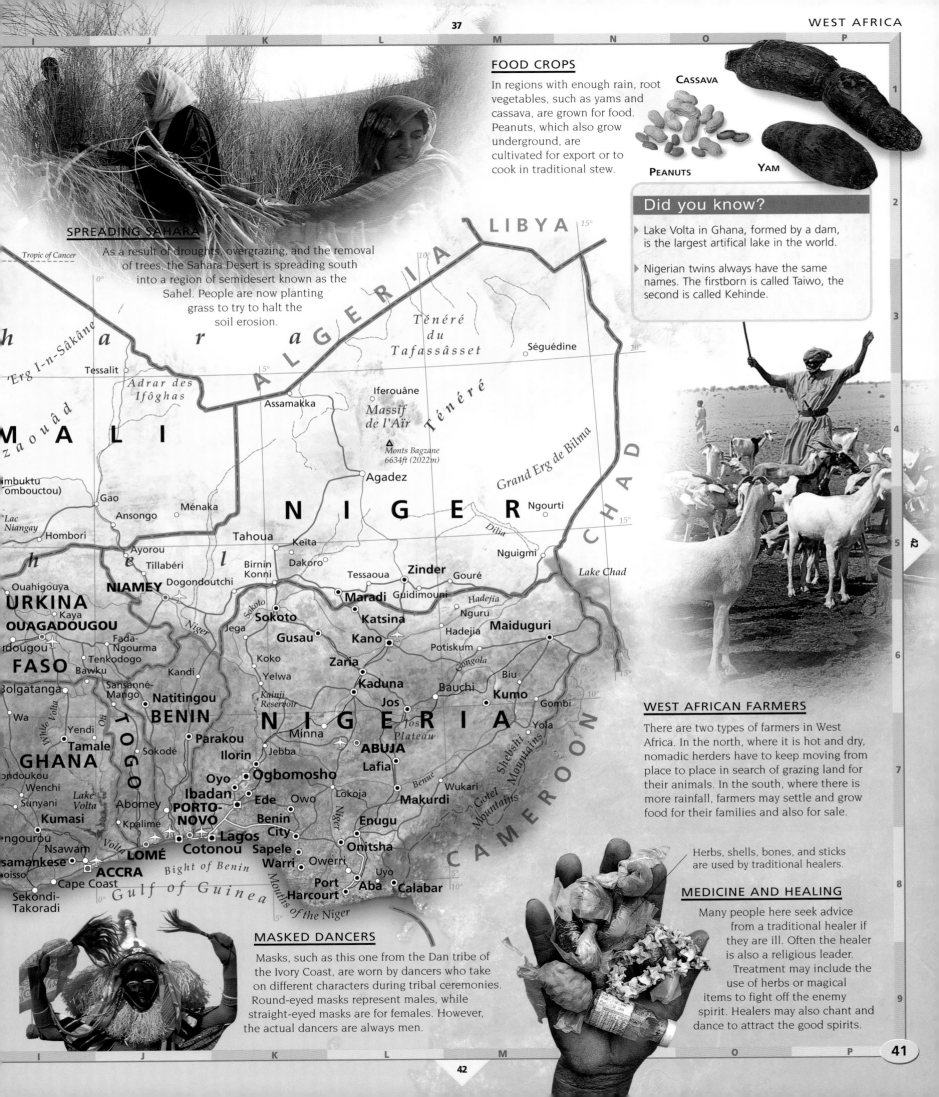

FOOD CROPS

In regions with enough rain, root vegetables, such as yams and cassava, are grown for food. Peanuts, which also grow underground, are cultivated for export or to cook in traditional stew.

CASSAVA

PEANUTS

YAM

Did you know?

▶ Lake Volta in Ghana, formed by a dam, is the largest artifical lake in the world.

▶ Nigerian twins always have the same names. The firstborn is called Taiwo, the second is called Kehinde.

SPREADING SAHARA

As a result of droughts, overgrazing, and the removal of trees, the Sahara Desert is spreading south into a region of semidesert known as the Sahel. People are now planting grass to try to halt the soil erosion.

WEST AFRICAN FARMERS

There are two types of farmers in West Africa. In the north, where it is hot and dry, nomadic herders have to keep moving from place to place in search of grazing land for their animals. In the south, where there is more rainfall, farmers may settle and grow food for their families and also for sale.

Herbs, shells, bones, and sticks are used by traditional healers.

MEDICINE AND HEALING

Many people here seek advice from a traditional healer if they are ill. Often the healer is also a religious leader. Treatment may include the use of herbs or magical items to fight off the enemy spirit. Healers may also chant and dance to attract the good spirits.

MASKED DANCERS

Masks, such as this one from the Dan tribe of the Ivory Coast, are worn by dancers who take on different characters during tribal ceremonies. Round-eyed masks represent males, while straight-eyed masks are for females. However, the actual dancers are always men.

Central Africa

ALL EIGHT COUNTRIES IN Central Africa were European colonies with a painful history of slavery. Since the 1960s, independence has brought them mixed success. Rich mineral deposits and the discovery of offshore oil have provided income for Cameroon, Congo, and Gabon, while civil war and repressive governments have damaged other countries in the region. These include Chad and the Central African Republic, two of the world's poorest countries. Although the north is mainly arid, Africa's largest tropical rain forest dominates the south, with the powerful Congo River linking the interior with the coast. The tiny, volcanic country of Sao Tome and Principe lies off the coast of Gabon.

RELIGIOUS BELIEFS

Although Christianity is the main religion here, many people also follow traditional beliefs. These suggest that natural objects, such as mountains and rivers, have a spirit. Masks, like this Bambuku head, are sometimes used to scare off evil spirits.

VILLAGE LIFE

Most people in rural areas live in villages or small towns. Some grow crops, such as cotton or cassava, for sale, but many exist just by growing food just for their families.

Mud-brick home

FISHING IN LAKE CHAD

Lake Chad is an important source of food, but it is shrinking at an alarming rate. A shallow lake, it is now only about 20 ft (6 m) deep. Its surface area has also reduced, due to droughts and the demand for water to irrigate the land.

PEOPLE OF CHAD

With almost half the country lying in the arid Sahara Desert, about 80 percent of Chadians work on farmland near the Chari River in the south. Across Chad there are large numbers of ethnic groups, speaking over 100 languages. Women here live an average of just 53 years and have 6.5 children.

| 0 km | 100 | 200 | 300 | 400 |
| 0 miles | 100 | 200 | 300 | 400 |

LIBYA

SUDAN

NIGER

NIGERIA

Sahara

Tibesti

Massif d'Abo

Bardaï   Aozou
Zouar

Tropic of Cancer

Erdi
Erdi Ma
Ounianga
Kébir
Dépression du Mourdi
Ennedi
Fada
Massif du Kapka

Faya

Koro Toro

Erg du Djourab

CHAD

Biltine
Abéché
Goz Beïda
Birao
Ouanda Djallé
Mangalmé
Abou-Déïa
Am Timan
Bahr Azoum

Ati

Moussoro

Bahr Aouk
Ndélé

Mongo

Kyabé
Sarh

Massenya
Chari
Ba Illi
Bongor
Fianga
Léré
Kélo
Laï
Koumra
Doba
Maro
Goré

NDJAMENA
Mao
Bol
Lac
Chad
Nokou
Lake
Chad

Kousséri

Baïbokoum
Markounda
Bossangoa
Bouar
Baoro
Bossembélé

CENTRAL AFRICAN REPUBLIC

Kaga Bandoro
Bria
Ippy
Bambari
Alindao
Mobaye
Bangassou
Bakala
Grimari
Dékoa
Sibut
Damara
Berbérati
Zongo
BANGUI

Kotto

Ubangi (Oubangui)

Obo
Bonu
Djema
Dembia

Maroua
Guider
Garoua

Mbé
Ngaoundéré
Adamaua Highlands
Djérem
Bertoua

CAMEROON

Banyo
Foumban
Bafoussam
Bamenda

Nkongsamba
Kumba
Douala

Sanaga

YAOUNDÉ

Map labels

TANZANIA
UGANDA
RWANDA
BURUNDI
ZAMBIA
ANGOLA
CONGO
GABON
EQUATORIAL GUINEA
SÃO TOMÉ & PRÍNCIPE
CABINDA (to Angola)

DEM. REP. CONGO

Great Rift Valley
Equator
Lake Albert
Lake Edward
Lake Kivu
Lake Tanganyika
Lake Mweru
Lake Bangweulu
Lake Rukwa
Congo Basin
Mitumba Range

Mungbere, Bunia, Beni, Nia-Nia, Butembo, Goma, Bukavu, Lubutu, Kisangani, Yangambi, Lualaba, Lomami, Kalima, Kindu, Kibombo, Kasongo, Kongolo, Kalemie, Moba, Manono, Mulongo, Kamina, Kabinda, Gandajika, Lubao, Kasaji, Dilolo, Kolwezi, Likasi, Kipushi, **Lubumbashi**, Kamina, Mwene-Ditu, Mbuji-Mayi, Kananga, Demba, Mweka, Luebo, Tshikapa, Ilebo, Kikwit, Mangai, Kenge, Kasongo-Lunda, Bandundu, Kwango, Kwilu, Kasai, Lulua, Sankuru, Lodja, Ikela, Lomela, Boende, Mbandaka, Lisala, Akula, Bumba, Buta, Impfondo, Dongou, Epéna, Ouesso, Souanké, Sembé, Bélinga, Makoua, Owando, Oyo, Gamboma, Ngo, Djambala, Etoumbi, Mpama, Mossendjo, Dolisie, Sibiti, Nkayi, Kibangou, Loubomou, Moanda, Franceville, Ndendé, Mouila, Fougamou, Lambaréné, Ndjolé, **LIBREVILLE**, Bitam, Oyem, Acalayong, Cocobeach, Bata, Ambam, Ndindi, Pointe-Noire, Boma, Matadi, Tshela, Mbanza-Ngungu, **KINSHASA**, **BRAZZAVILLE**, Port-Gentil, Omboué, Setté Cama, Ndendé, Ombio, Lukenie, Lac Mai-Ndombe, Lac Tumba, Lac Ntomba, Lulonga, Ubangi (Oubangui), Congo, Zaïre, Plateaux Batéké, Massif du Chaillu

Principe, São Tomé, **SÃO TOMÉ**

Lukuga, Luvua, Luapula, Lufira, Lualaba, Lomami, Zambezi, Lualaba

ATLANTIC OCEAN

CONGO

The Congo River, also called the Zaire, is a crucial part of the area's transport system. Dugout canoes and motorized boats take people, goods, and even health clinics from cities to the villages and back. The river is home to many species of fish, as well as crocodiles.

Did you know?

▶ The waters of the Congo River have the capacity to provide electrical power for all of Africa.

▶ Cameroon's soccer team is one of the best in Africa, with great performances in recent World Cup events.

▶ The wooden masks of Central Africa inspired the Spanish painter Pablo Picasso.

REFUGEES

There are more than 5.4 million African refugees south of the Sahara—more than 40 percent of the world's total. Conflict, such as the civil war in Chad, and corrupt government, such as in the Central African Republic, have resulted in huge numbers of Africans leaving their homes.

MINING FOR COPPER

The Democratic Republic of Congo has vast reserves of copper, and was once one of the world's major exporters. More recently, however, competition from lower-cost producers, such as Chile, has seen a dramatic downturn in the industry.

COPPER

LOGGING IN GABON

Timber provides valuable income for Gabon, with much of the demand for okoumé—a softwood used to make plywood. Hardwoods, such as mahogany and ebony, are also felled. Because logging poses a threat to the future of the forests, the government is now setting up conservation programs.

Southern Africa

FROM THE DRAMATIC Namibian and Kalahari deserts in the west, to the tropical forests in the north, Southern Africa is a region of contrasts. Oil, diamonds, gold and other precious metals are all found here. There are huge inland plains that are home to a variety of wildlife, and large areas devoted to agriculture. But flooding and droughts, together with civil unrest, have hampered development so that despite an abundance of natural resources, many countries remain poor.

SAN HUNTER uses a poison-tipped arrow.

SAN BUSHMEN

One of the few groups of hunter-gatherers left in Africa, the San people roam the Kalahari Desert. Also known as Bush people, many San are now changing to a more settled life, often working on cattle ranches.

Tunnels transport water between dams.

Did you know?

▶ The Okavango River does not run out to sea, like most rivers, but runs inland into the Kalahari Desert.

Dams are marked in black.

LESOTHO

Water is a valuable resource in Southern Africa, and Lesotho makes good use of its mountainous land and numerous rivers. The Highlands Water Scheme uses dams and tunnels to transport water to neighboring South Africa.

JOHANNESBURG

With a population of more than nine million, Johannesburg is the second-largest city in Africa, after Cairo. Many people have moved here from the surrounding countryside in search of work.

GOLD MINING

Gold, first discovered near Johannesburg in 1886, brought a great deal of wealth to the region. South Africa currently produces about one-third of the world's gold.

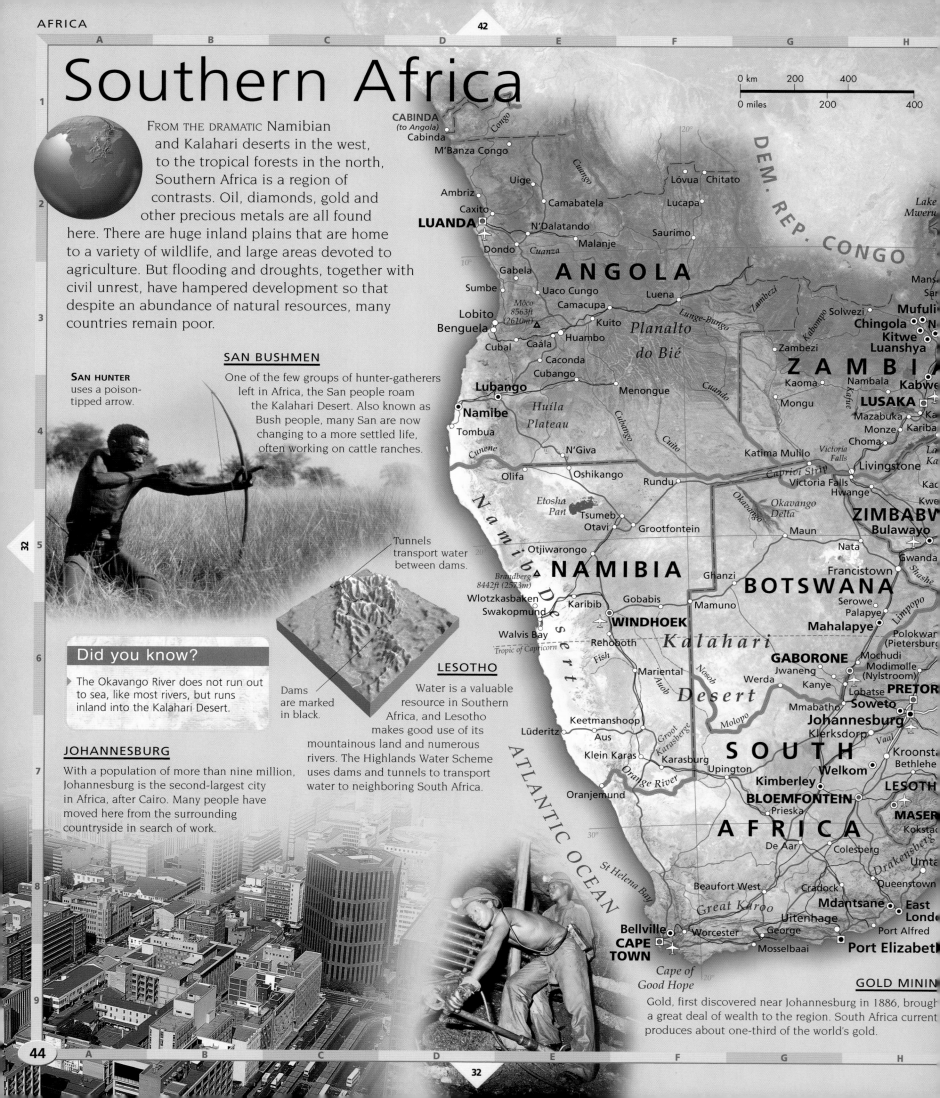

Map labels:

0 km 200 400
0 miles 200 400

CABINDA (to Angola)
Cabinda
M'Banza Congo
Congo
Uige
Ambriz
Camabatela
Lóvua Chitato
Caxito
Lucapa
LUANDA
N'Dalatando
Saurimo
Dondo
Cuanza
Malanje
Gabela
ANGOLA
Sumbe
Uaco Cungo
Luena
Lobito
Môco 8563ft (2610m)
Camacupa
Benguela
Kuito
Huambo
Planalto do Bié
Cubal
Caála
Caconda
Zambezi
Cubango
Lubango
Menongue
Huila Plateau
Namibe
Tombua
N'Giva
Olifa
Oshikango
Rundu
Etosha Pan
Tsumeb
Otavi
Grootfontein
Okavango Delta
Otjiwarongo
Brandberg 8442ft (2573m)
NAMIBIA
Ghanzi
BOTSWANA
Wlotzkasbaken
Karibib
Gobabis
Mamuno
Serowe
Swakopmund
WINDHOEK
Kalahari
Mahalapye
Walvis Bay
Rehoboth
Desert
Tropic of Capricorn
GABORONE
Mariental
Werda
Jwaneng
Kanye
Lüderitz
Keetmanshoop
Aus
Klein Karas
Karasburg
Upington
Oranjemund
Orange River
De Aar
ATLANTIC OCEAN
St Helena Bay
Beaufort West
Cradock
Great Karoo
Uitenhage
Bellville
CAPE TOWN
Worcester
George
Mosselbaai
Cape of Good Hope

M'Banza Congo
DEM. REP. CONGO
Lake Mweru
Solwezi
Mufuli
Chingola
Kitwe
Luanshya
Zambezi
ZAMBI
Kaoma
Nambala
Kabwe
Mongu
LUSAKA
Mazabuka
Monze
Kariba
Choma
Katima Mulilo
Victoria Falls
Livingstone
Caprivi Strip
Victoria Falls
Hwange
ZIMBABW
Maun
Bulawayo
Nata
Gwanda
Francistown
Polokwar (Pietersburg)
Mochudi
Modimolle (Nylstroom)
Lobatse
PRETOR
Mmabatho
Soweto
Johannesburg
Klerksdorp
SOUTH
Kroonsta
Bethlehe
Welkom
LESOTH
Kimberley
BLOEMFONTEIN
MASER
Prieska
Kokstad
AFRICA
Colesberg
Drakensberg
Umta
Queenstown
Mdantsane
East London
Port Alfred
Port Elizabet

MOZAMBIQUE FLOODS

In Mozambique, floods in 2000 and again in 2001 ruined crops, swept away livestock, and left millions homeless and vulnerable. Many people now rely on foreign aid to stay alive.

TOBACCO PLANTATION

VICTORIA FALLS

At Victoria Falls, situated on the Zambia–Zimbabwe border, the Zambezi River drops 420 ft (128 m) down a narrow chasm. The sound of crashing water can be heard 25 miles (40 km) away.

WORKING ON THE LAND

In both Malawi and Mozambique, agriculture employs more than four out of every five workers. Important crops include cotton, tea, tobacco, and sugar.

MADAGASCAN MAMMALS

Madagascar has an unusual range of mammals that developed in isolation after the island split from the African mainland. It is the only place where lemurs, members of the primate family, live in the wild.

RING-TAILED LEMUR

APARTHEID

In 1994, Nelson Mandela (below) became the first black president to govern South Africa. This historic event marked the end of white rule and the first fair elections in the new "Rainbow Nation." Apartheid was a policy of racial segregation and restricted the rights of black people.

WILDLIFE

Southern Africa is home to a huge variety of animals. Numerous parks have been created to protect the animals and their habitat. The Gaza–Kruger–Gonarezhou Transfrontier Park joins parks in Mozambique, South Africa, and Zimbabwe to form the largest conservation and ecotourism park in Africa.

Map labels

TANZANIA

Lake Rukwa
Mbala
sama
Isoka
Mpika
Serenje
Chipata
Nyamapanda
Tete
Masvingo
shavane
sina
essina)

Lake Nyasa
MALAWI
Mzuzu
LILONGWE
Salima
Monkey Bay
Zomba
Blantyre
Milange
Nsanje
Mocuba

Mocimboa da Praia
Rio Rovuma
Negomane
Rio Lugenda
Rio Messalo
Mucojo
Pemba
Lúrio
Rio Lúrio
Nacala
Lumbo
Nampula

Albufeira de Cahora Bassa
Vila do Zumbo
Zambezi
HARARE
Inyangani 8504ft (2592m)
Chitungwiza
Mutare
Chimoio
Beira
Machanga
Rio Save
Quelimane

MOZAMBIQUE

Mozambique Channel

Changane
Inhambane
Quissico
Xai-Xai
MAPUTO
MBABANE
SWAZILAND
ndee
etermaritzburg
Durban

INDIAN OCEAN

MORONI **COMOROS**
Grande Comore
Anjouan
Mohéli
MAMOUDZOU
MAYOTTE (to France)

Tanjona Bobaomby
Antsiranana
Ambanja
Analalava
Antsohihy
Sambava
Maromokotro 7795ft (2376m)
Antalaha
Mahajanga
Maroantsetra

MADAGASCAR

Bemaraha
Fenoarivo
Toamasina
ANTANANARIVO
Betafo
Morondava
Ambositra
Makay
Mananjary
Fianarantsoa
Mangoky
Ihosy
Manakara
Toliara
Farafangana
Vangaindrano
Amboasary
Tanjona Vohimena

Tropic of Capricorn

ST-DENIS
RÉUNION (to France)
PORT LOUIS
MAURITIUS
Mascarene Islands

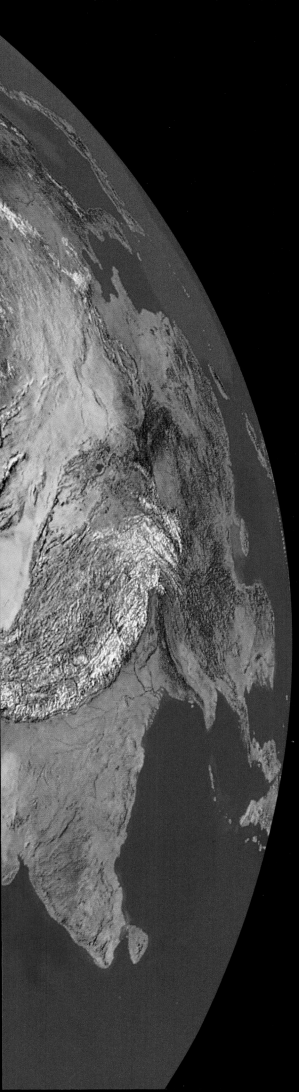

EUROPE

EUROPE IS THE SECOND-smallest continent in the world,

but it is one of the most densely populated, with

more than 727 million people living in its 44 countries. Most Europeans

live in cities. They watch TV, use cell phones, surf the

Internet, drive cars, and in comparison with many

other people in the world, are quite prosperous. The European climate

is mild, although winters are cold in the north and east and summers

are hot in the south. Over the past 500 years,

Europeans have conquered much of the world, setting

up huge empires in every continent. These empires are now gone,

but their influences remain. Many people around

the world still speak a European language, such as

English, French, or Spanish, and European culture has been exported

to many parts of the globe. As members of the European Union,

many countries are forging closer economic and political links.

Scandinavia and Finland

THE THREE SCANDINAVIAN countries of Norway, Sweden, and Denmark, along with neighboring Finland, are among the most northerly countries in Europe. Here the winters are long and cold. In the far north above the Arctic Circle, the Sun remains below the horizon for up to two months a year. Because of the harsh winter climate and the geographical isolation, Scandinavia has attracted little immigration, so the population is not very ethnically diverse. Finland is the most densely forested country in Europe, and wood accounts for 30 percent of its exports. All four countries are highly industrialized and are among the wealthiest in the world.

URBAN POPULATIONS

Scandinavia has a high urban population. Many people live in towns and cities, with less than a fifth living in the countryside. Since it is an area covered in lakes, fjords, and surrounded by sea, many people also live near the water.

COPENHAGEN IN Denmark is the largest city in Scandinavia.

SKIING

During the winter months, much of Scandinavia is covered with snow, so skiing is one of the easiest forms of transportation. It is also a very popular sport.

LAPLAND

Northern Sweden and Finland are known as Lapland. Here the local Sami people survive the cold and inhospitable climate by herding reindeer, which they breed for their meat, milk, and skins.

SAMI man in traditional costume

RUSSIAN FEDERATION

FINLAND

SWEDEN

NORWAY

ARCTIC OCEAN

Barents Sea

Norwegian Sea

Gulf of Bothnia

Lapland

0 km   100   200
0 miles   100   200

INDUSTRIAL STRENGTH

Manufacturing is an important source of employment and wealth throughout Scandinavia. Many of the goods produced, such as cars in Sweden, electronic goods in Denmark (above), and mobile phones in Finland, are exported all over the world. In Denmark, many people also work in agriculture, fish processing, and brewing.

Did you know?

- *Ski* is Norwegian for "strip of wood."
- Two-thirds of all Danish people have surnames that end in "sen," such as Hansen, meaning "son."
- Sweden recycles more aluminum cans than any other country in the world.

THE SAUNA

The sauna, or steam bath, was invented in Finland about 1,000 years ago as a way of cleaning and relaxing the body. After a hot sauna, many Finns cool off by plunging into an icy pool (above) or a snowdrift.

NORWEGIAN FJORDS

The west coast of Norway has thousands of deep inlets, known as fjords, gouged out of the mountains by glaciers during the last Ice Age and then flooded by the sea. The fjords run inland between high mountains and are a favorite destination for cruise ships bringing tourists to admire the stunning scenery.

BUILDING WITH WOOD

Much of Norway and Sweden, and two-thirds of Finland, is covered by dense forests of birch, pine, spruce, and other trees. Many people work in the forestry industry, producing wood for the construction and furniture industries. This great natural resource is also used to build homes and churches, like this medieval stave church (left) in Norway.

SAVING THE ENVIRONMENT

The people of Scandinavia are very environmentally conscious and recycle as many household items as they can. Strict national laws protect the environment from industrial waste and pollution, although there is growing concern about the levels of pollution in the Baltic Sea.

The British Isles

FOR SUCH A SMALL GROUP OF ISLANDS, the British Isles have a very rich history. This is evident from their legacy of ancient ruins, medieval castles, dramatic cathedrals, and grand country houses. Once a leading industrial and colonial power, British monarchs ruled an empire that circled the globe. As a result, English is still widely spoken around the world. Today, many traditional industries, such as shipbuilding, mining, and engineering, have declined, and the emphasis is now on banking and insurance, as well as pharmaceuticals. The British Isles consist of two countries: the United Kingdom of Great Britain and Northern Ireland (the UK), and the Republic of Ireland.

Did you know?

- Edinburgh, in Scotland, is built on the core of an extinct volcano.

- The Romans founded London in AD 43. They named it Londinium.

- Wales has more than 200 castles.

IRELAND

Tourists visit Ireland every year, attracted by its unspoiled countryside and lively cities, such as Dublin (left). Once part of Britain, Ireland gained independence in 1922. It is now one of the fastest-growing economies in Europe.

HORSE BREEDING

Lush pastures and a mild climate have encouraged the breeding of thoroughbred racehorses in Ireland. Stud farms here raise some of the best racehorses in the world.

IRISH HORSE and rider on a training run.

SCOTLAND

Scotland and England united as a single country in 1707. Today, however, Scotland is a self-governing part of the UK, with its own parliament and distinct legal and educational systems. Edinburgh, above, is a popular city with a magnificent castle. Each summer, it hosts an international arts festival.

NORTH SEA ENERGY

Beneath the shallow seas around Britain, there are supplies of oil and natural gas. Large oil rigs raise oil and gas to the surface, where it is pumped by pipeline to be refined on the mainland. Supplies are now beginning to run low, and new, more distant areas are being explored.

MONEY MATTERS

The City of London is the UK's financial center with more than 500 banks. Lloyd's Insurance Building (right) is one of the city's modern skyscrapers. Built of steel and glass, it has elevators outside.

ATLANTIC OCEAN

North Sea

Shetland Islands
Unst
Yell
Fetlar
Mainland
Lerwick
Fair Isle

Orkney Islands
Sanday
Mainland
Kirkwall
Hoy

Cape Wrath
Thurso
Wick
John o'Groats

Outer Hebrides
St Kilda
Isle of Lewis
Stornoway
Harris
North Uist
South Uist
Barra

The Minch
Ullapool
The Little Minch

North West Highlands
Isle of Skye
Stromeferry
Mallaig
Rhum
Eigg
Coll
Tiree
Isle of Mull
Oban
Fort William
Ben Nevis 4406ft (1344m)

Inner Hebrides
Islay
Jura
Kintyre
Isle of Arran

Inverness
Loch Ness
Aviemore
Spey
Dee
Elgin
Moray Firth

Grampian Mountains
Ben Hope 3041ft (927m)

Peterhead
Fraserburgh
Aberdeen
Montrose
Arbroath
Forfar
Dundee
Perth
St Andrews
Firth of Tay
Firth of Forth
Dunfermline
Stirling
Loch Lomond
Glasgow
Greenock
Paisley
Hamilton
Clyde
Edinburgh
Galashiels
Hawick
SCOTLAND

Southern Uplands
East Kilbride
Kilmarnock
Prestwick
Ayr
Dumfries
Stranraer

Berwick-upon-Tweed
Cheviot Hills
Newcastle upon Tyne
South Shields
Sunderland
Durham
Hartlepool
Middlesbrough
Whitby
Scarborough
Bridlington
Beverley
Darlington
Northallerton
Harrogate
Leeds
York
Ouse
Ribble

Pennines
Carlisle
Penrith
Workington
Whitehaven
Lake District
Kendal
Barrow-in-Furness
Lancaster
UNITED KINGDOM

NORTHERN IRELAND
Coleraine
Londonderry
Strabane
Stranorlar
Omagh
Enniskillen
Lough Erne
Lower Lough Erne
Upper Lough Erne
Belfast
Newtownabbey
Lough Neagh
Bangor
Newtownards
Downpatrick
Armagh
Portadown
Newry
Dundalk

Sligo
Donegal
Donegal Bay
Colloney
Boyle
Cavan
Castlebar

DOUGLAS
ISLE OF MAN

LONDON

The capital of the UK is London, a sprawling city on the banks of the Thames River. It is the political and financial center of the country, as well as home to more than 7 million people. One of its most recent attractions is the London Eye—a giant ferris wheel, 443 ft (135 m) high.

When the pods reach the top, you can see all of the city beneath you.

BRITISH LANDMARKS

Tourism is a major industry in Britain. Visitors come from all over the world to see the many churches, castles, and ancient monuments, such as Stonehenge (above), and to admire the pretty villages. Many also come for the theaters, galleries, and shops in Britain's vibrant cities.

STONEHENGE in southern England, was built from about 3000 BC onward.

WALES

Wales was formally united with England in 1536, but retains its own language and traditions. Welsh is spoken widely in some parts, and public signs appear in both Welsh and English. Coal mining and steel production were important in the south, but have both declined. Rugby is the national game.

MULTICULTURAL SOCIETY

Britain once controlled a world empire with colonies in every continent. Many people—from the Indian subcontinent, Africa, and the Caribbean in particular—came here and brought their cultures with them. Today, about one in 20 British people are from ethnic minorities, but are integrated into British life.

WALES PLAYS IRELAND at rugby in the Millennium Stadium, Cardiff, Wales.

Map labels

North Sea

Great Yarmouth
Lowestoft
Felixstowe
Harwich
Colchester
Southend-on-Sea
Margate
Dover
Channel Tunnel
Canterbury
Folkestone
Hastings
Eastbourne
Brighton
Hove
Portsmouth
Isle of Wight
Newport
Bournemouth
Poole
Weymouth
Lyme Bay
Torquay
Exeter
Exmouth
Plymouth
Saltash
Dartmoor
Exmoor
Biddeford
Barnstaple
Ilfracombe
Tamar
Exe
Bodmin
Newquay
St Austell
Truro
Falmouth
Penzance
Land's End
Isles of Scilly

English Channel

Norwich
Ipswich
Skegness
Louth
Lincoln
Boston
King's Lynn
The Wash
Newmarket
Cambridge
Peterborough
Bedford
Stevenage
Harlow
St Albans
Watford
LONDON
Croydon
Crawley
Woking
Guildford
Winchester
Havant
Eastleigh
Southampton
Salisbury
Andover
Cotswold Hills
Cheltenham
Swindon
Reading
Oxford
Luton
Milton Keynes
Northampton
Coventry
Leicester
Nottingham
Derby
Sheffield
ENGLAND
Trent
Mersey
Stoke-on-Trent
Crewe
Chester
Birkenhead
Kettering
Muneaton
Birmingham
Wolverhampton
Stafford
Shrewsbury
Worcester
Kidderminster
Gloucester
Bristol
Bath
Newport
Cardiff
Swansea
Llanelli
Carmarthen
Weston-super-Mare
Port Talbot
Bristol Channel
Yeovil
Taunton
Tiverton
Bridport
Cambrian Mountains
Brecon Beacons
WALES
Wye
Snowdonia
Bangor
Holyhead
Barmouth
Tywyn
Aberystwyth
Cardigan Bay
Fishguard
Haverfordwest
Milford Haven

Irish Sea

DUBLIN
Dún Laoghaire
Lucan
Liffey
Wicklow Mts
Newbridge
Arklow
Wexford
Carlow
Kilkenny
Port Laoise
Athlone
Shannon
Leinster
Barrow
Waterford
Youghal
Clonmel
Cashel
Nenagh
Limerick
Ennis
Munster
Blackwater
Cork
Bantry
Killarney
Tralee
Abbeyfeale
Rathkeale
Loughrea
Galway
Galway Bay
Lough Derg
Dingle Bay
Bantry Bay

Celtic Sea

St George's Channel

Scale

0 km 50 100
0 miles 50 100

ST PETER PORT
Guernsey
Alderney
Sark
ST HELIER
Jersey
CHANNEL ISLANDS (to UK)

The Low Countries

THE NETHERLANDS, BELGIUM, AND LUXEMBOURG are known as the Low Countries because the land is so flat and low-lying. In the case of the Netherlands, much of the land is below sea level—Netherlands is Dutch for "under lands." The three countries are among the richest in Europe, and, while farming still plays an important part, they all have strong, modern economies based on manufacturing and trade.

Luxembourg in particular is known as a tax haven and is a major center for international finance. Their location at the mouth of the Rhine River and other major European rivers places the three countries at the heart of western European trade and politics—all three were founder members of the European Economic Community (now the European Union or EU), established in 1957.

Did you know?

▶ Tulips were introduced into the Netherlands from Turkey in 1562. Black tulips were the most valuable.

▶ Belgium combines two cultures: the French-speaking Walloons and the Dutch-speaking Flemings.

▶ In Belgium, French fries, known as *frites*, are served in a paper cone or dish, with a dollop of mayonnaise. They are generally eaten using a small wooden fork.

RECLAIMING THE LAND

Over the centuries, the Dutch have reclaimed land from the sea. They did this by building huge dykes, or dams, to keep out the sea, and then draining the surface water into canals. Windmills originally pumped out the water, but electric pumps are now used.

  ▭ Land below sea
     level on main map

DUTCH PEOPLE

The Dutch once ruled a vast empire in Indonesia, the Caribbean, and South America. As a result, many nationalities now live here. Ethnic minorities make up about 45 percent of the people, and the majority of primary school children have a non-Dutch background.

ROTTERDAM

Every year, more than 30,000 seagoing ships and 110,000 barges call at the port of Rotterdam. Lying at the mouth of the Rhine River, this port is the largest in the world, and is where vast container ships from all over the world load or unload their cargoes. The smaller barges help to transport goods further inland. With the port's ultramodern Vessel Traffic System (VTS) it's possible to track ships on a radar sceen up to 37 miles (60 km) off the coast and 25 miles (40 km) inland.

DUTCH TULIP

CROPS

Fertile soil and good irrigation have helped the Netherlands become a major exporter of agricultural products, with vegetables and tomatoes forming important crops. It is also famous for its bulbs and cut flowers, notably tulips.

Map labels

GERMANY

NETHERLANDS

West Frisian Islands (Waddeneilanden)

Schiermonnikoog
Ameland
Schiermonnikoog
Terschelling
Vlieland
Texel

Wadden Zee

IJsselmeer
Flevoland
IJssel

Delfzijl
Appingedam
Groningen
Zuidborn
Haren
Zuidlaren
Vlagtwedde
Borger
Emmen
Coevorden
Hardenberg
Den Ham
Denekamp
Tubbergen
Almelo
Rijssen
Hengelo
Goor
Enschede
Deventer
Zutphen
Haaksbergen

Eemshaven
Loppersum
Zuidborn
Leek
Beilen
Hoogeveen
Staphorst
Assen
Steenwijk
Wolvega
Heerenveen
Zwolle
Meppel
Emmeloord
Nunspeet
Apeldoorn
Vaassen
Zeewolde
Baarn
Amersfoort

Dokkum
Winsum
Leeuwarden
Drachten
Joure
Sneek
Harlingen
Menaldum
Lelystad

Schagen
Opmeer
Hoorn
Purmerend
Almere
Amstelveen
Hilversum
Zaanstad
AMSTERDAM

Den Helder
Alkmaar
Castricum
Velsen-Noord
Haarlem
Noordwijk aan Zee
Leiden
Sassenheim
Zoetermeer
Utrecht
THE HAGUE

AMSTERDAM

The old architecture and picturesque canals make Amsterdam one of the most-visited cities in Europe. Occasionally the canals freeze over, and city officials may decide it's safe for people to go skating. Amsterdam is also home to some of the world's best museums, including the Van Gogh Museum and the Rijksmuseum.

Cyclists have their own traffic lights—this one is green for "go."

BELGIAN QUALITY

Belgium is renowned for its beautiful historic buildings, and for its excellent food, especially chocolates. Belgians have been making top-quality chocolates for more than 100 years and pralines, a type of filled chocolate, are a specialty. Brussels even boasts a chocolate museum.

TRILINGUAL

The Grand Duchy of Luxembourg lies between Germany, France, and Belgium. As a result, the majority of the people are trilingual—German and French are widely spoken, as is Letzebugesch, the national language. The capital, also known as Luxembourg, has more than 200 banks.

FLAGS of the member states of the European Union

CYCLING

The flatness of the land makes the Netherlands ideal for cycling, and more than half a million people cycle to school or work each day. Most of the roads have special cycle lanes, and bicycles are often the quickest form of transportation to get around the crowded towns and cities. The use of bicycles also reduces car use and thus cuts down the amount of air pollution.

GERMANY

BELGIUM

FRANCE

LUXEMBOURG

LUXEMBOURG

North Sea

0 km 25 50 75
0 miles 25 50 75

France

IN DIRECT CONTRAST TO ITS mainly rural landscape, France is a modern nation with most people now living in towns and cities. It has flourishing industries and is the fifth-richest economy in the world, after the US, Japan, Germany, and the UK. A country of varied scenery, from gently rolling farmland in the north to a stretch of dry, warm Mediterranean coast in the south, France also shares two mountain ranges—the Pyrenees and the Alps. Each of the 22 regions within France, which includes the island of Corsica, has its own distinct identity and culture. The tiny countries of Andorra and Monaco lie next to France.

Did you know?

▶ Some of the world's finest perfumes come from southern France, where fields of lavender, roses, and jasmine are grown. As many as 300 oils may be used to make one perfume.

▶ Boules, the national game of France, is still played in village squares around the country.

▶ *Poisson d'avril*, or April fish, is the name given to anyone who is fooled on April 1st. Confectionery shops sell fish-shaped chocolate, and people send funny cards with fish on them.

HIGH-SPEED TRAVEL

France has the world's fastest train, the TGV—*train à grande vitesse*—which travels at an average speed of 186 mph (300 km/h). The TGV network connects Paris with all the country's major regional cities, which makes it easier to commute or visit relatives. It also extends to Germany, Italy, Belgium, Switzerland, and through the Channel Tunnel to Britain.

NUCLEAR POWER

Three-quarters of France's electricity is produced by nuclear power plants (above), making the country largely self-sufficient in energy and one of the main producers of nuclear power in Europe. Hydroelectric plants are also an important source of power.

STREETS OF PARIS

Tourists flock to Paris to visit its world-famous museums and art galleries, shop in its elegant stores, and soak up its vibrant atmosphere. Montmartre, which overlooks the city, is famous for its artists. Close by, in the Place du Tertre (above), visitors can have their portrait painted.

FRENCH CHEESE

The French generally like strong-smelling cheese. Among the best known are Brie, Camembert, and Roquefort. Made from either cow, sheep, or goat's milk, cheese is often named after the French town or region where it is made.

AVIATION INDUSTRY

The French were pioneers of aviation. They co-built the Concorde and, in 1970, joined forces with German, Spanish, and UK companies to produce short-to-medium-range aircraft that were both economic to run and carried up to 300 passengers. Called Airbus, these aircraft filled a vital gap in the market and changed the face of the aviation industry.

HISTORIC HOMES

During the 15th and 16th centuries, French aristocrats built beautiful chateaus, such as Chenonceau (above), in the Loire Valley, Bordeaux, and other regions of France. These houses were elaborately decorated by the best artists and craftsmen. Today, most are state-owned and open to the public.

TOUR DE FRANCE

The Tour de France cycle race was first held in 1903 and is the most important sports event in France. Every July, thousands of people line the route to support their favorite team or cheer on the winner. The race covers about 2,500 miles (4,000 km) and is divided up into 20 or more daily stages.

VINEYARDS

The Romans first planted grapevines in southern France about 2,000 years ago. Today, France is the world's major wine-producing country, selling a range of wines for the home market and for export. The type of wine produced depends on the soil, location, and climate where the vine is planted. Wines from Burgundy, Champagne, and the Rhone valley are sold worldwide.

Ligurian Sea

ITALY

Mont-Blanc 15771ft (4807m)

Col du Mont Cenis 6831ft (2083m)

Corsica (Corse)
Monte Cinto 8878ft (2706m)
Monte Incudine 7064ft (2136m)
Bastia
Ajaccio
Sartène
Bonifacio
Strait of Bonifacio

Mediterranean Sea

Côte d'Azur

MONACO
MONACO
Nice
Antibes
Cannes

Toulon
Hyères
Îles d'Hyères
La Ciotat
Aubagne

Marseille
Martigues
Sète
Aix-en-Provence
le Cannet
Salon-de-Provence
Arles
Tarascon
Camargue
Avignon
Orange
Bollène
Montélimar
Privas
Valence
Le Puy

Nîmes
Montpellier
Béziers
Narbonne
Agde
Frontignan

Perpignan

ANDORRA LA VELLA
ANDORRA

Grenoble
Briançon
Digne
Manosque
Gap
Voiron
St-Egrève
Vienne
Villeurbanne
Lyon
St-Chamond
St-Étienne
Chambéry
Annecy
Aix-les-Bains
Thonon-les-Bains
Bourg-en-Bresse
Ambérieu-en-Bugey
Tarare
Roanne
Mâcon

Dauphiné
Durance
Drôme
Rhône

Provence
Languedoc

SPAIN

Pyrénées

Gascogne
Aquitaine
Bordeaux
Libourne
Arcachon
Pessac
Mérignac
Cenon
la Teste
Médoc

Toulouse
Montauban
Castelsarrasin
Moissac
Agen
Auch
Cahors
Figeac
Rodez
Albi
Carmaux
Gaillac
Graulhet
Castelnaudary
Carcassonne
Limoux
Foix
Pamiers
St-Gaudens

Clermont-Ferrand
Montluçon
Vichy
Riom
Issoire
Thiers
Cusset
Guéret
Ussel
Tulle
Brive-la-Gaillarde
Aurillac
St-Flour
Mende

Limoges
Angoulême
Périgueux
Bergerac
Marmande
Houilles

Massif Central
Auvergne
Limousin

St-Claude

Île d'Oléron
Rochefort
Royan
Saintes
Cognac

Mont-de-Marsan
Dax
Orthez
Pau
Tarbes
Lourdes
Anglet
Bayonne
Biarritz
Landes

0 km 50 100 150
0 miles 50 100 150

Germany and the Alpine States

LYING AT THE VERY HEART OF EUROPE, Germany is one of the world's wealthiest nations. It is also Europe's leading industrial power. An extensive network of rivers and canals forms an important waterway for transporting goods around Germany and also to other European countries. To the south lie the Alpine states of Switzerland, Austria, Liechtenstein, and Slovenia. Although German is the main language in all but Slovenia, each of the five countries has its own distinct history, culture, and sense of national identity. The entire region boasts beautiful alpine scenery, forests, mountains, and lakes.

THE BERLIN WALL

After World War II, Germany was split, with a US-backed capitalist state in the west and a Russian-backed communist state in the east. The wall was built in 1961 to stop East Germans from leaving for a better life in the West. The wall divided Berlin and separated families, friends, and a nation for 28 years. When Germany was reunited in 1990, the Berlin Wall was finally demolished.

THE WALL consisted of 96 miles (155 km) of barbed-wire barricade and a concrete wall with an average height of 11.8 ft (3.6 m).

GERMAN INDUSTRY

The Ruhr Valley used to be the powerhouse of the German economy, with vast coal and iron mines and a massive steel industry. Today, its economy is more diverse, ranging from heavy engineering to high-tech goods. It is the world's third-largest car producer (above).

FOOD AND DRINK

Traditional German food and drinks include smoked sausage, *sauerkraut* (pickled cabbage), and beer. The annual Munich *Oktoberfest* is Germany's biggest beer festival.

GENEVA

The Swiss city of Geneva lies on the shores of Lake Geneva, Europe's largest alpine lake. This orderly city is a global center for banking and finance. It is also a base for many international organizations, such as the Red Cross.

SWISS WATCHES

The Swiss invented the first wristwatch, the first quartz watch, and the first water-resistant watch. With their worldwide reputation for quality and style, timepieces make up the country's third largest export.

ALPINE SCENERY

The Alps run from southeast France and spread eastward through Switzerland and northern Italy into Austria and Slovenia. A popular tourist destination, the Alps are famous for dramatic scenery and winter sports. Cable cars carry skiers and hill-walkers higher up the mountains.

Did you know?

- Germany is famous for its Christmas markets, and the one held in Nuremberg is the oldest.
- From 1961–89, 171 people died trying to climb the Berlin Wall.
- Liechtenstein is so small that it only has 12 miles (19 km) of single-track railroad.

SLOVENIA

Independent since 1991, Slovenia has retained a strong national culture and identity, despite centuries of rule by overlords. Colorful embroidery and distinctive headwear (right) are part of their folk culture.

VIENNA

Vienna is a city of music, cafes, and delicious pastries. It has many baroque buildings, palaces, cathedrals, and famous concert halls. These are a reminder of when the city was the center of the Austro-Hungarian Empire that controlled much of eastern and central Europe.

St. Stephen's Cathedral, generally known as Stephansdom

Map labels (selection): CZECH REPUBLIC, SLOVAKIA, HUNGARY, CROATIA, AUSTRIA, SLOVENIA, ITALY, SWITZERLAND, FRANCE, LIECHTENSTEIN

VIENNA (WIEN), Linz, Salzburg, Graz, Klagenfurt, Maribor, LJUBLJANA, Innsbruck, Munich (München), Nuremberg, Regensburg, Augsburg, Ulm, Stuttgart, Heidelberg, Mannheim, Karlsruhe, BERN, Zürich, Basel, Geneva (Genève), Lausanne, VADUZ

Spain and Portugal

THE COUNTRIES OF SPAIN AND PORTUGAL share an area of land called the Iberian Peninsula. In the north, this land is cut off from the rest of Europe by the Pyrenees Mountains, while to the south, it is separated from Africa by the Strait of Gibraltar. The region was once ruled by Islamic people from North Africa, known as the Moors. Evidence of their occupation can still be seen from buildings in the cities of Andalucía. The Moors were eventually defeated in 1492, and for a while, Portugal came under Spanish control, as did much of Europe. During the 20th century, both countries were ruled by brutal dictatorships, which were overthrown in the 1970s. They are now modern democracies.

Did you know?

▶ In Spain, it is customary for families to eat dinner late in the evening, usually around 9 p.m. So after school, children eat a snack called *merienda*.

▶ Bullfights, known as *touradas*, are still popular in Portugal, despite opposition from local and international animal welfare groups.

HARVESTING CORK

Cork is made from the outer bark of the evergreen cork oak tree. The bark is carefully stripped off, flattened, laid out in sheets, and then left to dry. The cork is used for many products, such as stoppers for wine bottles, matting, and tiles. Portugal is the world's leading exporter of cork.

LISBON

The capital city of Portugal is Lisbon, which is situated at the mouth of the Tagus River on a series of steep hills and valleys. In 1755, two-thirds of the city was completely destroyed by an earthquake and tidal wave, but was rebuilt with beautiful squares and public buildings. Many explorers set sail from Lisbon in their quest to find new lands.

TRAMS are a feature of Lisbon streets, and a popular form of transportation for both residents and tourists.

FISHING

Spain and Portugal have well-developed fishing industries—with large-scale fleets and many smaller local fleets. However, overfishing along Portugal's coastline and out in the North Atlantic, plus a massive oil spill in 2002 off the coast of Galicia, have put many people's livelihood's at risk.

32

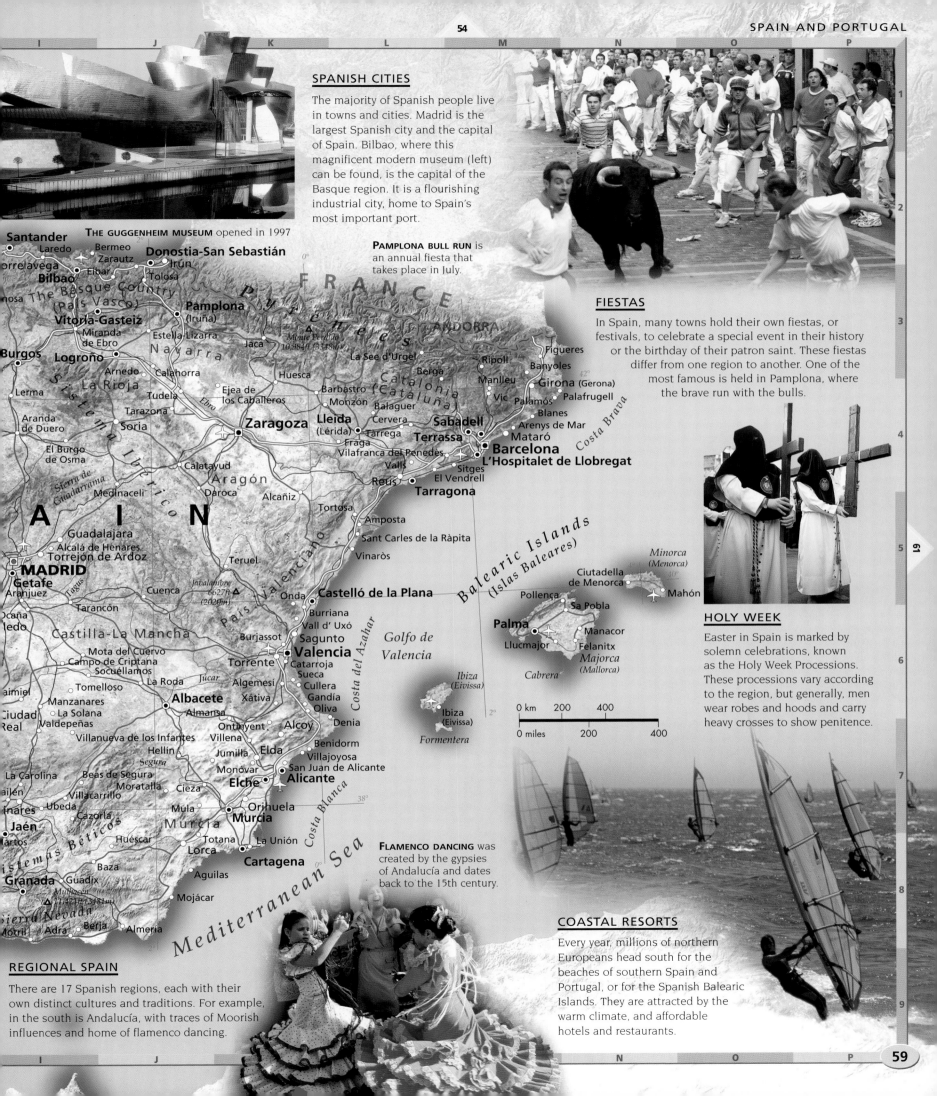

SPANISH CITIES

The majority of Spanish people live in towns and cities. Madrid is the largest Spanish city and the capital of Spain. Bilbao, where this magnificent modern museum (left) can be found, is the capital of the Basque region. It is a flourishing industrial city, home to Spain's most important port.

THE GUGGENHEIM MUSEUM opened in 1997

PAMPLONA BULL RUN is an annual fiesta that takes place in July.

FIESTAS

In Spain, many towns hold their own fiestas, or festivals, to celebrate a special event in their history or the birthday of their patron saint. These fiestas differ from one region to another. One of the most famous is held in Pamplona, where the brave run with the bulls.

HOLY WEEK

Easter in Spain is marked by solemn celebrations, known as the Holy Week Processions. These processions vary according to the region, but generally, men wear robes and hoods and carry heavy crosses to show penitence.

FLAMENCO DANCING was created by the gypsies of Andalucía and dates back to the 15th century.

COASTAL RESORTS

Every year, millions of northern Europeans head south for the beaches of southern Spain and Portugal, or for the Spanish Balearic Islands. They are attracted by the warm climate, and affordable hotels and restaurants.

REGIONAL SPAIN

There are 17 Spanish regions, each with their own distinct cultures and traditions. For example, in the south is Andalucía, with traces of Moorish influences and home of flamenco dancing.

Map labels:

Santander, Laredo, Bermeo, Zarautz, Donostia-San Sebastián, Irún, Torrelavega, Eibar, Tolosa, Bilbao, The Basque Country (País Vasco), Pamplona (Iruña), Vitoria-Gasteiz, Miranda de Ebro, Estella-Lizarra, Jaca, Navarra, Burgos, Logroño, Arnedo, Calahorra, Huesca, La See d'Urgel, Ripoll, Figueres, Lerma, La Rioja, Tudela, Tarazona, Barbastro, Berga, Banyoles, Catalonia (Cataluña), Manlleu, Girona (Gerona), Aranda de Duero, Soria, Ejea de los Caballeros, Monzón, Balaguer, Vic, Palamós, Palafrugell, El Burgo de Osma, Sistema Ibérico, Zaragoza, Lleida (Lérida), Cervera, Tàrrega, Sabadell, Arenys de Mar, Blanes, Fraga, Terrassa, Mataró, Costa Brava, Medinaceli, Sierra de Guadarrama, Calatayud, Aragón, Daroca, Alcañiz, Vilafranca del Penedès, Barcelona, L'Hospitalet de Llobregat, Valls, Sitges, Reus, El Vendrell, Tarragona, Tortosa, Guadalajara, Alcalá de Henares, Torrejón de Ardoz, Teruel, Javalambre 6627ft (2020m), Amposta, Sant Carles de la Ràpita, Balearic Islands (Islas Baleares), Minorca (Menorca), MADRID, Getafe, Aranjuez, Cuenca, Vinaròs, Ciutadella de Menorca, Mahón, Tarancón, País Valenciano, Castelló de la Plana, Onda, Pollença, Sa Pobla, Ocaña, Castilla-La Mancha, Burriana, Vall d'Uxó, Sagunto, Golfo de Valencia, Palma, Manacor, Mota del Cuervo, Burjassot, Felanitx, Campo de Criptana, Socuéllamos, La Roda, Torrente, Valencia, Catarroja, Sueca, Cullera, Majorca (Mallorca), Cabrera, Tomelloso, Manzanares, La Solana, Valdepeñas, Albacete, Almansa, Algemesí, Gandía, Oliva, Ibiza (Eivissa), Villanueva de los Infantes, Ciudad Real, Onteniyent, Xàtiva, Villena, Denia, Costa del Azahar, Almería, La Carolina, Hellín, Jumilla, Elda, Benidorm, Beas de Segura, Villajoyosa, Moratalla, Monóvar, San Juan de Alicante, Jaén, Villacarrillo, Cieza, Elche, Alicante, Úbeda, Cazorla, Mula, Orihuela, Murcia, Costa Blanca, Sistemas Béticos, Huéscar, Totana, La Unión, Lorca, Cartagena, Baza, Aguilas, Granada, Guadix, Mojácar, Sierra Nevada, Mulhacén 11,421ft (3481m), Motril, Adra, Berja, Almería, Mediterranean Sea

FRANCE, ANDORRA, Pyrenees, Monte Perdido 10,984ft (3348m), SPAIN, Ebro, Tagus, Júcar, Segura

0 km 200 400
0 miles 200 400

Italy

THE BOOT-SHAPED COUNTRY of Italy stretches from the mountainous north down to the Mediterranean Sea. For much of its history, Italy consisted of city-states—such as Florence and Venice—and was only united in 1870. Regional differences in Italy are huge; each region has its own cuisine, customs, and dialect, and is geographically quite distinct. As a result, many Italians identify themselves first by region and then by country. The national division, however, is between the rich north and the poorer south, a rugged region with several active volcanoes and the occasional severe earthquake. The mainland of Italy includes two tiny independent states—San Marino and Vatican City.

COLOSSEUM

One of Rome's greatest sights is the Colosseum, which opened in AD 80. Deadly gladiatorial combats and animal fights were staged here before crowds of up to 55,000 people

The oval-shaped Colosseum stood 620 ft (189 m) high.

Did you know?

The *Sartiglia* of Oristano is a festival in Sardinia. Before the tournament, masked horsemen must pierce the center of a silver star with their swords while riding past at high speed.

Vatican City has a permanent population of only about 1,000 people, although a further 3,400 come to work in the city-state each day.

More than 600 different types of pasta are eaten in Italy.

CARNIVAL MASKS

ANDREA BOCELLI

HOME OF OPERA

The idea of setting drama to music originated in Italy during the 16th century. Since then, Italian composers, such as Rossini, Verdi, and Puccini, have made opera the most popular musical form in Italy. Many cities have their own opera houses.

CITY OF CANALS

The beautiful city of Venice is made up of 118 islands, 177 canals, and 400 bridges. The only way to get around is to walk or take a boat: a *vaporetto*, *motoscafo*, or *motonave*. The most familiar boat, however, is the gondola. Each year, in the days before Ash Wednesday, Venice hosts a carnival: the city celebrates with fireworks, and everyone wears spectacular masks.

SOCCER FANS

Italians are crazy about soccer and fanatically follow the performance of teams such as Juventus, Milan, Roma, and Lazio. Italian teams have regularly won major European championships, and the national team has won the World Cup three times—in 1934, 1938, and 1982.

Adriatic Sea

Brindisi
Lecce
Maglie
Taranto
Manduria
Gallipoli
Golfo di
Taranto
Strait of Otranto

Bari
Molfetta
Barletta
Manfredonia
San Severo
Foggia
Cerignola
Andria
Bitonto
Benevento
Altamura
Matera
Potenza
Puglia
Campobasso
Isernia

Ciro Marino
Crotone
Catanzaro
Rossano
La
Sila
Siderno

Cosenza
Castrovillari
Amantea
Lamezia
Reggio
di Calabria
Palmi
Strait of
Messina

Ionian
Sea

Sala
Consilina
Sapri
Lauria

Tyrrhenian
Sea

Isola
Stromboli
Isole Eolie
Isola Lipari
Isola Vulcano

Messina
Catania
Siracusa
Modica
Ragusa
Vittoria
Gela
Caltanissetta
Pozzallo
Catania
Mount Etna
10,958ft (3340m)
Simeto

Palermo
Cefalù
Falù
Castelvetrano
Marsala
Alcamo
Trapani
Agrigento

Sicily
(Sicilia)

Malta Channel
Gozo
MALTA
VALLETTA
Malta

Strait of Sicily

Isola di
Pantelleria

Isole
Pelagie

M e d i t e r r a n e a n   S e a

Salerno
Avellino
Torre del Greco
Battipaglia
Agropoli
Caserta
Naples
(Napoli)
Isola
di Capri
Gulf of
Salerno
Campania
Vesuvius
Latina
Anzio
Terracina
Gaeta
Golfo di
Gaeta
Isole
Ponziane

VATICAN CITY ROME
(ROMA)

Sardinia
(Sardegna)
Isola Asinara
la Maddalena
Tempio Pausania
Porto Torres
Olbia
Sassari
Ozieri
Siniscola
Alghero
Nuoro
Macomer
Punta La Marmora
6017ft (1834m)
Villacidro
Oristano
Iglesias
Cagliari
Quartu
Sant' Elena
Carbonia

OLIVE HARVEST

Italy is the world's largest producer of olive oil, followed by
Spain and Greece. The oil is produced by first pressing the fruits
of the olive tree between steel or stone rollers, then squeezing
the oil from the pulp using a press. Olive trees flourish in the fertile
soils and the mild, frost-free climate of southern Italy.

Olives are gathered
in large nets.

VATICAN CITY

This tiny state in Rome is the
center of the Roman Catholic
church and home to the Pope.
As well as St. Peter's basilica
and the surrounding buildings
and gardens, the Vatican boasts
Michelangelo's Sistine Chapel.
The state has its
own flag, postage
stamps, and coins.

SWISS GUARDS, in their red, yellow,
and blue striped costumes, stand at
the gates into Vatican City.

RENAISSANCE ITALY

Florence (below) sits on either side of the Arno River. During the
14th century, a new movement in art and architecture, known as
the Renaissance, or rebirth, began in Italy. Painters and sculptors
such as Leonardo da Vinci, Michelangelo, and Raphael created
beautiful works of art often based on religious themes. Many of
these can still be seen in the galleries and churches of Florence.

HOME LIFE

Family life is
important in Italy,
and most people live
at home until they
marry. This is partly
due to lack of cheap
housing. Lunch
(pranzo) is often the
main meal of the day.

Central Europe

FOUR COUNTRIES LIE AT THE heart of Central Europe—Poland, the Czech Republic, Slovakia, and Hungary. The region is characterized by wide plains, broken by gentle hills and the Carpathian Mountain range in the south. In the late 1980s, these countries broke from years of communist rule. The new democratic governments were faced with the problems of trying to modernize their country. These changes are ongoing, but in some of the countries, such as the Czech Republic, there are signs of improvement and a rise in living standards.

GOLDEN PRAGUE

Prague, capital of the Czech Republic, is one of Europe's most beautiful cities. It contains many old buildings with golden roofs and grand squares. Unlike other Central European cities, Prague escaped serious damage during both world wars, and thus retains much of its charm.

PART OF PRAGUE'S colorful history is preserved in buildings around the Old Town Square.

FAMILY FARMS

Poland has one of the largest agricultural sectors in Europe, with more than a quarter of the workforce employed on the land. Most farms are still small, family-run businesses, growing grains, sugar beet, and potatoes. Large numbers of pigs and other animals are also kept.

TRADITIONAL TRADES

The countries of Central Europe, except Slovakia, are heavily industrialized. Vast coal mines, steel works (above), and engineering works dominate the urban landscape. Although some of the sites are old and poorly equipped, these countries are trying to update machinery and introduce measures to improve standards on environmental pollution.

RELIGION

The Roman Catholic Church is very strong throughout Central Europe. Attending mass on Sunday and observing religious holidays, such as Christmas and Easter, are important features of family life.

FOLK CULTURE

Traditional folk culture is still preserved in Slovakia, and is seen as an essential part of regional identity. Throughout the year, especially during the summer months, folk festivals are held in many towns. The people dress up in their colorful regional folk costumes, play traditional instruments, and sing and dance.

LANDSCAPE OF SLOVAKIA

Slovakia is divided between a fertile southern lowland and a more rugged, mountainous north. The country is far more rural than its industrial neighbor, the Czech Republic. Most Slovaks live in small towns and mountain villages. The Tatra Mountains in the north are popular with skiers and hikers, who bring in much-needed tourist income.

Did you know?

In 1993, Czechoslovakia was divided into two countries—the Czech Republic and Slovakia.

Budapest was once two cities—Buda on the right bank of the Danube River, and Pest on the left bank.

Poland has the oldest operating salt mine, now a World Heritage Site, in Wieliczka, near Kraków. The layers of salt go down 1,073 ft (327 m).

INDUSTRIAL LIFE

The Czech Republic is Central Europe's most industrialized country. It is renowned for its centuries-old glass industry. The region also produces some of the world's best-known beers. Pilsener beer, for example, originated in the town of Plzeň, while Budweiser beer has been brewed at České Budějovice for over a century.

HOT SPRINGS

A land of fertile plains, Hungary is also famous for its numerous hot springs. In the capital city of Budapest, there are more than 100 hot springs. The warm waters rise naturally from the ground, and the spas and baths are centered on these springs. They are as popular today as they were centuries ago, when the Romans used the hot springs on the Buda side of the city.

SZÉCHENYI BATHS has the hottest spa water in Budapest.

Southeast Europe

UNTIL 1991 CROATIA, Bosnia and Herzegovina, Serbia and Montenegro, and Macedonia were all part of Yugoslavia. Ethnic tensions between the Serbs and other peoples in Yugoslavia caused a series of bloody wars that broke the country up. Peace was eventually restored in 1999, but all four countries have suffered intense economic problems as a result. The five nations do, however, have huge potential, with considerable agricultural and mineral resources. In the north, the Danube River is an important trading route for both Croatia and Serbia, while Croatia has a flourishing tourist industry along its beautiful Adriatic coast.

SPORTING ACHIEVEMENT

Croatia is a great sporting nation. Skier Janica Kostelic became Croatia's first triple Olympic champion, after winning three gold medals at the 2002 Winter Games. In January 2003, Janica and her brother, Ivica, both won World Cup Alpine Races.

JANICA KOSTELIC

THE ADRIATIC

The long Adriatic coastline of Croatia is one of the most beautiful in Europe. The wooded hillsides, pretty beaches, such as Markarska (right), islands, and historic towns once attracted tourists from all over Europe. Now that the country is no longer involved in the war, tourists are returning, contributing vital income to the national economy.

Did you know?

The Dalmatian dog is named after the coastal region of Dalmatia in Croatia, its first known home.

In the mountains of Albania, announcements of a death, birth, or marriage are passed from one house to another by a gunshot or a shout that echoes through the mountains.

Bosnia and Herzegovina hosts the Sarajevo annual film festival.

GROWING FOOD

The most fertile area in this region lies along the Danube River in northern Serbia and eastern Croatia. Here, vegetables, fruit, corn, and cereals are grown, as are grapes for wine-making. Most farms are small-scale family businesses, growing a wide range of crops.

FAMILY-RUN PLOTS

SERBO-CROAT

The people of Croatia, Bosnia and Herzegovina, and Serbia all speak the same language, Serbo-Croat, but write it in different scripts. Croatians are predominantly Roman Catholic and write the language in the Roman script, as do the people of Bosnia. Serbians, however, are mainly Eastern Orthodox, and write using the Russian Cyrillic script.

POSTAGE STAMP WITH CYRILLIC SCRIPT

POSTAGE STAMP WITH ROMAN SCRIPT

THE SHELL of an impressive temple still stands at Apollonia, Albania.

100

100

50

50

0 km

0 miles

BULGARIA

MONTENEGRO (YUGOSLAVIA)

Batkan Mountains

Knjaževac

Aleksinac

Niš

Južna Morava

Pirot

Vlasotince

Surdulica

Leskovac

Prokuplje

Kruševac

Podujevo

Vranje

Bujanovac

Preševo

Kumanovo

Kriva Reka

Bregalnica

Štip

Radoviš

Strumica

Vardar

Kavadarci

Gevgelija

Prilep

Kičevo

Crna Reka

Veles

Prizren

Gostivar

SKOPJE

MACEDONIA

Ohrid

Struga

Lake Ohrid

Lake Prespa

Bitola

Pogradec

Lumi i Devollit

GREECE

Korçë

Elbasan

Berat

Lumi i Osumit

Lumi i Vjosës

ALBANIA

TIRANA (TIRANË)

Kukës

Peshkopi

Burrel

Debar

Black Drin

North Albanian Alps

Krujë

Lezhë

Lumi i Shkumbit

Kuçovë

Fier

Apollonia

Lushnjë

Vlorë

Tepelenë

Gjirokastër

Sarandë

Konispol

Corfu (Kérkyra)

20°

Strait of Otranto

Durrës

Kavajë

Shkodër

Lake Scutari

Bar

Bajram Curri

Lumi i Drinit

Deravica 8720ft (2658m)

Đakovica

Peć

Prizren

Uroševac

Orahovac

KOSOVO

Kosovska Mitrovica

Vučitrn

Kosovo Polje

Priština

Gnjilane

Tetovo

Kočani

North Albanian Alps

MONTENEGRO

Nikšić

Cetinje

Kotor

Trebinje

Podgorica

Bijelo Polje

Berane

Sjenica

Novi Pazar

Ibar

Kopaonik

Pljevlja

Prijepolje

Mostar

Metković

Ploče

Dubrovnik

Vis

Hvar

Korčula

Mljet

DUBROVNIK

The medieval walled city of Dubrovnik, at the very southern tip of Croatia on the Adriatic Sea, is one of the architectural gems of Europe. In 1991, Serb troops shelled the city, causing immense damage. The city was restored after the end of the war. Other historic cities damaged during the fighting, notably Sarajevo and Mostar, have yet to be fully restored.

GREAT LAKES

Macedonia contains two huge lakes—Ohrid and Prespa. The latter has clear water, fed by underground streams, and is a popular tourist destination. In 2002, the first Prespa boat regatta took place here. Both lakes have substantial fish stocks, especially of trout and eel, which are used to make local dishes.

LAKE PRESPA

EEL

LIFE IN ALBANIA

Albania is the poorest country in Europe. Most people are ethnic Albanian, with a sizable Greek minority in the south of the country. Loyalty to one's family or clan is more important than national identity, and married sons often live with their parents and look after them in old age.

AN ALBANIAN FAMILY

APOLLONIA

About 8 miles (13 km) outside the city of Fier, Albania, lie the ruins of an ancient city called Apollonia. Founded in 588 BC by Greeks from Corinth, it is one of 30 cities named after the Greek god Apollo. Austrian archaeologists began excavating the site during World War II, and this was continued by the French in the 1930s. However, much of the city still remains buried in the surrounding hill.

Bulgaria and Greece

FOR MORE THAN FOUR CENTURIES Bulgaria and Greece were ruled by the Ottoman Turks. Bulgaria gained independence in 1908, while southern Greece became independent in 1832, and was joined by northern Greece in 1913. After World War II, Bulgaria became a communist state, and Greece was ruled by the military from 1967 until 1974. Both states are now democracies, although Bulgaria remains relatively poor and underdeveloped in comparison with Greece, which is a member of the European Union. Although they share a common border, the two countries are quite different. The Greek mainland is mountainous, with only one-third of the land suitable for cultivation. By contrast, Bulgaria is more fertile, with a strong agricultural tradition. Tourism is an important source of income to both countries, with visitors flocking to the Black Sea resorts in Bulgaria, to the Greek mainland to see the ancient ruins, and to the Greek islands in search of sandy beaches.

BULGARIAN AGRICULTURE

Wheat, corn, and other cereals grow in the fertile Danube river valley in the north of the country. Tobacco (right) grows in the Maritsa river valley in the southeast, while grapes for the wine industry flourish on the slopes of the Balkan Mountains. The festival of Kukerov Dan, with traditional processions, celebrates the start of the agricultural year.

CITY LIFE

Bulgarians make up about 85 percent of the total population of the country. The rest are Turkish, Macedonian, or Roma. Most people live in apartment blocks in the main towns and cities. They are more likely to use public transportation, since not all families have a car.

TRAMS provide an efficient way for people to get around the city of Sofia.

Did you know?

▶ Every June, Bulgaria holds a Festival of the Roses to celebrate the flowers harvested for their oils.

▶ First held in Athens in 1896, the modern Olympic Games will be staged there again in 2004.

▶ Melbourne, Australia, has the second largest number of Greek-speakers in the world after Athens.

ARCHITECTURE

Bulgaria contains many fine old churches, monasteries, and mosques, despite the damage done to the country during World War II. Rila Monastery (above) was founded by a hermit monk who took to the mountains in search of solitude in 927 AD. After a fire in 1833, Rila was rebuilt and the magnificent church now boasts three great domes, a museum, and 1,200 frescoes.

LANGUAGE

The 24 characters in the Greek alphabet date from the 8th century BC, when the first texts were written in classical Greek. Since then, the language has evolved and is now spoken by 11 million people around the world.

Κέντρο Centre
Λαμία Lamia
Θεσσαλονίκη Thessaloniki

Map labels

Black Sea

Durankulak
Kavarna
Zlatni Pyasŭtsi
Varnenski Zaliv
Varna
Banya
Burgaski Zaliv

Dobrich
Karapelit
Khitrino Vetrino
Shumen
Rudnik
Evlyakovo
Aytos
Burgas
Sredets
Primorsko
Tsarevo
Kondolovo
Malko Tŭrnovo
Rezovo

Silistra
Alfatar
Dulovo
Tervel
Gara
Razgrad
Polikrayshte
Veselinovo
Luda Kamchiya
Karnobat
Yambol
Bolyarovo

Tutrakan
Pravda
Zavet
Polsko
Kosovo
Veliko
Sliven
Kazanlŭk
Stara Zagora
Sredets
Topolovgrad
Oreshada
Soufli

Ruse
Dralfa
Pavikeni
Sevlievo
Troyan
Gabrovo
Dimitrovgrad
Kharmanli
Kŭrdzhali
Komotini
Sapes
Alexandroúpoli

ROMANIA
Gulyantsi
Telish
Lovech
Mikre
Kisura
Brezovo
Khaskovo
Chepelare
Ardino
Momchilgrad
Didymóteicho
Féres
Thracian

Pleven
Lukovit
Roman
Plovdiv
Pazardzhik
Velingrad
Yakoruda
Dospat
Smolyan
Néa
Xánthi
Komotiní
Thásos

Lom
Miziya
Borovan
Vratsa
Novi Iskur
Kostenets
Simitli
Dupnitsa
Krasna
Strumyani
Sandanski
Serres
Dráma

Vidin
Borovan
Berkovitsa
Montana
Dragoman
Slivnitsa
SOFIA (SOFIYA)
Pernik
Iskŭr
Blagoevgrad
Petrich
Sidirókastro
Kilkís
Salonica (Thessaloníki)

Bregovo
Belogradchik
Vinishte
Lekhchevo
Trŭn
Izvor
Kyustendil
MACEDONIA
Lachanás
Giannitsá

Dimovo

Danube (Dunav)

Dunavska Ravnina

Balkan Mountains

Rila

Rodopi Mountains

SERB. & MON. (YUGOSLAVIA)

Tundzha
Maritsa
Arda
Nestos
Strymónas

Lake Prespa
Flórina
Atídara
Polýkastro
Amýntaio

BULGARIA

TURKEY

GREEK ISLANDS

More than 2,000 islands lie off the mainland of Greece. The Cyclades and Dodecanese in the Aegean Sea are often rocky and arid, while the Ionian Islands, such as Zakynthos (below), are more fertile. Tourists often travel from one island to another by ferry or hovercraft.

GREEK WEDDING

About 94 percent of Greeks follow the Greek Orthodox religion, and weddings follow the rites of the Orthodox Church. At the ceremony, it is traditional for the best man to place wreaths of orange blossom, linked by a silk ribbon, on the heads of the bride and the groom (above).

ATHENS

The capital city of Greece is dominated by the Parthenon, a temple built in 447–438 BC on a rocky hill known as the Acropolis. Modern-day Athens is a sprawling city where the large number of cars cause serious air pollution.

EARTHQUAKES

The idyllic landscape of the Greek Islands, such as Santorini (left), can be rocked by earthquakes. This is because the islands and mainland of Greece, as well as Bulgaria, sit on a plate boundary. There is now a Greek Seismic Code that outlines regulations on all new buildings.

CORINTH CANAL

The Corinth Canal was built to provide a shortcut for ships between the Aegean and Ionian Seas. Dug through solid limestone, the steep-sided canal was begun in 1882 by the French and completed in 1893 by the Greeks.

Aegean Sea

Northern Sporades (Vóreioi Sporádes)

Sea of Crete (Kritikó Pélagos)

Mediterranean Sea

Mirtóo Pelagos

Ionian Sea

Ionian Islands (Iónioi Nísoi)

Dodecanese (Dodekánisos)

Cyclades (Kykládes)

GREECE

Pindus Mountains (Pindos)

Peloponnese (Pelopónnisos)

Crete (Kríti)

ALBANIA

Thermaic Gulf

Gulf of Corinth

Lakonikós Kólpos

Rhodes (Ródos)

Lindos

Kárpathos

Kásos

Saría

Kos

Tílos

Nísyros

Chálki

Astypálaia

Sými

Léros

Agía Marína

Lepsoí

Arkoí

Agathónisi

Pátmos

Ikaría

Sámos

Sámos

Thérma

Amorgós

Anáfi

Ákra Floúda

Náxos

Íos

Íos

Thíra

Santorini (Thíra)

Páros

Mýkonos

Ermoúpoli

Tínos

Tínos

Ándros

Ándros

Kéa

Kéa

Kýthnos

Sýros

Kástro

Sérifos

Sífnos

Mílos

Mílos

Folégandros

Sikinos

Iráklio

Neápoli

Sitía

Ágios Nikólaos

Díkti

Mýrtos

Ierápetra

Kántanos

Kastélli

Pánormos

Zarós

Spíli

Tympáki

Sfákia

Lefká Ori

Chaniá

Gávdos

Antikýthira

Potamós

Kýthira

Neápoli

Daimoniá

Geráki

Gýtheio

Spárti

Areópoli

Gerolimenas

Karavás

Kýthira

Leonídi

Ýdra

Ermióni

Póros

Palaiá Epidavros

Náfplio

Tripoli

Argos

Nemea

Kalamáta

Messíni

Koróni

Pylos

Kyparissía

Zácharo

Pyrgos

Lampeia

Gastoúni

Lechainá

Kerí

Zákynthos

Kefalloniá (Kefalliniá)

Lixoúri

Argostóli

Vasilikí

Lefkáda

Lefkáda

Préveza

Paxoí

Antipaxoi

Párga

Lefkimmi

Kleisoúra

Ioánnina

Igoumenítsa

Corfu (Kérkyra)

Sidári

Kálpaki

Kónitsa

Grevená

Métsovo

Kranéa

Ioánnina

Árta

Amfilochía

Neochóri

Póros

Katoúna

Thérmo

Agrínio

Náfpaktos

Pátra

Káto Achaía

Xylókastro

Corinth (Kórinthos)

Corinth Canal

Aígio

Liódoriki

Aliartos

Chalkída

Vília

Mándra

ATHENS (ATHÍNA)

Piraeus (Peiraiás)

Aígina

Lávrio

Keratéa

Marathónas

Kárystos

Euboea (Évvoia)

Kými

Alivéri

Kálamos

Lamía

Karpenísi

Domokós

Karpenísi

Renína

Mólos

Agriovótano

Strofyliá

Skópelos

Skiathos

Alónnisos

Kyrá Panagía

Skýros

Skýros

Ágios Efstrátios

Límnos

Myrina

Akrotírio Drépano

Antissa

Kalloní

Mytilíni

Plomári

Lesbos (Lésvos)

Psará

Chíos

Chíos

Antipsara

Volos

Agía

Argalastí

Stómio

Soúrpi

Litóchoro

Litóchoro

Agiá

Lárisa

Tyrnavos

Trikala

Karditsa

Kalampáka

Pláka

Gónnoi

Velvendós

Olympus 2917m

Kateríni

Kozáni

Néa Moudaniá

Sárti

Thermaïc Gulf

Akrotírio Pínes

Akrotírio Pínes

Karyés

Simonpetra

Pélagos

Ukraine, Moldova & Romania

THROUGHOUT MUCH OF THE last century, Ukraine and Moldova formed part of the Soviet Union, while Romania was ruled for 20 years by the dictator Nicolae Ceausescu. In 1989 Ceausescu was overthrown, while Ukraine and Moldova became independent in 1991. Today the three countries are struggling to come to terms with their communist inheritance and transform themselves into modern democracies. All three lack modern technology and face serious economic and environmental problems arising from outdated industry. They also face increasing ethnic tensions with their minority populations – Hungarians in Romania, and Russians left behind in Ukraine and Moldova after the collapse of the Soviet Union.

CITY LIFE

Romania has many cities and towns with a mix of old and new buildings. Sibiu (left) was founded in the 12th century and, at one time, had 19 guilds—each representing a different craft—within its city walls. Much remains from this colorful history, especially in the painted buildings of the old town.

FOLK CUSTOMS

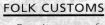

Despite years of communist rule, folk customs thrived in the rural areas of Romania and Ukraine. In Ukraine, singers perform *dumas*, historical epics that tell of slavery under the Turks. One of the traditional instruments is a *bandura* (left), a stringed instrument that sounds like a harpsichord.

DRACULA'S CASTLE

Situated in Transylvania—and a favorite tourist destination—is Bran Castle. This is where author Bram Stoker's fictional blood-drinking Count Dracula lived. The story is probably based on 15th-century Romanian prince Vlad Dracul, who reigned for less than 10 years but caused more than 50,000 deaths.

Did you know?

▶ The word Transylvania means "land beyond the forests."

▶ Russia's famous beet soup—*borscht*—comes from Ukraine.

▶ Built entirely underground, Crivoca winery north of Chisinau, Moldova, stretches over 37 miles (60 km).

EASTER BREAD

In Romania, Easter is celebrated with a meal of roast lamb served with a bread called *cozonac*. This is made by pounding nuts, raisins, and even cocoa, into the dough.

INDUSTRY IN THE UKRAINE

Ukraine is the world's fourth-largest producer of steel and has a large coal industry as well as reserves of oil and gas. Today, however, much of its industry is outdated and inefficient. Most of the heavy industry is situated in the central Dnieper river valley.

Liquid iron ore

HOLIDAYS BY THE SEA

The Black Sea resorts of the Crimea, in southern Ukraine, were once a favorite vacation destination for Russians heading south for the summer sun. Today, resorts here, such as Yalta (below), are still popular, although the facilities are poor when compared with similar places around the Mediterranean Sea.

PEOPLE OF ROMANIA

Romanians speak Romansch—a language closely related to French, Italian, and Spanish. The country also has sizable Hungarian and Roma minorities, which have both been discriminated against in recent years. Most Hungarian-speakers live in the region of Romania known as Transylvania.

CHILDREN from the Maramures region of Transylvania.

RICH SOILS OF MOLDOVA

Moldova consists of partially wooded plains intercut with rivers and streams. About 75 percent of the land is rich in chernozem (black) soil, which is very fertile. Wine and sunflower production is important here. Fruit and vegetables, such as pumpkins (left), also grow well.

Map labels:

RUSSIAN FEDERATION

0 km 50 100
0 miles 50 100

Horodnya, Shostka, Shchors, Krolevets', Hlukhiv, Chernihiv, Konotop, Bakhmach, Nizhyn, Oster, Nosivka, Romny, Sumy, Brovary, Pryluky, Yahotyn, Lebedyn, KIEV (KYIV), Pyryatyn, Okhtyrka, Zolochiv, Derhachi, Fastiv, Hrebinka, Lubny, Myrhorod, Lyubotyn, Kharkiv, Bila Tserkva, Merefa, Kup''yans'k, Poltava, Hlobyne, Izyum, Starobil's'k, Horodyshche, Cherkasy, Kreminna, Rubizhne, Tal'ne, Shpola, Chyhyryn, Kremenchuk, Slov''yans'k, Syeverodonets'k, Uman', Oleksandrivka, Kramators'k, Lysychans'k, Mala Vyska, Znam''yanka, Oleksandriya, Novomoskovs'k, Pavlohrad, Kostyantynivka, Zolote, Luhans'k, Kirovohrad, Dniprodzerzhyns'k, Dnipropetrovs'k, Horlivka, Stakhanov, Ulyanivka, Zhovti Vody, P''yatykhatky, Synel'nykove, Yenakiyeve, Krasnodon, Vil'shanka, Dolyns'ka, Pokrovs'ke, Makiyivka, Krasnyy Luch, Pervomays'k, Kryvyy Rih, Donets'k, Torez, Arbyzynka, Inhulets', Zaporizhzhya, Orikhiv, Volnovakha, Dokuchayevs'k, Amvrosiyivka, Novyy Buh, Voznesens'k, Nikopol', Ordzhonikidze, Marhanets', Polohy, Novovazovs'k, Kam''yanka-Dniprovs'ka, Dniprorudne, Tokmak, Mariupol', Mykolayiv, Molochans'k, Zhovtneve, Kakhovka, Melitopol', Ochakiv, Kherson, Akinovka, Prymors'k, Berdyans'k, Hola Prystan', Tsyurupyns'k, Novotroyits'ke, Odesa, Chaplynka, Kalanchak, Henishes'k, Illichivs'k, Armyans'k, Krasnoperekops'k, Chornomors'ke, Rozdol'ne, Dzhankoy, Krasnohvardiys'ke, Kerch, Nyzhn'ohirs'kyy, Lenine, Yevpatoriya, Saky, Feodosiya, Simferopol', Bakhchysaray, Alushta, Sevastopol', Yalta, Alupka

Dnieper Lowland, Russian Federation, Black Sea, Sea of Azov, Crimea (Kryms'kyy Pivostriv), Kerch Strait, Gulf of Taganrog, Kremenchuts'ke Vodoskhovyshche, Dniprodzerzhyns'ke Vodoskhovyshche, Kakhovs'ka Vodoskhovyshche, Kaniys'ke Vodoskhovyshche, Dnieper (Dnipro), Desna, Psel, Donets, Oskil, Karkinits'ka Zatoka, Zatoka Syvash, Pivdennyy Buh, Kryms'ki Hory

Baltic States & Belarus

THE THREE BALTIC STATES, Estonia, Latvia, and Lithuania, all share a small stretch of coast on the Baltic Sea. Belarus lies between Poland, Ukraine, and the Russian Federation. Following independence from the Soviet Union in 1991, all these countries faced problems such as price rises, food shortages, and pollution. However, the Baltic States have since tried to reform their societies and economies along western lines. Belarus has kept close links with Russia and has been the slowest to reform. This mainly rural country remains isolated from the rest of Europe and, with few natural resources, remains one of its poorest nations.

SINGING REVOLUTION

Estonia is known for its classical music tradition, most notably its choirs. This love of music was most powerful when people raised their voices during the Singing Revolution in 1988 (right), part of their move toward independence.

POLITICAL RALLY IN TALLINN

TALLINN OLD TOWN

With its colorful buildings, turreted walls, and gabled roofs, Tallinn is one of the best-preserved capital cities in Europe. All the winding, cobbled streets lead to the Town Hall Square (left).

AMBER

Two-thirds of the world's amber, the fossilized resin of pine trees, is washed up from the seabed along the Baltic coast. Amber is used to make jewelry, among other things.

Gulf of Finland

Narva Bay

RUSSIAN FEDERATION

ESTONIA

LATVIA

LITHUANIA

POLAND

Baltic Sea

Gulf of Riga

TALLINN
Tartu
RĪGA
VILNIUS
Kaunas
Šiauliai
Panevėžys
Liepāja
Ventspils
Klaipėda
KALININGRAD (to Russian Federation)
Navapolatsk
Polatsk

Lake Peipus
Lake Pskov

Narva Reservoir

MINSK CITY

The capital of Belarus, Minsk, was destroyed during World War II and was then rebuilt in a starkly modern style.

Minsk is the country's economic center—cars, trucks and tractors, chemicals, timber products, and a range of high-tech goods are all produced here. Farm produce (above) is also sold in the markets.

RUSSIAN FEDERATION

Vitsyebsk
Lyozna
Chashniki
Bahushewsk
Lyadchyn
Krupki
Talachyn
Orsha
Horki
Khodasy
Krychaw
Klimavichy
Mahilyow
Harbavichy
Sava
Kastsyukovichy
Cherykaw
Slawharad
Baron'ki
Shklow
Chavusy
Myekulavichy
Buda-
Kashalyova
Zhlobin
Rahachow
Dobrush
Kastsyukowka
Uvaravichy
Tsyerakhowka
Babruysk
Abidavichy
Homyel
Loyew
Byval'ki

Barysaw
Zhodzina
Byerezino
MINSK
Krasnaye
Plyeshchanitsy
Valozhyn
Shchuchyn
Orlya
Navahrudak
Masty
Vawkavysk
Zel'va
Slonim
Ruzhany
Pruzhany
Novy Dvor
Zhabinka
Brest
Kobryn
Damachava
Makrany

BELARUS
Minskaya
Wzvyshsha
Baranavichy
Nyasvizh
Kapyl'
Slutsk
Salihorsk
Starobyn
Luninyets
Pinsk
Drahichyn
Lyusina
Ivanava
Yasyel'da
Pripet Marshes

POLAND
Bug

UKRAINE

FARMING

The fertile soils and flat landscapes make this region good for farming. The Baltic States, particularly Latvia (left), have large dairy farms. Belarus is a major producer of flax, used to make linen and other products. Potatoes—used to make vodka—sugar beet, and other root crops are also grown here.

TEXTILES

Development of the textile industry in these countries is strong, with foreign investment from Sweden (for Latvia) and Indonesia (for Lithuania) helping growth. Clothes, bedlinen, curtains, and towels are just some of the items made for export.

GYMNASTICS

The former Soviet Union worked its young athletes and gymnasts extremely hard in order to win Olympic medals and thus national glory. Many of the most famous gymnasts came from Belarus, notably Olga Korbut and, more recently, Svetlana Boginskya (right), who has won 3 gold, 1 silver, and 1 bronze Olympic medals.

FERNS THRIVE in this Latvian forest.

FORESTS AND LAKES

All four countries are low-lying with many moors, bogs, unspoiled lakes, and fir and pine forests. Forestry is an important industry, providing wood pulp for paper-making, and timber for furniture and houses.

LITHUANIAN COSTUME

In some Lithuanian villages, people still wear traditional folk costume, especially for festive occasions. Women's clothing is generally colorful (left) and might include a white linen shirt, a skirt, and an apron. The decoration and style of the costume shows which region of Lithuania the wearer comes from.

0 km   50   100
0 miles   50   100

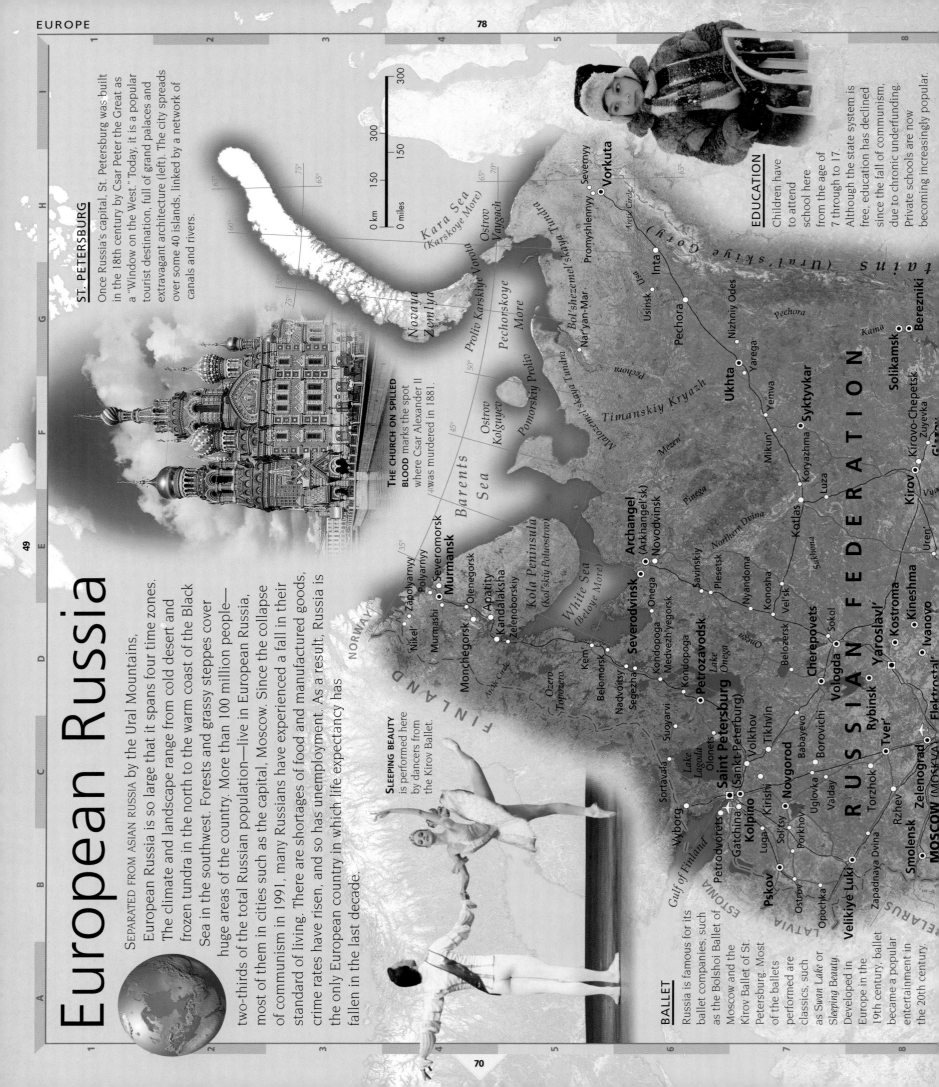

European Russia

SEPARATED FROM ASIAN RUSSIA by the Ural Mountains, European Russia is so large that it spans four time zones. The climate and landscape range from cold desert and frozen tundra in the north to the warm coast of the Black Sea in the southwest. Forests and grassy steppes cover huge areas of the country. More than 100 million people—two-thirds of the total Russian population—live in European Russia, most of them in cities such as the capital, Moscow. Since the collapse of communism in 1991, many Russians have experienced a fall in their standard of living. There are shortages of food and manufactured goods, crime rates have risen, and so has unemployment. As a result, Russia is the only European country in which life expectancy has fallen in the last decade.

ST. PETERSBURG

Once Russia's capital, St. Petersburg was built in the 18th century by Csar Peter the Great as a "Window on the West." Today, it is a popular tourist destination, full of grand palaces and extravagant architecture (left). The city spreads over some 40 islands, linked by a network of canals and rivers.

THE CHURCH ON SPILLED BLOOD marks the spot where Csar Alexander II was murdered in 1881.

EDUCATION

Children have to attend school here from the age of 7 through to 17. Although the state system is free, education has declined since the fall of communism, due to chronic underfunding. Private schools are now becoming increasingly popular.

BALLET

Russia is famous for its ballet companies, such as the Bolshoi Ballet of Moscow and the Kirov Ballet of St. Petersburg. Most of the ballets performed are classics, such as *Swan Lake* or *Sleeping Beauty*. Developed in Europe in the 19th century, ballet became a popular entertainment in the 20th century.

SLEEPING BEAUTY is performed here by dancers from the Kirov Ballet.

---

0 km   150   300

0 miles   150   300

Kara Sea (Karskoye More)

Novaya Zemlya

Ostrov Vaygach

Proliv Karskiye Vorota

Severnyy

Vorkuta

Promyshlennyy

Arctic Circle

Inta

Usa

Usinsk

Ust'

Bol'shezemel'skaya Tundra

Naryan-Mar

Pechora

Nizhniy Odes

(Ural'skiye Gory)

Pechora

Yarega

Berezniki

Kama

tains

Ukhta

Yemva

Mikun'

Solikamsk

Syktyvkar

Koryazhma

Kirovo-Chepetsk

Zuyevka

Kirov

Timanskiy Kryazh

Luza

Mezen'

Koslan

Malozemel'skaya Tundra

Ponorskiy Proliv

Pechorskoye More

Ostrov Kolguyev

Barents Sea

Ostrov Kolguyev

Pinega

Pechora

Savinskiy

Vel'sk

Arkhangel (Arkhangel'sk)

Plesetsk

Northern Dvina

Novodvinsk

Nyandoma

Konosha

Sukhona

Kotlas

Kola Peninsula (Kol'skiy Poluostrov)

Zapolyarnyy

Polyarnyy

Severomorsk

Murmansk

Monchegorsk

Olenegorsk

Apatity

Kandalaksha

Zelenoborskiy

White Sea (Beloye More)

Severodvinsk

Onega

Onega

Belozersk

Sokol

Vologda

Nel'sk

Konosha

Nikel'

Murmashi

Kem

Arctic Circle

Belomorsk

Kondopoga

Medvezh'yegorsk

Petrozavodsk

Lake Onega

Onega

Cherepovets

Babayevo

Borovichi

Ozero Topozero

Nadvoitsy

Segezha

Kondopoga

Suoyarvi

Belozersk

Yaroslavl'

Kostroma

Rybinsk

Kineshma

RUSSIAN FEDERATION

NORWAY

FINLAND

Sortavala

Lake Ladoga

Olonets

Volkhov

Tikhvin

Uglovka

Valday

Ivanovo

Vyborg

Luga

Kirishi

Novgorod

Torzhok

Rzhev

Tver'

Zelenograd

Elektrostal'

Saint Petersburg (Sankt-Peterburg)

Petrodvorets

Gatchina

Kolpino

Sol'tsy

MOSCOW (MOSKVA)

ESTONIA

Pskov

Ostrov

Velikiye Luki

Porkhov

Opochka

Zapadnaya Dvina

Smolensk

LATVIA

BELARUS

49

70

RURAL LIFE

Rural life has become extremely tough since the economic collapse of large-scale farms in the 1990s, with many people living in poverty. Smaller co-operatives and farms (above) have sprung up, and the agricultural industry is going through a painful period of reform. Because of the harsh climate, only 10 percent of the land is suitable for agriculture.

THE RUSSIAN CHURCH

The main religion in Russia is the Russian Orthodox Church. Under communism, all religion was banned. The new freedom means that many Russians now attend church services on a regular basis. New churches are being built, old ones restored, and seminaries reopened to train new priests.

RUSSIAN icons show religious scenes painted on wood.

THE TARTARS

Russia's largest ethnic minority, the Tartars (below), are an Islamic people descended from the Mongols. They live in the Tatarstan Republic, midway between Moscow and the Urals.

Did you know?

Ice cream is popular in Russia, even in winter. It can be bought from places marked *morozhenoe.*

The title csar, once used for Russian rulers, is a word meaning "emperor."

During the 20th century, St. Petersburg went through three revolutions, as well as a 900-day siege.

MOSCOW METRO

Not many subways can claim to be tourist attractions, but Moscow's metro can. Built in the 1930s, many of its stations are decorated with beautiful chandeliers, mosaics, paintings, and sculptures. One of the busiest, most efficient subways in the world, it is used by over seven million people daily.

POLLUTION

The communists invested heavily in industry, but their outdated methods of production have affected the environment. Rivers such as the Volga are badly polluted, and many cities are covered in a permanent and poisonous smog. Chest infections and other diseases related to air pollution are common.

INDUSTRIAL SMOG casts a haze over Moscow.

ASIA

Asia is the biggest continent in the world. From east to west it stretches

almost halfway around the globe; from north

to south it spreads from the frozen Arctic to the

sweltering, tropical heat of Southeast Asia. All 17 of the world's

 mountains over 26,246 ft (8,000 m) can be found in

Asia, as well as the largest and deepest lakes—the

Caspian Sea and Lake Baikal. The world's first civilizations started here,

many of the most important inventions were made here, and all the

world's major religions began here. Much of Asia is uninhabited, yet

its 48 countries are home to 3,672,342,000 people—

more than half the world's population. The discovery

 of oil in countries such as Saudi Arabia has made

some people very rich, while many of those who live

on the Indian subcontinent live in rural areas and are extremely poor.

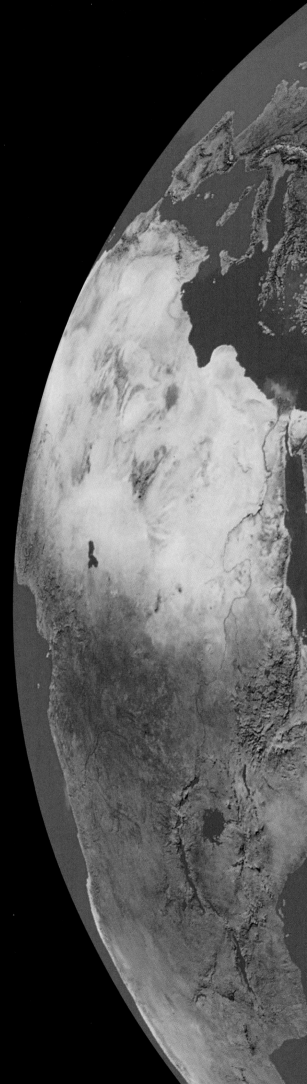

Turkey and the Caucasus

TURKEY LIES IN BOTH ASIA and Europe—separated by the Bosporus—and was once part of the powerful Ottoman Empire. Although the Turks are 99 percent Muslim, modern Turkey is a country with no official religion. Western Turkey is relatively industrialized, with a tourist industry along the Mediterranean coast that brings in considerable income. Many farmers and herders in the center and east, however, struggle to make a living in the harsh environment. To the northeast lie the Caucasus countries of Georgia, Azerbaijan, and Armenia. Once part of the USSR, they are now independent.

ISTANBUL

The different faces of Turkey can be seen in its former capital, Istanbul, which lies on both sides of the Bosporus waterway. Churches, mosques, and ancient buildings in both European and Islamic styles sit side by side with modern shops and offices. Bridges link the two parts of the city. In 1923, Ankara became the new capital.

TURKISH FOOD

Turkey is self-sufficient in food, and grows specialized crops such as eggplant, peppers, figs, and dates. A typical Turkish meal might consist of spiced lamb, often grilled on a skewer with onion and tomato to make a *shish kebab*. This would be served with rice or cracked wheat.

EPHESUS

Tourism is one of Turkey's major industries. As well as beach resorts, the country has many ancient sites. One of these is the old Greek city of Ephesus, which lies 35 miles (56 km) south of modern-day Izmir on the Aegean coast. The city was famous for its Temple of Artemis, which was considered one of the seven wonders of the world.

VISITORS to Ephesus admire the remains of the Library of Celsus.

FATHER OF THE TURKS

Mustafa Kemal Atatürk (1881–1939), founder of the modern Turkish state, became its first president in 1923. He introduced many reforms, including more equality for women and better education for all. He also declared that Islam was no longer to be the official religion.

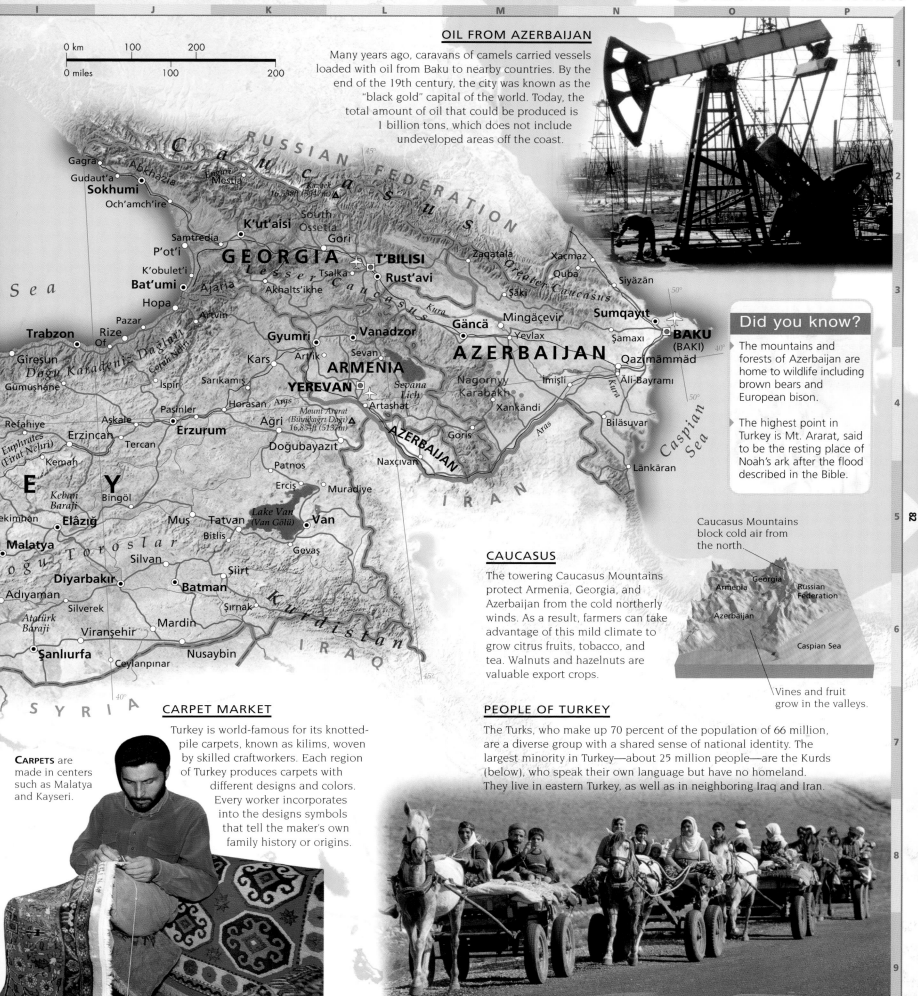

OIL FROM AZERBAIJAN

Many years ago, caravans of camels carried vessels loaded with oil from Baku to nearby countries. By the end of the 19th century, the city was known as the "black gold" capital of the world. Today, the total amount of oil that could be produced is 1 billion tons, which does not include undeveloped areas off the coast.

Did you know?

► The mountains and forests of Azerbaijan are home to wildlife including brown bears and European bison.

► The highest point in Turkey is Mt. Ararat, said to be the resting place of Noah's ark after the flood described in the Bible.

CAUCASUS

The towering Caucasus Mountains protect Armenia, Georgia, and Azerbaijan from the cold northerly winds. As a result, farmers can take advantage of this mild climate to grow citrus fruits, tobacco, and tea. Walnuts and hazelnuts are valuable export crops.

Caucasus Mountains block cold air from the north.

Vines and fruit grow in the valleys.

CARPET MARKET

Turkey is world-famous for its knotted-pile carpets, known as kilims, woven by skilled craftworkers. Each region of Turkey produces carpets with different designs and colors. Every worker incorporates into the designs symbols that tell the maker's own family history or origins.

CARPETS are made in centers such as Malatya and Kayseri.

PEOPLE OF TURKEY

The Turks, who make up 70 percent of the population of 66 million, are a diverse group with a shared sense of national identity. The largest minority in Turkey—about 25 million people—are the Kurds (below), who speak their own language but have no homeland. They live in eastern Turkey, as well as in neighboring Iraq and Iran.

Russia and Kazakhstan

THE RUSSIAN FEDERATION is the biggest country in the world, almost twice as big as either the US or China. It extends halfway around the world, crosses two continents, and spans 11 time zones. The vast region of Siberia alone is larger than Canada. Kazakhstan lies to its south and is a large but sparsely populated country. From 1917 to 1991, both countries were part of the Union of Soviet Socialist Republics (USSR), the world's first communist state. When the USSR collapsed, Russia, Kazakhstan, and the 13 other member republics gained independence. Since then, Russia and Kazakhstan have begun to transform themselves from communist states into democratic nations. Both countries have a lot of fertile land, huge mineral deposits, and many other natural resources. However, Russia still has the lowest life expectancy rate of all the industrialized countries.

Did you know?

▶ The Chukchi people of Siberia get their name from the Chukchi word *Chauchu*, meaning "rich in reindeer."

▶ Lake Baikal is up to 6,367 ft (1,940 m) deep. It is the world's largest freshwater lake, containing more than 20 percent of the world's supply of fresh water.

▶ The traditional home of the Kazakh is called the *yurt*. This is made of a collapsible framework with felt stretched over it.

▶ The native populations of Siberia are bilingual. They speak their own native languages as well as Russian.

A KAZAKH man hunts with a trained golden eagle.

KAZAKH CULTURE

The majority of people in Kazakhstan are Kazakh Muslims. They were once a nomadic people who traveled around on horseback, herding their sheep. Now the Kazakhs mainly live in the rural areas of the country, retaining a strong loyalty to their clan and family.

COAL MINERS IN SIBERIA

NATURAL WEALTH

Siberia contains one-third of the world's natural gas reserves and has vast deposits of oil, as well as abundant minerals, such as coal, and precious metals, including gold. However, many of these resources are inaccessible or in remote places, and the extreme winters make it difficult to extract them.

Map labels

Franz Josef Land
North Cape (Nordkapp)
Barents Sea
ARCTIC
Novaya Zemlya
Kara Sea (Karskoye More)
Ostrov Belyy
Dikson
FINLAND
Murmansk
Kandalaksha
Kola Peninsula
Arctic Circle
White Sea
Ostrov Kolguyev
Nar'yan-Mar
Pechora
EST.
LAT.
Gulf of Finland
Saint Petersburg (Sankt-Peterburg)
Lake Lagoda
Pskov
Novgorod
Petrozavodsk
Lake Onega
Severodvinsk
Arkhangel'sk
Severnaya Dvina
Vel'sk
Ukhta
Vorkuta
Yamal Peninsula
Obskaya Guba
Talnak
Noril's
BELARUS
Smolensk
Cherepovets
MOSCOW (MOSKVA)
Tver'
Vologda
Yaroslavl'
Kotlas
Syktyvkar
Salekhard
Ob'
Igarka
UKRAINE
Bryansk
Tula
Kineshma
Vladimir
Nizhniy Novgorod
Kirov
Glazov
Solikamsk
Perm'
Serov
Khanty-Mansiysk
Nadym
Nyagan'
West Siberian Plain
Yenisey
Belgorod
Ryazan
Voronezh
Tambov
Penza
Kazan'
Izhevsk
Ural Mountains
Yekaterinburg
Surgut
Nizhnevartovsk
Rostov-na-Donu
Ul'yanovsk
Saratov
Tol'yatti
Naberezhnyye Chelny
Samara
Tyumen'
Chelyabinsk
RUSSIAN
Black Sea
Krasnodar
Volgograd
Stavropol'
Sterlitamak
Ufa
Tobol'sk
Ishim
Ishim
Irtysh
Ob'
Sochi
Ural'sk
Orenburg
Magnitogorsk
Aktobe
Orsk
Kostanay
Petropavlovsk
Omsk
Tomsk
El'brus 18,510ft (5642m)
Nal'chik
Astrakhan'
Alga
Rudnyy
Kokshetau
Novosibirsk
Krasnoyars
GEORGIA
Caucasus
Vladikavkaz
Groznyy
Makhachkala
Atyrau
Kemerovo
Fort-Shevchenko
Emba
Atbasar
Shchuchinsk
KAZAKHSTAN
ASTANA
Barnaul
AZERBAIJAN
Aktau
Zhanaozen
Chelkar
Aral'sk
Temirtau
Pavlodar
Novokuznetsk
Abaka
Caspian Sea
Ustyurt Plateau
Aral Sea
Syr Darya
Novokazalinsk
Saran'
Karaganda
Semipalatinsk
Leninogorsk
Zyryanovsk
Zapad
Ky
TURKMENISTAN
Zhezkazgan
Dzhusaly
Kyzylorda
Kazakh Uplands
Shar
Ust'-Kamenogorsk
Gora Belukha 14,783ft (4506m)
Kazakh Steppe
Kyzyl Kum
Balkhash
Ayaguz
Ozero Zaysan
Altai Mountains
UZBEKISTAN
Turkestan
Kentau
Lake Balkhash
Taldykorgan
Arys
Karatau
Tekeli
CHINA
Shymkent
Taraz
Almaty (Alma-Ata)
Kirghiz Range
KYRGYZSTAN

Scale

0 km 400 800
0 miles 400 800

Taiga forest

Russia's forests cover more than two-fifths of the country's territory. The Taiga forest region extends across the Urals to cover much of Siberia. This type of forest is characterized by small, widely spaced trees, with large areas of poorly drained marsh grasses.

NENET man guiding a sled and reindeer

NATIVE PEOPLES

During the winter months, temperatures in Siberia regularly drop to below −45°F (−43°C). The native people who live here, such as the Nenet people of the Yamal Peninsula region, have adapted well to their environment and survive by herding reindeer, hunting, and fishing.

RUSSIAN LANGUAGE

Russian is the official language of the Russian Federation, but many of the 152 other nationalities inside the federation speak their own language as well. The Russian language uses the Cyrillic alphabet, which was devised by Greek missionaries.

OLD CUSTOMS

The communists tried to impose a Russian national culture on the native peoples of Siberia, but many of their customs survived in remote areas. Today, traditional costume, music, and dance are all flourishing throughout Siberia.

RUSSIAN dancer in traditional dress

SIBERIAN WILDLIFE

Siberia is home to a huge range of wildlife, including the rare Siberian tiger—the biggest in the world—wolves, reindeer, and black and brown bears. The Baikal seal—found only in Lake Baikal—is the world's only freshwater seal.

SIBERIAN TIGER

TRANS-SIBERIAN RAILROAD TRAIN

TRANS-SIBERIAN RAILROAD

The longest railroad in the world runs 5,785 miles (9,310 km) from Moscow's Yaroslavl Station in the west, across Siberia to the Pacific port of Vladivostok in the east. The railroad was started in 1891 and took 14 years to finish. Trains take eight days to complete the journey and cross eight time zones.

77

The Near East

ISRAEL, JORDAN, SYRIA, AND LEBANON are the countries collectively known as the Near East. This is a land that is dominated by desert but also has fertile coastal plains. Lack of water is a constant problem here, although Israel has introduced computerized irrigation systems to extend the land suitable for agriculture. The creation of the Jewish state of Israel in 1948, in what was previously Arab-dominated Palestine, has led to almost continuous conflict in the region. Arabs and Israelis have fought four major wars, which have cost many lives. The Mediterranean island of Cyprus has also suffered a violent recent history.

LEBANON REBUILT

Beirut, the capital of Lebanon, was once the commercial and banking center of the Arab world, but was devastated by the civil war that ravaged the country from 1975 to 1989. Today, the country is largely at peace and Beirut is regaining much of its former glory. Lebanon remains dominated, however, by its two powerful neighbors—Syria and Israel.

CYPRUS

Cyprus became independent from Britain in 1960. However, conflict between Greeks and Turks caused Turkey to invade the island in 1974. Since then, Cyprus has been split between a Turkish Cypriot north and a Greek Cypriot south. Most Cypriots make a living from farming grapes, citrus fruit, and olives. Women often sell hand-made lace items to tourists.

SYRIAN MARKET

Damascus is one of the oldest inhabited cities in the world. At its center is a massive souk (bazaar) where the streets are full of stalls and small shops selling everything from carpets, textiles, and jewelry to household goods and fresh produce.

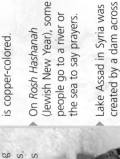

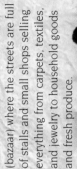

DAILY LIFE

Even in a war-torn country such as Israel, people continue to live as normal a life as possible. Children listen to pop music and watch their favorite sports stars, either live or on TV. In a peaceful break, these Palestinian boys play soccer in a Jerusalem street.

Map labels

TURKEY

IRAQ

I R A Q

S Y R I A

LEBANON

CYPRUS

TURKISH REPUBLIC OF NORTHERN CYPRUS (recognized only by Turkey)

Mediterranean Sea

Al Mālikīyah
Al Qāmishlī
Al Ḥasakah
Ash-Shadādah
Aş Şuwār
Subaykhān
Abū Ḥardān
Abū Kamāl
Al Jazīrah
Al Manāşif
Busayrah
Al Mayādīn
Al 'Ashārah
Ra's al 'Ayn
Jabal 'Abd al 'Azīz
Dayr az Zawr
Euphrates
At Tibnī
Jabal Bishrī
As Sukhnah
Ar Raqqah
As Sabkhah
Madīnat ath Thawrah
Lake Assad (Buḥayrat al Asad)
Sabkhat al Jabbūl
At Tall al Abyaḍ
Nahr Balīkh
Tudmur (Palmyra)
Ar Rāmī
Al Baridah
Manbij
Jarābulus
Euphrates
Aleppo (Halab)
Al Bāb
A'zāz
Afrin
Ḥārim
Idlib
Arīḥā
Abū aḍ Duhūr
Ma'arrat an Nu'mān
Salamiyah
Ḥamāh
Ḥimṣ
Al Quşayr
Tall Kalakh
Mazyaf
Orontes
Jibāl as Sāḩilīyah
Jebel Libnān
Quobāyāt
Banīyās
Jablah
Al Lādhiqīyah
Ţarţūs
Al Mina
Tripoli
Batroûn

Hirir Tigris
Tigris

Agialodsa (Yenierenköy)
Lápithos (Lapta)
Kerýneia (Girne)
Kythréa (Değirmenlik)
Mórfou (Güzelyurt)
NICOSIA
Dekéleia
Sovereign Base Area (to UK)
Ammóchostos (Gazimağusa) (Famagusta)
Lárnaka
Sovereign Base Area (to UK)
CYPRUS
Limassol (Lemesós)
Pólis (Πόλις)
Páfos (to UK)
Sovereign Base Area
Akrotírion

Scale

0 km 50 100
0 miles 50 100

ANCIENT CITY OF PETRA

Temples and tombs were cut out of the rock to form the spectacular city of Petra, in modern-day Jordan. Petra was built by the Nabataeans, an Arab tribe of the 4th century BC. The remains of the city are situated in a valley surrounded by cliffs with only one narrow entrance. Petra is Jordan's most famous historic site.

The Dome of
the Rock

Western
Wall

JERUSALEM

The old city of Jerusalem is sacred to three of the world's major religions: Judaism, Christianity, and Islam, each with their own holy sites and separate districts. Both Israelis and Palestinians claim Jerusalem as their capital. As a result, the city is a frequent source of conflict. The Dome of the Rock, sacred to Muslims, and the Western Wall, sacred to Jews, stand next to each other.

JORDANIAN DESERT police patrol the borders. Most are from Bedouin families.

REFUGEES LIVE in crowded conditions in this camp near Amman, Jordan.

PALESTINIAN REFUGEES

The frequent wars between Israel and its Arab neighbors have created a huge number of Palestinian refugees who have fled Israel to seek shelter in adjoining countries. Many live in poorly equipped refugee camps or settlements with few facilities and little chance of work. There are currently about 3.9 million registered refugees living in Jordan, Syria, Lebanon, and the West Bank.

THE KINGDOM OF JORDAN

Much of Jordan is hot, dry desert, with little land available for agriculture. Water is scarce and control of the Jordan River, which forms a border with Israel, is an important issue in peace talks. The desert is home to nomadic tribes of Bedouin who live in large tents woven from camel hair. Modern Bedouin use cars and trucks for transportation. Jordan has few natural resources other than phosphates, which it exports for use as fertilizer, and some limited oil reserves.

BEIRUT
(BEYROUTH)

DAMASCUS
(DIMASHQ)

S y r i a n

D e s e r t

SAUDI ARABIA

JORDAN

AMMAN
(AMMÄN)

Az Zarqä'

Irbid

Al Mafraq

Aş Şafāwī

Wāḥat al Azraq

Al 'Umarī

Ard aş Şawwän

Bāyir

Qā' al Jafr

Al-Jafr

Ra's an
Naqb

Al Quwayrah

Al Mudawwarah

SAUDI ARABIA

As Suwaydā'

Jabal ad Durūz
5899ft (1798m)

Muqaṭ

Dar'ā

Ar Ramthā

Mount
Hermon
9232ft (2814m)

Al Qunayṭirah

Qaṭanā

Dūmā

Damour

Şaïda

Soûr

En Nâqoûra

Nahariyya

Jbail

Bent
Jbail

Zefat
(Zefat)

Naḥr el Liṭānī

Golan
Heights

Lake
Tiberias

Teverya

Mifraẓ
Haifa
(Hefa)

Haifa
(Hefa)

Nazareth
(Nazerat)

Jenin

Nablus

Jordan

Hadera

Netanya

WEST
BANK

Petah Tiqwa

Tel Aviv-
Yafo

Holon

Rehovot

Jericho

Wadi as Sir

JERUSALEM

As Salt

Ma'daba

Al Karak

Al 'Aynā

Aṭ Ṭafīlah

Ash Shawbak

Ma'ān

Petra

Şāppir

Be'er Menuḥa

Gharandal

Elat

Al 'Aqabah

Gulf of Aqaba

ISRAEL

Negev
(Ha Negev)

Mizpe
Ramon

Be'ér
Sheva'

'Arad

Hebron

Bethlehem

Dead
Sea

Al Mazra'ah

Al Hịsā

Ash Sharāhız

Wadi al 'Arabá

EGYPT

Ashdod

Ashqelon

Gaza

Khān Yūnis

Rafaḥ

GAZA STRIP
(under Palestinian
administration)

32°

33°

33°

33°

38°

30°

31°

37°

36°

35°

30°

31°

32°

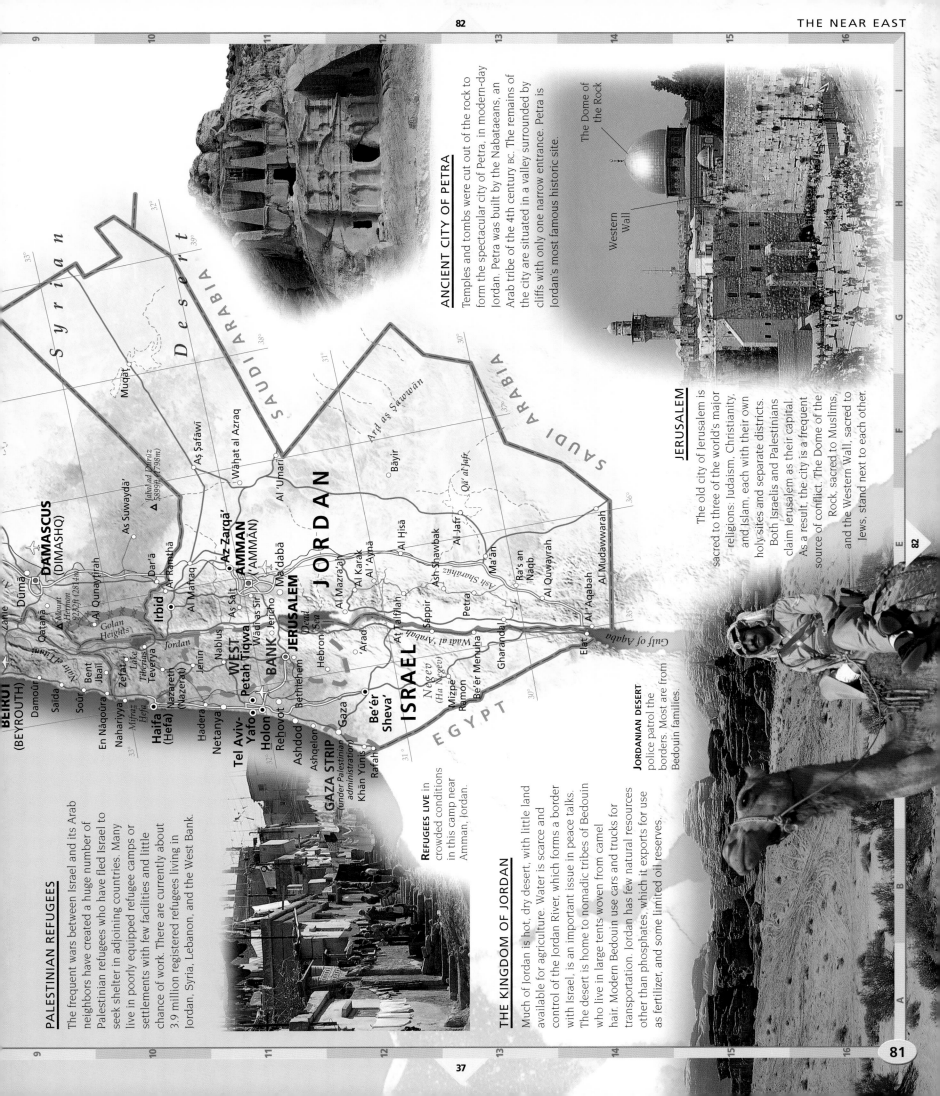

The Middle East

THE MIDDLE EAST IS HOME to the world's oldest civilizations, which grew up in the Tigris and Euphrates river valleys of present-day Iraq more than 6,000 years ago. The world's first towns and cities were built here. Since then, many powerful empires have dominated the region, all leaving a wealth of buildings and monuments behind them. Today, the Middle East is at the center of the Islamic world. The population of every country is Arab and speaks Arabic, except Iran, where half the population are Farsi-speaking Persians.

DESERT WARS

Most international boundaries in the Middle East are just lines drawn in the sand by the former European colonial powers, and have often caused conflict. Iraq and Iran fought a bitter eight-year war along their common border from 1980. Since then, further conflicts between Iraq and international forces have caused much suffering.

OIL PRODUCTION

The Middle East is the world's major oil producer—Saudi Arabia alone produces 10 percent of the world's supply. Oil has brought great wealth to the region, in particular to Saudi Arabia and the Gulf States.

THE IRANIANS

About half the total population of Iran are Persians, who live in the center and north of the country. Large numbers of Azeris live in the northwest, while Kurds live in the west and Baluchis in the southeast. The official language of Iran is Farsi, but many other languages are also spoken.

The Persian language is written in Arabic script.

ROLE OF WOMEN

Family life is important throughout the Muslim world. The role of women varies from country to country—traditionally, women stay at home and look after the family, but some now work. In public, many cover their head or whole body with a burqa.

Map labels

PAKISTAN
AFGHANISTAN
TURKMENISTAN
ARMENIA
AZERBAIJAN
AZ.
TURKEY
SYRIA
JORDAN
EGYPT

Sarakhs
Mashhad
Bojnūrd
Sabzevār
Mayamey
Shāhrūd
Semnān
Nehbandān
Birjand
Nosratābād
Zāhedān
Fahraj
Mīrjāveh
Hāmūn-e
Rīgān
Bam
Bāft
Sīrjān
Māhān
Kermān
Zarand
Bandar-e ʿAbbās
Bandar-e
Kangān
Deh Bid
Izad Khvāst
Shahr-e Kord
Eşfahān
Nā'īn
Ardakān
Anār
Yazd
Shīrāz
Kāzerūn
Bandar-e Būshehr
Rūd-e Mand
Koppeh Dāgh
Dasht-e Lūt
Dasht-e Kavīr
Iranian Plateau
Zagros Mountains (Kūhhā-ye Zāgros)
I R A N
Gorgān
Sārī
Āmol
Rasht
Ardabīl
Tabrīz
Qazvīn
Zanjān
Mīāneh
Qorveh
Saqqez
Marāgheh
Orūmīyeh
Daryācheh-ye Orūmīyeh
Maʿkū
Khvoy
Zākhō
Altin Köprü
Arbīl
Kirkūk
Al Mawṣil (Mosul)
Reshteh-ye Kūhhā-ye Alborz
△ Qolleh-ye Damāvand 18,606 ft (5671 m)
TEHRĀN
Qom
Kāshān
Arāk
Hamadān
Bākhtarān
Eslāmābād
Dezfūl
Ahvāz
Abādān
Khorramshahr
Al Amārah
Al Kūt
Kuwayt
Al Hillah
Al Hūrāh
As-Sulaymānīyah
Sanandaj
Caspian Sea
KUWAIT (AL KUWAYT)
KUWAIT (AL KUWAYT)
The G...
Baʿqūbah
BAGHDĀD
Karbalāʾ
An Najaf
As Samāwah
An Nāṣirīyah
Basra (Al Baṣrah)
Ar Rawdatayn
Al Jahrā'
Wādī al Bāţin
Al Wariʿah
Nişāb
Rafḥah
I R A Q
Ar Ramādī
Buḥayrat ar-Razāzah
Buḥayrat ath Tharthār
Al Baghdādī
ʿAnnah
Ar Ruţbah
Juday'idat Hāmīr
ʿArʿar
Sakākah
Rafḥah
Al Jawf
A n N a f ū d
Ḥāʾil
Taymaʾ
Tabūk
Jebel Ash Shifā
Tigris
Euphrates
Gulf of Aqaba

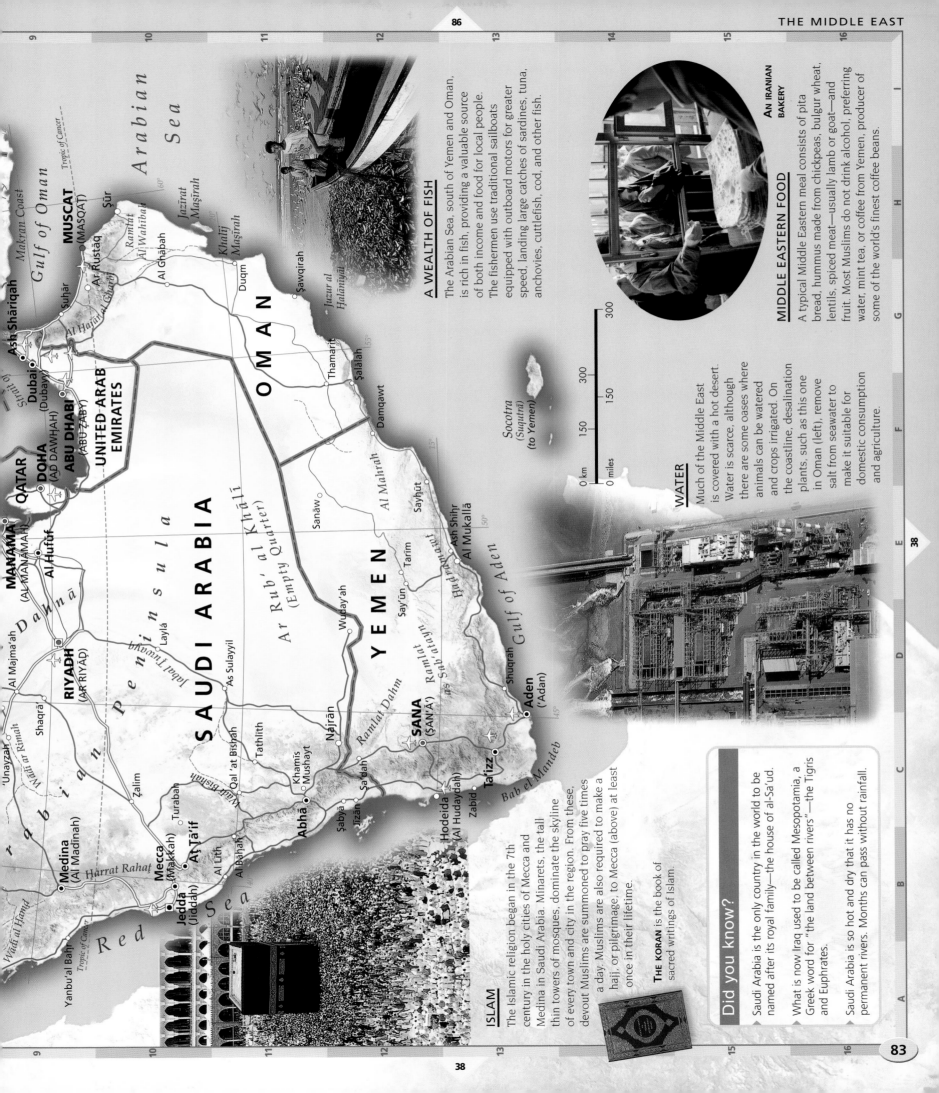

A WEALTH OF FISH

The Arabian Sea, south of Yemen and Oman, is rich in fish, providing a valuable source of both income and food for local people. The fishermen use traditional sailboats equipped with outboard motors for greater speed, landing large catches of sardines, tuna, anchovies, cuttlefish, cod, and other fish.

AN IRANIAN BAKERY

MIDDLE EASTERN FOOD

A typical Middle Eastern meal consists of pita bread, hummus made from chickpeas, bulgur wheat, lentils, spiced meat—usually lamb or goat—and fruit. Most Muslims do not drink alcohol, preferring water, mint tea, or coffee from Yemen, producer of some of the world's finest coffee beans.

WATER

Much of the Middle East is covered with a hot desert. Water is scarce, although there are some oases where animals can be watered and crops irrigated. On the coastline, desalination plants, such as this one in Oman (left), remove salt from seawater to make it suitable for domestic consumption and agriculture.

ISLAM

The Islamic religion began in the 7th century in the holy cities of Mecca and Medina in Saudi Arabia. Minarets, the tall thin towers of mosques, dominate the skyline of every town and city in the region. From these, devout Muslims are summoned to pray five times a day. Muslims are also required to make a hajj, or pilgrimage, to Mecca (above) at least once in their lifetime.

THE KORAN is the book of sacred writings of Islam.

Did you know?

Saudi Arabia is the only country in the world to be named after its royal family—the house of al-Sa'ud.

What is now Iraq used to be called Mesopotamia, a Greek word for "the land between rivers"—the Tigris and Euphrates.

Saudi Arabia is so hot and dry that it has no permanent rivers. Months can pass without rainfall.

0 km 150 300
0 miles 150 300

Map labels

Makran Coast
Gulf of Oman
Tropic of Cancer
Arabian Sea
MUSCAT (MASQAT)
Ash Shāriqah
Dubai (Dubayy)
Strait of...
UNITED ARAB EMIRATES
ABU DHABI (ABŪ ZABY)
DOHA (AD DAWḤAH)
QATAR
MANAMA (AL MANĀMAH)
Al Hufūf
Dahnā
Suḥār
Ar Rustāq
Ramlat Al Wahībah
Al Ghābah
Jazīrat Maṣīrah
Khalīj Maṣīrah
Duqm
OMAN
Al Hajar al Gharbī
Ṣawqirah
Juzur al Ḥalānīyāt
Thamarīt
Ṣalālah
Damqawt
Socotra (Suquṭrā) (to Yemen)
Al Mahrah
Sayḥūt
Sanāw
Ḥaḍramawt
Ash Shiḥr
Al Mukallā
Gulf of Aden
Tarīm
Say'ūn
Wudayʻah
Shuqrah
Aden ('Adan)
Bab el Mandeb
SANA (ṢAN'Ā')
YEMEN
Ta'izz
Hodeida (Al Ḥudaydah)
Zabīd
Sa'dah
Abhā
Jīzān
Ṣabyā
Khamīs Mushayt
Qal'at Bīshah
Najrān
Tathlīth
Nahr Bīshah
Ar Rub' al Khālī (Empty Quarter)
Ramlat Dahm
Ramlat as Sab'atayn
Layla
As Sulayyil
SAUDI ARABIA
Arabian Peninsula
Jabal Ṭuwayq
RIYADH (AR RIYĀḌ)
Shaqrā
Al Majma'ah
'Unayzah
Wādī ar Rimah
Zalim
Turabah
At Ṭā'if
Mecca (Makkah)
Medina (Al Madīnah)
Harrat Rahat
Al Līth
Al Birk
Jedda (Jiddah)
Red Sea
Yanbu' al Baḥr
Wādī al Ḥamḍ
Tropic of Cancer

Central Asia

THE FIVE CENTRAL ASIAN nations rise up from hot deserts in the west and south to cold, high mountain ranges in the east. The area has oil, gas, and mineral reserves, as well as other natural resources, but water is often scarce and agriculture is limited. The four northern nations were once part of the Soviet Union, and are now independent nations. Afghanistan is a landlocked country with three-quarters of its land being inaccessible terrain. It was invaded by the Soviet Union in 1979, prompting a civil war that has lasted for more than 20 years. In 2002, American and other western forces overthrew a fundamentalist Islamic regime in Afghanistan because of its support for international terrorism. The country, however, has been wrecked by these years of continuous warfare, making it one of the poorest and most deprived nations on Earth.

Did you know?

▶ Almost 90 percent of Turkmenistan consists of the Garagumy Desert, meaning "black sands" in Turkic.

▶ Tashkent in Uzbekistan is known as the "city of fountains" because it has so many water features.

▶ About 10 million land mines are buried in Afghanistan, making it one of the most heavily mined countries in the world. More than 90 people are maimed or killed every month.

▶ The world's largest gold mine is located in the Kyzyl Kum desert in Uzbekistan.

CHILDREN IN KABUL, Afghanistan, who have been made homeless by war.

FESTIVALS IN AFGHANISTAN

Despite the horrors of recent years, the Afghans still celebrate important Islamic festivals, notably Eid ul-Fitr, which marks the end of the holy month of Ramadan. People visit friends and family and eat a festive meal together. The art of storytelling still flourishes in Afghanistan, as does the *attan*, the national dance.

AN AFGHAN REFUGEE carries bread with which to break the Ramadan fast.

LIFE EXPECTANCY

As a result of war, drought, and poverty, people in Afghanistan can expect to live an average of only 46 years, one of the lowest life expectancy rates in the world. Infant mortality is extremely high. Health services have almost completely collapsed and few trained doctors and nurses are available to help the sick. There are not enough orphanages to cope with the increasing number of children who have no family.

Map labels: *Ustyurt Plateau*, *Aral Sea*, KAZAKHSTAN, Mŭynoq, Chimboy, Takhtakŭpir, *Sarykamyshkoye Ozero*, **Nukus**, Këneurgench, Takhiatosh, Uchquduq, *Kyzyl Kum*, Gubadag, Il'yaly, **Dashkhovuz**, **Urganch** UZBEKISTAN, Türtkŭl, Khiwa, Zarafshon, Gaz-Achak, Lebap, *Plato Kaplangky*, *Peski Uchtagan*, Turkmenbashi, *Krasnovodskiy Zaliv*, Nebitdag, *Zaunguzskiye Garagumy*, Gazli, Ghijduvon, **Bukhoro**, Cheleken, Darvaza, *Amu Darya*, Seydi, Kogon, Gazandzhyk, Gyzylarbat, *Kara Kum (Garagumy)*, Deynau, **Chardzhev**, *Kopetdag Gershi*, **TURKMENISTAN**, Sayat, Kara-Kala, Bakharden, *Caspian Sea*, Geok-Tepe, Byuzmeyin, *Kelifskiy Uzboy*, Amu-Dar, Kerk, **ASHGABAT**, *Gora Chapan 9478ft (2889)*, Kaakhka, Tedzhen, Mary, Bayramaly, *Kara Kum Canal*, Murgab, *Murgab*, Serakhs, Andkhvoy, *Vozvyshennost' Karabil'*, Meymaneh, Bālā Morghāb, *Torkesta*, Gushgy, *Darya-ye Morghāb*, Towraghoudī, *Selseleh-ye Safid Kŭh*, Ghūriān, **Herāt**, Han, **AFGHA**, Shīndand, *Farah Rūd*, Farāh, Delārām, Gereshk, *Dasht-e Khāsh*, Lashkar Gāh, **Kandaha**, *Hāmūn-e Sāberī*, Chakhānsūr, Zaranj, *Dasht-e Mārgow*, Kŭchnay Darweyshān, Deh Shū, *Darya-ye Helmand*, *Rigestān*, *Chāgai Hills*, PAKISTAN

ARAL SEA

The vast inland Aral Sea, between Uzbekistan and Kazakhstan, was once a thriving freshwater lake full of fish. Over the years, the rivers flowing into it were diverted or drained to provide irrigation for crops. The sea has now shrunk to half its original size, reducing the numbers of fish, and leaving former fishing villages stranded inland.

The fishing village of Muynoq is now over 30 miles (48 km) away from the Aral Sea.

A MAN in front of his home, called a *yurt*, in western Pamir, Tajikistan

MOUNTAIN LIFE

The two small eastern republics of Kyrgyzstan and Tajikistan are both very mountainous and are subject to earthquakes and landslides. Only about six percent of Tajikistan can be used for agriculture, while Kyrgyzstan is more fertile.

LOCAL WEALTH

Uzbekistan, Turkmenistan, and Kyrgyzstan all grow considerable crops of cotton—Uzbekistan is the world's fourth-largest producer—as well as fruit and vegetables. The three countries are also rich in mineral deposits, such as gold, mercury, sulfur, and uranium, and have reserves of coal, oil, and natural gas.

HARVESTING cotton in Uzbekistan

THE TAJIKS

The majority of people of Tajikistan are Iranian in origin and speak Tajik, which is related to Farsi. The minority Uzbeks are made up mainly of descendents of Turkic-speaking (related to Turkish) nomads. This division has led to ethnic tension between the two groups. Civil war between the government and Islamic rebels in the east of the country during the 1990s led to an exodus of Uzbeks and Russians, who had moved into the country when it was part of the Soviet Union.

TAJIK HORSEMEN in Pamir, Tajikistan

TILLA-KARI, a 17th-century Islamic religious school in Samarqand, Uzbekistan

THE SILK ROAD

The Silk Road is the ancient trading route that brought silks and other fine goods from China through central Asia and the Middle East to Europe. Many cities were built along its route, including Bukhoro, an important place of pilgrimage for Muslims, and Samarqand (right), which contains some of the finest Islamic architecture in the world. Many of these cities are now UNESCO-designated World Heritage Sites.

0 km   100   200

0 miles   100   200

Indian Subcontinent

SEPARATED FROM THE rest of Asia by the Himalayas, the Indian subcontinent is home to more than one-fifth of the world's population—a staggering one billion people. They have a long and complex history, form many different ethnic groups, speak a wide variety of languages, and worship many different gods. Some of these countries are relatively wealthy, but many people live in poverty. Tensions between and within countries in this region have sometimes erupted in warfare. The Indian subcontinent is often affected by natural disasters, notably cyclones in the Bay of Bengal, and earthquakes. However, India, the most heavily populated state and once prone to famine, is now more than self-sufficient in food. All but Nepal and Bhutan were once ruled by the British, whose legacy can be seen in the common language of English, in the architecture, the vast railroad system, and in sport—most notably cricket.

Monsoon

From May–June to September, warm, moist southerly winds sweep up from the Indian Ocean and the Bay of Bengal across the subcontinent. Once these winds meet dry land, moisture falls as monsoon rainfall. Although this irrigates the land and replenishes the water supply, it can also cause severe flooding.

SRI LANKA

In 1983, civil war erupted in Sri Lanka between the Buddhist majority Sinhalese, who dominate the government, and the Hindu minority Tamils, who want to establish their own independent state in the north of the island. The civil war has cost many lives and disrupted the island's economy, yet Sri Lanka still has one of the highest literacy rates in the world and high levels of health care.

FAMILY LIFE IN PAKISTAN

Pakistanis have strong ties to their extended families, and often many generations live and work together in family-run businesses. Smaller family units, however, are becoming more common in urban areas. Although some women hold prominent positions in public and commercial life—Benazir Bhutto has twice been prime minister—most women do not work outside the home.

SCHOOLCHILD in Sri Lanka

Map labels:

Hindu Kush
Khyber Pass 3543ft (1080m)
Mingãora
Mardãn
ISLAMABAD
Peshãwar
Wãh
Rãwalpindi
Jhelum
Jammi
AFGHANISTAN
Pottwar Plateau
Sargodha Gujrãt
Gujrãnwa
Chaman
Toba Kãkar Range
Lahore
Amrit
Faisalãbãd
Ludhiãr
Quetta
Dera Ghãzi Khan
Multan Okãra
Chandi
Kãlat
Sibi
Bathinda
Haryãna
PAKISTAN
Karnã
Chãgai Hills
Bahãwalpur
Delh
Baluchistãn
Jacobãbãd
NEW DEL
Shikãrpur
Rahïmyãr Khãn
Lãrkãna
Sukkur
Bïkãner
Khairpur
Thar Desert
Alwar
Turbat
Nawãbshãh
Jaisalmer
Jaipur
Gwãdar
Pasni
Jodhpur
Hyderãbãd
Mïrpur Khãs
Pãli
Beãwar
Karãchi
Rãjasthãn Shiv
Sind
Sujawal
Udaipur
Kota
Rann of Kachchh
Pãlanpur
Tropic of Cancer
Gãndhïdhãm
Gujarãt
Gulf of Kachchh
Ahmadãbãd
Ratlãm
Godhra
Vindhya R
Jãmnagar
Bho
Rãjkot
Indore
Vadodara
Porbandar
Bhãvnagar
Satpura Ra
Gulf of Khambhãt
Sürat
Bhusãwal
Dãmãn
Mãnmãd
Nãshik
Aurangãbã
Kalyãn
Maharãshtra
Mumbai
(Bombay)
Pune
Nãnde
Arabian Sea
Bãrãmati
Solãpur
Gulbar
Kolhãpur
Rãïc
Karnãtaka
Belgaum
Gadag
Panaji
Hubli
Dãvang
Shimoga
Udupi
Mangalore
Bangalore
Kãsargod
Mysore
Cannanore
Kerala
Erod
Calicut
Coimbatore
Ernãku
Cochin
Quilon
Trivandrum
Nãgercoi

0 km   150   300
0 miles   150   300

IRAN

"line of control" as agreed between India and Pakistan (1972)

AKSAI CHIN
(administered by China, claimed by India)

DEMCHOK/ DÊMQOG
(administered by China, claimed by India)

THE HIMALAYAS

The highest chain of mountains in the world, the Himalayas have eight peaks that are more than 26,247 ft (8,000 m) high. Everest, the world's highest mountain at 29,035 ft (8,850 m), is on the border of Nepal and Tibet. Mountaineers come from far and wide to scale these massive peaks.

BHUTANESE PEOPLE

BHUTAN

Hidden away in the Himalayas, the people of Bhutan are devoutly Buddhist and have little contact with the outside world. A minority of the population are Nepalese Hindus who came to the country in the first half of the last century. Most Bhutanese live in the fertile river valleys of the center and south of the country. Traditional dress—the *kira* for women and the *gho* for men—is widely worn.

Did you know?

▶ The name Bhutan means "land of the Thunder Dragon" in Dzongkha, the country's official language.

▶ India has the second largest population in the world after China, officially passing the one billion mark in the year 2000.

Map labels

NEPAL
CHINA
Himalayas
ARUNACHAI PRADESH *(claimed by China)*
Dibrugarh
Meerut
Bareilly
Salyan
Pokhara
Annapurna 26,545ft (8091m)
Mount Everest 29,035ft (8850m)
Kula Kangri 24,783ft (7554m)
KATHMANDU
Bhaktapur
Lalitpur
THIMPHU
BHUTAN
Darjiling
Bongaigaon
Brahmaputra
Jorhât
MYANMAR (BURMA)
Lucknow
Faizābād
Gorakhpur
Biratnagar
Shiliguri
Guwāhāti
Kohima
Gwalior
Kānpur
Chhapra
Dinajpur
Rangpur
Assam
Imphâl
Allahābād
Patna
Jamalpur
Sylhet
Silchar
Jhānsi
Uttar Pradesh
Varanasi
Ganges
BANGLADESH
Madhya Pradesh
Gaya
Bihar
Rajshahi
Pabna
DHAKA
Tropic of Cancer
Sāgar
Murwāra
Dhanbād
Āsānsol
Ganges
Jessore
Comilla
Jabalpur
Chota Nāgpur
Rānchi
West-Bengal
Khulna
Barisal
Chittagong
Jamshedpur
Rāulakela
Kharagpur
Calcutta (Kolkatta)
Bilāspur
Korba
INDIA
Mouths of the Ganges
Nāgpur
Gondia
Raipur
Sambalpur
Bāleshwar
Orissa
Mahānadi
Bay of Bengal
Chandrapur
Bhubaneshwar
Cuttack
Puri
Jagdalpur
Brahmapur
zāmābād
Andhra Pradesh
Karimnagar
Vizianagaram
Eastern Ghats
Warangal
Rājahmundry
Visākhapatnam
Hyderābād
Godāvari
Krishna
Vijayawāda
Chīrala
rnool
Ongole
dpatri
Kāvali
ddapah
Nellore
Chennai (Madras)
ellore
Kānchipuram
lem
Pondicherry
du
Tiruchchirāppalli
adurai
Palk Strait
Jaffna
ticorin
SRI LANKA
Mannar
Trincomalee
ulf of annar
Puttalam
Batticaloa
egombo
Kandy
COLOMBO
Kalutara
Galle
Matara
INDIAN OCEAN
North Andaman
Middle Andaman
Port Blair
South Andaman
Andaman Islands *(to India)*
Little Andaman
Nicobar Islands *(to India)*
Car Nicobar
Andaman Sea
Katchall Island
Little Nicobar
Great Nicobar
Indira Point

RELIGION

Two of the world's great religions—Hinduism and Buddhism—began in India more than 2,500 years ago. Most Pakistanis and Bangladeshis are Muslim, most Indians and Nepalese are Hindu, and most Sri Lankans and Bhutanese are Buddhist.

HINDUS BATHE in the Ganges River, considered sacred.

TEA IN SRI LANKA

Sri Lanka is the world's largest exporter of tea. The plantations are located mainly in the center of the island, and employ women to pick the delicate, green shoots of the bushes.

BOLLYWOOD

More films are produced in Mumbai (Bombay)—more than 800 a year—than in the US, turning "Bollywood," as it is known, into a major cultural center. Bollywood films generally have historical, religious, or social themes, and are famous for their song and dance routines and glamorous stars. These films are an important export to central Asia, the Middle East, and Africa.

Western China and Mongolia

CHINA IS A LAND of great geographical diversity and amazing landscapes. More than 90 percent of the population is Han Chinese—descendants of people who settled here more than 5,000 years ago. This region includes Western China, Mongolia, and Tibet. Mongolia gained its independence from China in 1911, and is now an independent democracy. Tibet is currently governed by China. Compared with Eastern China, this region is sparsely populated and characterized by vast deserts, remote mountains, and extreme temperatures.

DESERT LANDS

The cold, rocky Gobi Desert (right) covers more than 400,000 sq miles (1,000,000 sq km) through Mongolia and northeast China. Many dinosaur bones and eggs have been found here, making it one of the richest dinosaur fossil regions in the world.

THE MONGOLIANS

Most of the people living in Mongolia are Khalkh Mongols. About half of these people now live in urban areas, but some still lead traditional lives as nomadic herders. They live in large felt tents, called *yurts*. Smoke from the central iron stove escapes through a chimney in the roof.

Did you know?

▶ In traditional Mongolian *khoomi* singing, male singers produce harmonic overtones deep in their throats. They are able to sing several notes at once.

▶ Prayer flags are a Tibetan tradition symbolizing the Buddhist faith. Before the Chinese occupation, they flew from every home as a symbol of good luck.

CHINESE WRITING

The Chinese alphabet is not made up of letters. Instead, separate symbols stand for individual words or parts of words. There are more than 40,000 characters in the Chinese language. The same symbols are used everywhere in China, and no matter what Chinese language or dialect people speak, they can all read the same script.

兒童百科全書

The strokes in each symbol are written in a certain order.

MONASTERIES IN MONGOLIA

Under communism, Mongolians were forbidden to practice their traditional Buddhist faith, which was viewed as superstitious and unscientific. Since the democratic government was set up in 1990, about 100 monasteries have reopened. Most people, however, no longer follow any religion.

Map labels

KAZAKHSTAN
Altai Mountains
Hövsgöl Nuur
Uvs Nuur
Ulaangom
Ölgiy
Hyargas Nuur
Halban
Mö
Altay
Charus Nuur
Har Nuur
Hangayn Nuur
Hovd
Tsets
Ulungur Hu
M O
Karamay
Gurbantünggüt Shamo
Altay
Bayanhor
Kuytun
Aj Bogd Uul 12,474ft (3802m)
Shihezi
Fukang
Jimsar
Yining
Ürümqi
Qitai
Turpan
Atas Bogd 8865ft (2702m)
Bohoro Shan
Hami
G
Tien Shan
Pik Pobedy 24,406ft (7439m)
Turpan Pendi
Bosten Hu
Xingxingxia
Korla
Kuruktag
GANSU
Kashi
Tarim He Tarim Basin
Yengisar
Yumen
Shache
XINJIANG
Qilian Sha
Yecheng
Ruoqiang
Altun Shan
Danghe Nanshan
Pishan
Takla Makan Desert
Moyu
(claimed by India)
Hotan
Qira
CHIN
K2 28,251ft (8611m)
Kunlun Shan
Qaidam Pendi
Golmud
Qin
Karakoram Range
AKSAI CHIN
Burhan Budai Shan
Dulan
AKSAI CHIN (administered by China, claimed by India)
QINGHAI
Plateau of Tibet (Qingzang Gaoyuan)
PAKISTAN
INDIA
Rutog
Tongtian He
Bayan Har Sha
DEMCHOK/DÊMQOG (administered by China, claimed by India)
Gar
TIBET
Yushu
Zanda
Tanggula Shan
Mekong
Nyima
Siling Co
Amdo
Tangra Yumco
Gyaring Co
Nagqu
Qamdo
Ngangzê Co
Nam Co
Damxung
Brahmaputra
Nyainqêntanglha Shan
NEPAL
Lhazê
Xigazê
Maizhokunggar
ARUNACHAL PRADESH (claimed by China)
Mount Everest 29,035ft (8850m)
Gyangzê
Lhasa
Gonggar
BHUTAN
INDIA
MYANMAR (BURMA)

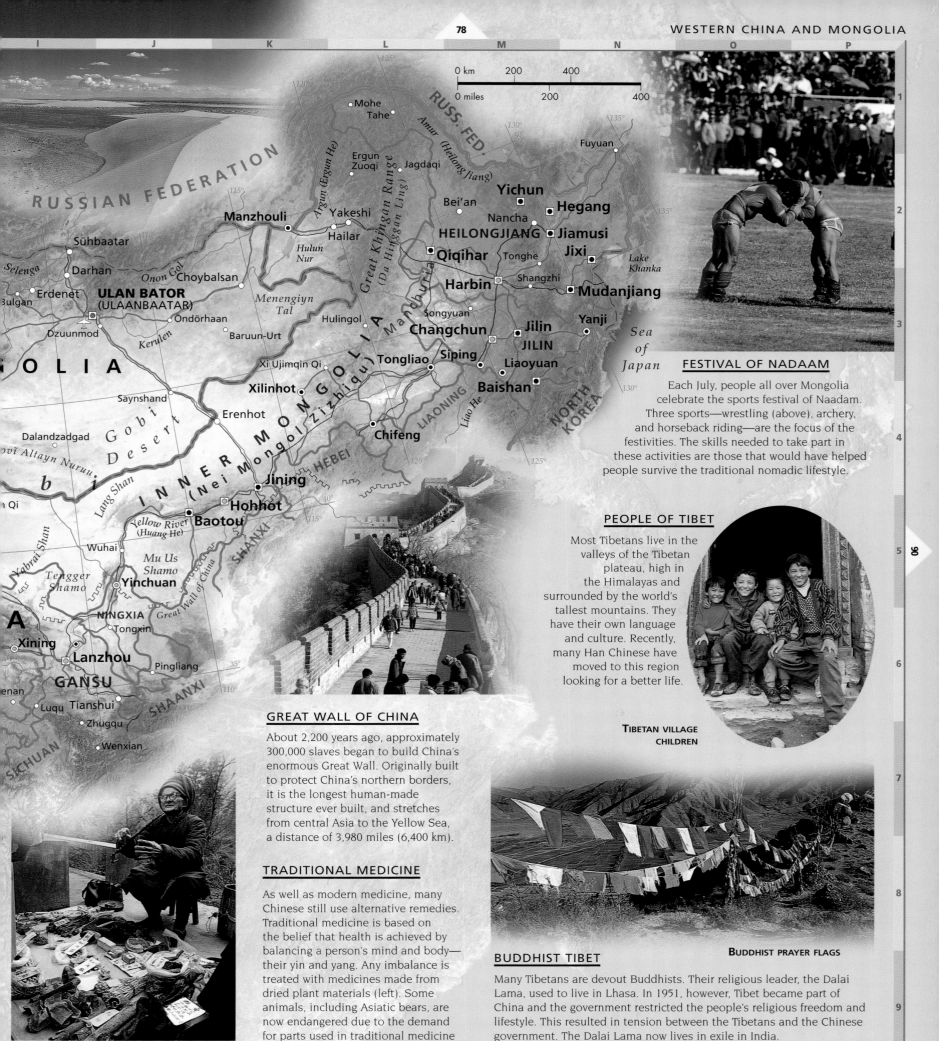

0 km 200   400

0 miles   200   400

FESTIVAL OF NADAAM

Each July, people all over Mongolia celebrate the sports festival of Naadam. Three sports—wrestling (above), archery, and horseback riding—are the focus of the festivities. The skills needed to take part in these activities are those that would have helped people survive the traditional nomadic lifestyle.

PEOPLE OF TIBET

Most Tibetans live in the valleys of the Tibetan plateau, high in the Himalayas and surrounded by the world's tallest mountains. They have their own language and culture. Recently, many Han Chinese have moved to this region looking for a better life.

TIBETAN VILLAGE CHILDREN

GREAT WALL OF CHINA

About 2,200 years ago, approximately 300,000 slaves began to build China's enormous Great Wall. Originally built to protect China's northern borders, it is the longest human-made structure ever built, and stretches from central Asia to the Yellow Sea, a distance of 3,980 miles (6,400 km).

TRADITIONAL MEDICINE

As well as modern medicine, many Chinese still use alternative remedies. Traditional medicine is based on the belief that health is achieved by balancing a person's mind and body— their yin and yang. Any imbalance is treated with medicines made from dried plant materials (left). Some animals, including Asiatic bears, are now endangered due to the demand for parts used in traditional medicine

BUDDHIST PRAYER FLAGS

BUDDHIST TIBET

Many Tibetans are devout Buddhists. Their religious leader, the Dalai Lama, used to live in Lhasa. In 1951, however, Tibet became part of China and the government restricted the people's religious freedom and lifestyle. This resulted in tension between the Tibetans and the Chinese government. The Dalai Lama now lives in exile in India.

Eastern China and Korea

CHINA HAS A LARGE population of 1.3 billion, with two-thirds living in Eastern China. For thousands of years, powerful emperors ruled China. During this period, Chinese civilization was very advanced, but much of the population lived in poverty. In 1949, after a communist revolution, the People's Republic of China was established. Food, education, and health care became available to more people, but there was also a loss of freedom. Today, Chinese people have more freedom, but the government still has tight control over their lives. The Korean peninsula is divided politically into north and south, and attempts are being made to restore peace between the two governments. Since 1949, the mountainous island of Taiwan has been in dispute with China over who governs it.

NEW YEAR CELEBRATIONS

Chinese New Year, also known as the Spring Festival, is the country's most important festival. It is usually held in January or February. Good-luck messages decorate buildings and there are feasts, fireworks, fairs, and processions. People wear red clothes for good luck and give gifts of coins to symbolize wealth.

CHINESE NEW YEAR PARADE

HONG KONG

For 100 years, Hong Kong was a British colony; then, in 1997, it was returned to China. These small islands are some of the most densely populated parts of the world. Most people live and work in high-rise buildings. Hong Kong has a prosperous economy and the people have one of the world's highest life expectancies.

THE SKYLINE OF HONG KONG with a Chinese junk in the foreground

ONE-CHILD FAMILIES

Many Chinese children do not have brothers or sisters. This is due to policies brought in by the Chinese goverment in 1979. To try to control the rising population, the government offers special benefits to couples with only one child. Although this has slowed down the rate of growth, China's population still grows by millions each year.

PADDY FIELDS

Rice forms the basis of most Chinese meals. It grows in paddy fields in the southeast of the country. During the growing season, fields are flooded so farmers can grow more rice more quickly. In the drier regions, wheat is grown and used to make noodles, buns, and dumplings. Rice or wheat is often combined with local vegetables, meats, and spices to create regional dishes.

Bayan Har Shan
QINGHAI
NINGXIA
GANSU
Tongchuan
Baoji · Xianyan
Xi'an
Hanzhong SHAANX
Hongyuan
Guangyuan
TIBET
Yalong Jiang
Luhuo
SICHUAN
Mianyang
Nanchong
Wany
Litang
Chengdu
Sichuan Pendi
Wanxi
Ya'an
Hengduan Shan
Yinsha Jiang
Leshan
Neijiang
Lichuan
CHONGQING
CHI
Zigong
Chongqing
Xichang
Zhongdian
Tongzi
Zunyi
Huaih
Yangtze Chang Jiang
Zhoatong
GUIZHOU
Panzhihua
Guiyang
MYANMAR (BURMA)
Dali
Anshun
Kaili
Duyun
Salween
Baoshan
Guanling
Dushan
Kunming
Xingxi
YUNNAN
Yuxi
Wuliang Shan
Kaiyuan
Liuzhou
Mekong
Wenshan
Bose
Gejiu
GUANGXI
Tropic of Cancer
Nanning
Jinghong
VIETNAM
Ya
Qinzhou
LAOS
Beihai
Gulf of Tongking
Danzhou
Dongfang
HAINA

0 km   150   300
0 miles   150   300

35°   105°
100°
25°
105°
100°
20°

NORTH KOREA

North Korea is an independent communist country, but since the breakup of the Soviet Union, it has lost many of its trading partners and is now very poor. However, the country has a good education system and a high literacy rate. Schooling is free and compulsory for all children for 10 years.

SOUTH KOREA

South Korea is a democratic nation with a thriving electronics and machinery industry. A quarter of the population lives in or near the capital city, Seoul. The Internet has developed quickly in South Korea and plays an important role in work and leisure. The children below are using computers at an Internet cafe in the central city, of Taejon.

INNER MONGOLIA

Najin

Ch'ŏngjin

Sea of Japan

Shenyang

Fuxin   Fushun

Chaoyang   LIAONING   Kanggye   Hyesan

Chengde   Jinzhou   Anshan   Kimch'aek

Zhangjiakou   Haicheng   NORTH

Huailai   Fengcheng   Sinŭiju   KOREA

Datong   BEIJING   Qinhuangdao   Dandong   Hamhŭng

(PEKING)   Chŏngju

Langfang   Tangshan   East

Shouzhou   Rengiu   P'YŎNGYANG   Korea

Tianjin   Dalian   Wŏnsan   Bay

TIANJIN SHI   Bo Hai   Sariwŏn

Shijiazhuang   HEBEI   Ch'unch'ŏn

Taiyuan   Botou   Cangzhou   Korea   Haeju

Yuci   Dezhou   Bay   Inch'ŏn   SEOUL   SOUTH

SHANXI   Binzhou   Yantai   (SŎUL)   KOREA

Handan   Zibo   Jinan   (North and South Korea   Taejŏn   Taegu

Changzhi   SHANDONG   Weifang   have been divided   Ulsan

Anyang   by a ceasefire   Chŏnju

nmenxia   Xinxiang   Jining   agreement since 1953)   Chinju   Pusan

Kaifeng   Rizhao   Kwangju   Mokp'o   Yŏsu

Luoyang   Zhengzhou   Xuzhou   Yellow   Cheju Strait   Korea Strait

Pingdingshan   Lianyungang   Sea

HENAN   Suzhou   JIANGSU   Cheju-do

Nanyang   Bengbu

Xiangfang   Huainan   Yangzhou

Xinyang   Nanjing   Suzhou

HUBEI   Hefei   Wuxi   Shanghai

Yichang   ANHUI   Wuhu

N   A   Wuhan   Anqing   Jiaxing

Jingzhou   Huangshi   Hangzhou   East China Sea

Jiujiang   Ningbo

Yueyang   Jingdezhen   Quzhou   Jinhua

Changde   Nanchang   ZHEJIANG   Wenzhou

Changsha   Shangrao

Loudi   Xiangtan   Linchuan

HUNAN   JIANGXI   FUJIAN   Chilung

gjiang   Hengyang   Nanfeng   Nanping   TAIPEI

Lengshuitan   Sanming   Fu'an   T'aichung

anzhou   Ganzhou   Yong'an   Fuzhou   Hualien   (China and Taiwan

Chenzhou   Longyan   Quanzhou   Chiai   claim all of each

uilin   Shaoguan   Zhangzhou   T'ainan   other's territory)

Hexian   Xiamen   TAIWAN

ou   GUANGDONG   Chaozhou   Kaohsiung   Tropic of Cancer

Guangzhou   Shantou

haoqing   Dongguan

Jiangmen   Hong Kong

Macao   (Xianggang)

(Aomen)

Maoming   Taiwan Strait

anjiang   South China Sea

ikou

Hainan

Dao

Yellow River (Huang He)

Yangtze

Did you know?

▶ Many of the world's inventions and technological advances originally came from China, including paper, money, compasses, fireworks, and silk.

▶ North Korean students are required to work for the government during part of their summer vacation as payment for their free education.

▶ The majority of the Chinese population lives in just 15 percent of the total land area.

MODERN SHANGHAI

China's largest city is Shanghai. More than eight million people live in this wealthy east coast port. International trade has recently transformed Shanghai's skyline, which is now crowded with high-rise buildings and modern shopping malls. The center of town still has some old western-style buildings that have survived from the days before the revolution.

BEAUTY OF TAIWAN

Taiwan's mountainous countryside is famous for its natural beauty, scenic lakes, and many ornate Buddhist temples. This peaceful environment contrasts sharply with Taiwan's capital city, Taipei, which is one of the fastest-growing cities in Asia.

CHINESE INDUSTRY

After the revolutionary leader Mao Zedong died in 1976, China's economy opened up. New industry is now encouraged, and many people are moving from the country to cities where there are relatively well-paid jobs.

BICYCLE FACTORY

92

Japan

JAPAN IS SITUATED in the north Pacific Ocean off the coast of the Asian continent. It is made up of four main islands and more than 3,000 smaller ones, The Japanese people have a distinctive culture based on traditions built up over thousands of years. They have their own language and script. Schoolchildren all learn to read and write both in the traditional script and using letters. Social rules in Japan are strict, and respect and politeness are considered very important. Most people bow when greeting one another, for example. Japan is a very modern country, however, with one of the world's most technologically advanced societies. Its economy is based on the development and production of cutting-edge electronics and vehicles, and most families have the latest consumer goods.

RELIGIONS OF JAPAN

Many Japanese people follow a mix of the Shinto and Buddhist religions, attending wedding blessings in Shinto shrines and funerals in Buddhist temples. Buddhism originated in India, and arrived in Japan in the 6th century, while the Shinto faith is native to Japan. Respect for nature is especially important in the Shinto religion. Many natural locations, such as Mount Fuji, are considered sacred.

JAPANESE TEMPLE

MOUNT FUJI is a dormant volcano.

Earthquakes

The islands of Japan are situated in an area where four of the Earth's tectonic plates meet. This causes frequent earthquakes. Japanese schoolchildren are taught how to keep safe during an earthquake by sheltering in a doorway or under a table.

OVERCROWDING

Most of the country's 126 million people live in cities in the flatter, coastal areas. Tokyo and Osaka are very crowded, and homes here are usually very small and are designed to make the most of the limited space.

FASHION IN JAPAN

On ordinary days, Japanese people usually wear western-style clothes. Most children have a school uniform. On festival days, such as Children's Day, many people prefer to wear the traditional kimono. Women's kimonos are often made of colorful silk, decorated with beautiful designs.

Traditional and modern dress side-by-side

Kurile Islands

○ Kuril'sk

Ostrov Iturup

Ostrov Shikotan

Ostrov Kunashir

(Kurile Islands administered by Russian Federation, claimed by Japan)

Nemuro

Sea of Okhotsk

La Perouse Strait

Akkeshi

Shari

Bekkai

Kushiro

Kitami

Abashiri

Shintoku

Obihiro

Hiroo

△ Asahi-dake 7613t (2290m)

△ Horoshiri-dake 6731t (2052m)

Hokkaidō

Shirataki

Monbetsu

Nakagawa

Nayoro

Shibetsu

Asahikawa

Takikawa

Ebetsu

Chitose

Tomakomai

Noboribetsu

Muroran

Uchiura-wan

Mutsu

Mutsu -wan

Kuji

Fudi

Miyako

Ishikari-wan

Otaru

Sapporo

Iwanai

Esashi

Setana

Okushiri-tō

Hakodate

Tsugaru-kaikyō

Fukushima

Mutsu

Aomori

Goshogawara

Kuroishi

Hiroshaki

Noshiro

Towada

Hachinohe

Iwate

Odate

Gojome

Morioka

Akita

Honjō

Yokote

Yuzawa

Shizugawa

Hanamaki

Kesennuma

Shinjo

Ishinomaki

Sakata

Tsuruoka

Furukawa

Wakkanai

Rebun-tō

Rishiri-tō

200

200

100

100

0 km 100

0 miles

BASEBALL

Baseball, known as *yakyu*, is fast becoming Japan's most popular sport. As well as two professional leagues, the game is played in colleges and high schools. It was introduced to Japan in the late 1800s.

A HEALTHY DIET

Rice is the major crop grown on the small amount of flat land in Japan. Along with rice, fish is an important part of most meals, and Japan has one of the world's largest fishing fleets. This healthy diet may be part of the reason why Japanese people have the world's longest life expectancy.

A **DISH** of raw fish and rice, known as sushi

MODERN TECHNOLOGY

Japan's economy is based on high-tech research, development, and production. The country has built up a reputation for providing the latest technology in vehicles and electronic goods, such as televisions, computers, and stereo systems. Their products are usually of a high quality but are still affordable.

A **PROTOTYPE** of a Mazda car produced in Hiroshima.

MARTIAL ARTS

Kendo is a popular martial art in Japan. It was developed (in its modern form) about 200 years ago, and teaches the art of Japanese Samurai swordsmanship. Children train using bamboo swords (above).

BULLET TRAIN

One of the fastest ways to travel around Japan is on their high-speed train system, known as the bullet trains, or Shinkansen. This network connects Tokyo with most of the country's other major cities, such as Sapporo and Nagasaki. The trains reach speeds of over 186 mph (300 km/h). Japan ran the world's first high-speed train in 1964.

JAPAN

Map labels

JAPAN
Honshū
Shikoku
Kyūshū

Niigata · Niitsu · Aizu · Fukushima · Kōriyama · Iwaki · Hitachi · Mito · Sukagawa · Chōshi
Intanashiro-ko · Utsunomiya · Otawara · Kasumiga-ura
Nagaoka · Kashiwazaki · Oyama · Narita · Chiba · Yokohama · Kawagoe · TŌKYŌ · Kawasaki · Fujisawa
Jōetsu · Maebashi · Nagano · Takasaki · Matsumoto · Kōfu · Fuji · Bōsō-hantō
Shinano-gawa · Toyama · Takaoka · Kanazawa · Toyota · Shizuoka · Hamamatsu · Suruga-wa · Izu hantō
Itoigawa · Komatsu · Gifu · Ogaki · Nagoya · Okazaki · Ise · Ise-wan · Kōzu-shima
Fukui · Nakatsugawa · Ōtsu · Kyōto · Ōsaka · Sakai · Tsu · Owase · Shingū
Tsuruga · Maizuru · Himeji · Kōbe · Wakayama · Gobō · Tanabe
Tottori · Yonago · Matsue · Okayama · Kurashiki · Fukuyama · Kure · Tokushima · Niihama
Izumo · Chūgoku-sanchi · Hiroshima · Iwakuni · Matsuyama · Kōchi · Nakamura
Hamada · Masuda · Hōfu · Ube · Ōita · Saiki · Nobeoka
Shimonoseki · Yamaguchi · Kitakyūshū · Fukuoka · Kurume · Ōmuta · Kumamoto · Yatsushiro · Miyazaki · Miyakonojō
Karatsu · Sasebo · Nagasaki · Hitoyoshi · Sendai · Kagoshima · Kanoya
Nagato · Iki · Tsushima · Kō-saki

Sado · Oki-shotō · Dōgo · Dōzen
Sea of Japan
Izu-shotō · Miyake-jima · Mikura-jima · Hachijō-jima · Ō-shima · Nii-jima · Sagami-nada
PACIFIC OCEAN
Shikoku · Tosa-wan · Kii-suidō · Bungo-suidō · Hyūga-nada
Kyūshū · Ōsumi-hantō · Tanega-shima · Yaku-shima · Ōsumi-shotō
Korea Strait · East China Sea · Amakusa-nada · Gotō-rettō · Koshikijima-rettō · Satsunan-shotō
Ryukyu Islands (Nansei-shotō) · Ōsumi-shotō · Amami-guntō · Naze · Amami-ō-shima · Okinawa · Naha · Okinawa-shotō · Satsunan-shotō

0 km 100
0 miles 100

Mainland SE Asia

THE PENINSULA of Southeast Asia lies directly below India and China, between the Pacific and Indian oceans. It is made up of Myanmar (Burma), Thailand, Vietnam, Cambodia, and Laos. Over thousands of years, the influence of people from nearby Indian, Chinese, and Arab cultures has helped to give this region a diverse mix of cultures and religions. Much of the land here is mountainous, with half the region covered in forest. Most people live in coastal or lowland regions, where they can grow crops such as rice, raise cattle, and catch fish. In recent years, the electronics industry has also become an important part of Southeast Asian economies, especially in Thailand.

ORPHANS IN CAMBODIA

Cambodia has the highest percentage of widows and orphans of any country in the world. Many men were killed in civil wars in recent decades.

CAMBODIAN ORPHANAGE

GROWING RICE

Rice is the most important crop in Southeast Asia. It grows well in wet lowland areas, such as the Mekong river delta in Vietnam, where the plants can be grown in paddy fields. Most rice is planted and harvested by women.

RURAL LIVING

Most people in Southeast Asia live in rural areas rather than cities, and farming is the most common occupation. The steep mountainous regions are often unsuitable for growing crops or raising cattle, however, and many farming communities are based in the fertile river valleys and deltas. There are over 200 villages on and around this lake (right) in Myanmar.

PADAUNG women, who are part of the Karen tribe, wear distinctive gold neck rings.

KAREN TRIBE

There are 600,000 tribespeople living in the northeastern hills of Thailand. The Karen are the largest hilltribe. They originated from Myanmar, but moved into Thailand to escape political unrest.

Scale bar:
0 km 100 200
0 miles 100 200

MYANMAR (BURMA)

CHINA

INDIA

LAOS

VIETNAM

THAILAND

BANGLADESH

Bay of Bengal

Gulf of Tongking

Tropic of Cancer

HA NÔI

VIENTIANE (VIANGCHAN)

Chiang Mai

Mandalay

96

98

THAILAND

CAMBODIA

VIETNAM

MALAYSIA

Gulf of Thailand

South China Sea

Andaman Sea

Mergui Archipelago

Mouths of the Irrawaddy

Mouths of the Mekong

ANGKOR WAT

The impressive temple complex of Angkor Wat in Cambodia attracts visitors interested in its history and architecture. This combination of temples and palaces was built in AD 1113 by the Khmer king Suryavarman II. The buildings are made of stone and brick and are decorated with relief sculptures showing mythical scenes of Hindu gods and great royal processions. The complex was uncovered in 1861 by French naturalist Henri Mouhot, following stories of a "lost city" in the jungle.

TEMPLE AT ANGKOR WAT

MONASTIC LIFE

The main religion in mainland Southeast Asia is Buddhism. Nearly all Thai villages have their own temple, or *wat*, which is the center of village life. Most young men spend some time in a monastery, where they have few possessions and spend much of their time in meditation.

FLOATING MARKET

The capital of Thailand, Bangkok, is a busy, crowded city with about six million inhabitants. The city was built on an island in the river, and has many canals. Boats known as *sampans* (above) act as floating markets from which traders sell fresh fruit and vegetables.

Did you know?

- A traditional greeting in Thailand is the "wai." The hands are placed together in prayer position and slightly raised, as the head is bowed.

- A large, previously unknown mammal, the vu quang ox, was only recently discovered in the forests of northern Vietnam.

THAI BEACHES

Tourism is now a major industry for Thailand. Popular tourist destinations include the lively capital, Bangkok, and the country's beautiful island beach resorts (below). Phuket, Thailand's largest island, is often referred to as the "Pearl of the South."

Maritime SE Asia

TO THE SOUTH OF THE Asian mainland lies maritime Southeast Asia. It includes Malaysia, Indonesia, East Timor, Singapore, and the Philippines. Part of Malaysia is connected to the mainland, but the rest of the region is made up of more than 20,000 islands that stretch across the Pacific and Indian Oceans. Lying near the Equator, the climate is mostly hot, wet, and humid. Most of the larger islands are mountainous and covered in dense forest, and many people live in villages near rivers or on the coast. Like the rest of Southeast Asia, the population is made up of people from many different cultural backgrounds, and hundreds of different languages are spoken. The most common religion is Islam, except in the Philippines, where most people are Roman Catholic.

GREAT APES

The orangutans are great apes that live only in Borneo and the northern corner of Sumatra. They spend most of their time in the trees, even building treetop nests in which to sleep. The orangutan is endangered because of deforestation.

PEOPLE OF MALAYSIA

Ethnic Malaysians make up 59 percent of the population, and are known as *bumiputera*, meaning "sons of the soil." Most Malaysians are Muslim. Ethnic Chinese form 26 percent of the population.

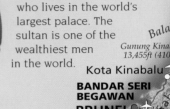

SULTAN OF BRUNEI

THE SULTAN OF BRUNEI

Brunei is ruled by a sultan who lives in the world's largest palace. The sultan is one of the wealthiest men in the world.

UBADIAH MOSQUE, MALAYSIA

SINGAPORE

As the financial and industrial center of Southeast Asia, Singapore is one of the wealthiest countries in this region. It has a thriving high-tech industry and a high standard of living. There are strictly enforced laws forbidding littering and other minor crimes. The death penalty is imposed for drug smuggling. The government also controls the press and restricts the Internet.

SKYSCRAPERS in Singapore's financial district

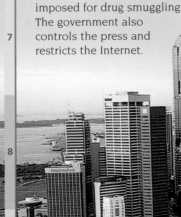

KITE-FLYING

After the harvest, the people of Malaysia celebrate with the Wau-flying (kite-flying) Festival. Here, skilled people demonstrate the traditional Malaysian sport.

Map labels

Andaman Sea
THAILAND
South China Sea
Strait of Malacca
Bandaaceh
Sigli
George Town
Butterworth
Kota Bharu
Kuala Terengganu
Meulaboh
Langsa
Taiping
Ipoh
Dungun
Cukai
Pulau Pinang
Kuala Lipis
Medan
Tebingtinggi
Kuantan
Kota Kinabalu
BANDAR SERI BEGAWAN
BRUNEI
Miri
Pulau Simeulue
Klang
KUALA LUMPUR
MALAYSIA
Pematangsiantar
Seremban
Melaka
Keluang
Bintulu
Kepulauan Banyak
Sibolga
Muar
Batu Pahat
Johor Bahru
SINGAPORE
Sibu
Sri Aman
Pulau Nias
Panyabungan
Pekanbaru
Singkawang
Sidas
Kuching
Sarawak
Kepulauan Lingga
Pontianak
Sungai Kapuas
Pegunungan Muller
Solok
Rengat
Borneo
Balikpapan
Padang
Kualatungkal
Selat Karimata
INDIAN OCEAN
Batang Hari
Jambi
Bangka
Kalimantan
Pulau Siberut
Pangkalpinang
Sampit
Sungaipenuh
Sumatra (Sumatera)
Palembang
Kandangan
Equator
INDO
Banjarmasin
Kepulauan Mentawai
Lahat
Pulau Belitung
Bengkulu
Kotabumi
Java Sea
Bandarlampung
Cirebon
Serang
JAKARTA
Tegal
Pekalongan
Semarang
Pulau Madura
Surabaya
Selat Sunda
Bogor
Sukabumi
Kudus
Probolinggo
Bandung
Java (Jawa)
Jember
Mataram
Tasikmalaya
Malang
Cilacap
Kediri
Denpasar
Magelang
Madiun
Yogyakarta
Surakarta
Gunung Kinabalu 13,455ft (410...)

Did you know?

▶ Indonesia is the world's biggest island chain. It has more than 17,000 islands and covers three time zones.

▶ In Malay, orangutan means "man of the jungle."

STORMS AND VOLCANOES

The islands of the Philippines are on a fault line and form part of the "Pacific Ring of Fire"—an area prone to volcanic activity and earthquakes. When Mount Pinatubo, on the island of Luzon, erupted in 1991, it destroyed more than 40,000 homes.

THE PHILIPPINES

The people of the Philippines are called Filipinos, and are mostly of Malay descent. It is estimated that about 40 percent of the population live in poverty. Since income is higher in the cities, many people move there in the hope of escaping poverty. However, lack of adequate housing means that many poorer families have to live in crowded slums.

THESE CHILDREN live and work in an area of Manila known as "Smokey Mountain."

MOUNT PINATUBO ERUPTING IN 1991

Machine replants rice seedlings.

RICE RESEARCH

Rice is the primary food source for half the world's population. Near Manila, in the Philippines, scientists are now experimenting with ways of creating rice plants that produce greater yields. New varieties are also being developed to grow faster, allowing farmers to harvest and replant several times during one growing season.

OIL RICHES

Oil was first discovered in Brunei in 1929. Since then, oil has also been drilled offshore (right). Brunei's most important natural resource has made the country very wealthy. Its people enjoy free health care and education, and pay no taxes.

Map labels:

Babuyan Island, Babuyan Channel, Laoag, Tuguegarao, Ilagan, Baguio, Cordillera, Luzon, Dagupan, Angeles, Cabanatuan, Mt. Pinatubo 4872ft (1485m), PHILIPPINES, MANILA, Lucena, Batangas, Naga, Legaspi, Mindoro, Mindoro Strait, Sibuyan Sea, Calbayog, Roxas City, Samar, Panay Island, Cadiz, Tacloban, Iloilo, Leyte, Bacolod City, Cebu, Palawan, Puerto Princesa, Negros, Bohol Sea, Butuan, Cagayan de Oro, Iligan, Bislig, Mindanao, Sulu Sea, Zamboanga, Moro Gulf, Basilan, Digos, Davao, Sandakan, Lebak, Davao Gulf, General Santos, Sulu Archipelago, Kepulauan Talaud, Celebes Sea, Kepulauan Sangir, Pulau Morotai, Pulau Halmahera, Manado, Bitung, Tolitoli, Gorontalo, Ternate, Molucca Sea, Pulau Waigeo, Equator, Pulau Biak, amarinda, Gulf of Tomini, Halmahera Sea, Selat Dampier, Sorong, Jazirah Doberai, Manokwari, Pulau Yapen, Palu, Kepulauan Banggai, Moluccas (Maluku), Pulau Misool, Teluk Cenderawasih, Jayapura, Poso, Celebes (Sulawesi), Kepulauan Sula, Ceram Sea, Wahai, Teluk Berau, Maniwori, Sungai Mamberamo, Wotu, Danau Towuti, Waflia, Pulau Seram, Obome, Peguunungan Maoke, Wahia, Puncak Jaya 16,503ft (5030m), Parepare, NESIA, Tifu, Ambon, Papua (Irian Jaya), Singkang, Kendari, Pulau Buru, New Guinea, Watampone, Kolaka, Pulau Buton, Amamapare, Ujungpandang, Kepulauan Kai, Kepulauan Aru, Bulukumba, Banda Sea, Flores Sea, Kepulauan Tanimbar, Sungai Digul, esser Sunda Islands (Nusa Tenggara), Kepulauan Alor, Pulau Wetar, Pulau Yamdena, Alotip, Flores, DILI, Tutuala, Arafura Sea, Selat Sumba, Endeh, Savu Sea, EAST TIMOR, Timor, Pulau Sumba, Kupang, Nikiniki, Timor Sea, PAPUA NEW GUINEA

0 km 200 400
0 miles 200 400

Indian Ocean

THE THIRD LARGEST ocean in the world, the Indian Ocean is bounded by Africa, Asia, Australasia, and Antarctica. The ocean contains some 5,000 islands. Madagascar and Sri Lanka are large, but most of the islands are small and ringed by coral reefs. The people of the Maldives have very mixed origins, incorporating Indian, Sinhalese, Arab, and African heritage, while two-thirds of those living on Mauritius are Indian immigrants and their descendants. Altogether, about one-fifth of the world's population live on this ocean's warm shores. Those along the northern coasts are often threatened by monsoon rain and tropical storms, which can cause severe flooding.

THE MALDIVES

The Maldives is a low-lying archipelago of 1,300 small, coral islands, of which 202 are inhabited. The main industries are fishing—still carried out by traditional pole and line methods (above) to conserve stocks—and tourism. Vacation resorts are on separate islands from those inhabited by the locals, so as not to disturb the Maldive peoples' traditional Muslim lifestyles.

Coral islands

Coral is a living organism formed in warm water by tiny sea creatures known as polyps. These creatures build limestone skeletons around themselves, which accumulate over thousands of years. As sea levels change, this coral can be exposed as low-lying islands or submerged as reefs.

THE SEYCHELLES

The Seychelles consists of 115 islands, some of which are coral islands, while others are mountainous and made of granite. Most Seychellois people are Creoles—people of mixed African, Asian, and European ancestry. There are also small Chinese and Indian communities.

MARKET in the Seychelles capital, Mahé

ENVIRONMENT

Beautiful shells are for sale on this beach in South Africa. If the trader only collects empty shells, no harm is done, but in many parts of the world, dealers hunt live shellfish, sea turtles, and rare species of starfish and sea urchins. Nations such as the Maldives take great care to protect their environment.

LIMITED TOURISM

The tropical climate, sandy beaches, beautiful coral reefs, and abundant marine life make both the Seychelles and the Maldives ideal tourist destinations. These same features also make them extremely attractive to scuba divers. However, the fragile environment of both island nations means that they have deliberately tried to make them exclusive, attracting only limited numbers of wealthy visitors, instead of pursuing mass tourism.

Mediterranean Sea

Black Sea

Arabian Peninsula

Red Sea

Gulf of Aden

Ethiopian Highlands

Horn of Africa

Andrew Tablemoun

AFRICA

Somali B

COMORO

MAYOT (to Franc

MADAGASCAR

Mozambique Channel

Davie Ridge

Mozambique Plateau

Natal Basin

Africana Seamount △

Agulhas Agulhas Plateau Basin

Prince Edward Islands (to South Africa)

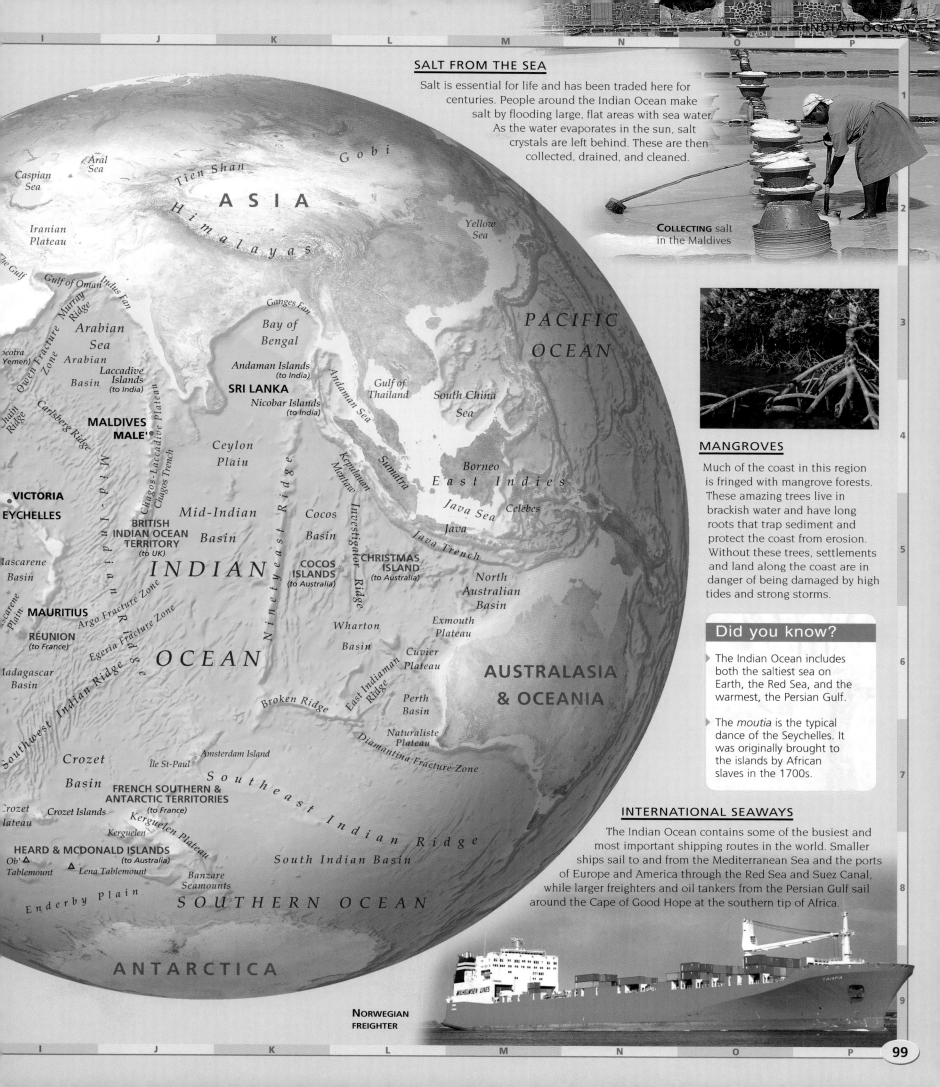

Map Labels

Caspian Sea
Aral Sea
Gobi
Tien Shan
ASIA
Himalayas
Yellow Sea
Iranian Plateau
The Gulf
Gulf of Oman
Murray Ridge
Indus Fan
Ganges Fan
Bay of Bengal
PACIFIC OCEAN
Scotra (to Yemen)
Owen Fracture Zone
Arabian Sea
Arabian Basin
Laccadive Islands (to India)
Andaman Islands (to India)
Gulf of Thailand
South China Sea
Carlsberg Ridge
Chain Ridge
MALDIVES
MALE'
SRI LANKA
Nicobar Islands (to India)
Andaman Sea
Chagos-Laccadive Plateau
Chagos Trench
Ceylon Plain
Kepulauan Mentawi
Sumatra
Borneo
East Indies
Celebes
Java Sea
Java
VICTORIA
EYCHELLES
Mid-Indian Basin
Cocos Basin
Java Trench
BRITISH INDIAN OCEAN TERRITORY (to UK)
CHRISTMAS ISLAND (to Australia)
North Australian Basin
INDIAN
COCOS ISLANDS (to Australia)
Mascarene Basin
Mascarene Plain
MAURITIUS
RÉUNION (to France)
Argo Fracture Zone
Egeria Fracture Zone
Wharton Basin
Exmouth Plateau
Cuvier Plateau
AUSTRALASIA & OCEANIA
Madagascar Basin
OCEAN
Ninetyeast Ridge
Investigator Ridge
East Indiaman Ridge
Perth Basin
Southwest Indian Ridge
Broken Ridge
Naturaliste Plateau
Diamantina Fracture Zone
Crozet Basin
Île St-Paul
Amsterdam Island
Southeast Indian Ridge
FRENCH SOUTHERN & ANTARCTIC TERRITORIES (to France)
Crozet Islands
Crozet Plateau
Kerguelen
Kerguelen Plateau
South Indian Basin
HEARD & MCDONALD ISLANDS (to Australia)
Ob' Tablemount
Lena Tablemount
Banzare Seamounts
Enderby Plain
SOUTHERN OCEAN
ANTARCTICA

SALT FROM THE SEA

Salt is essential for life and has been traded here for centuries. People around the Indian Ocean make salt by flooding large, flat areas with sea water. As the water evaporates in the sun, salt crystals are left behind. These are then collected, drained, and cleaned.

COLLECTING salt in the Maldives

MANGROVES

Much of the coast in this region is fringed with mangrove forests. These amazing trees live in brackish water and have long roots that trap sediment and protect the coast from erosion. Without these trees, settlements and land along the coast are in danger of being damaged by high tides and strong storms.

Did you know?

▶ The Indian Ocean includes both the saltiest sea on Earth, the Red Sea, and the warmest, the Persian Gulf.

▶ The *moutia* is the typical dance of the Seychelles. It was originally brought to the islands by African slaves in the 1700s.

INTERNATIONAL SEAWAYS

The Indian Ocean contains some of the busiest and most important shipping routes in the world. Smaller ships sail to and from the Mediterranean Sea and the ports of Europe and America through the Red Sea and Suez Canal, while larger freighters and oil tankers from the Persian Gulf sail around the Cape of Good Hope at the southern tip of Africa.

NORWEGIAN FREIGHTER

AUSTRALASIA & OCEANIA

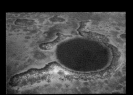

THE CONTINENT OF AUSTRALIA—the smallest of the

world's seven continents—lies between the Indian

and Pacific oceans. It forms part of a much larger region known

as Oceania that includes numerous small islands

and stretches across the southern half of the Pacific,

the world's deepest and biggest ocean. Australia is by far the biggest

island in Oceania. Nine out of every 10 Australians live next

to the coast, as the interior is hot, inhospitable

desert. New Zealand is mountainous and temperate

in climate, while Papua New Guinea is largely rain

forest. The rest of Oceania consists of thousands of

small coral atolls and island outcrops of solid rock. In all, the region

comprises 14 countries with a population of almost 31 million people

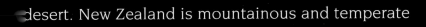

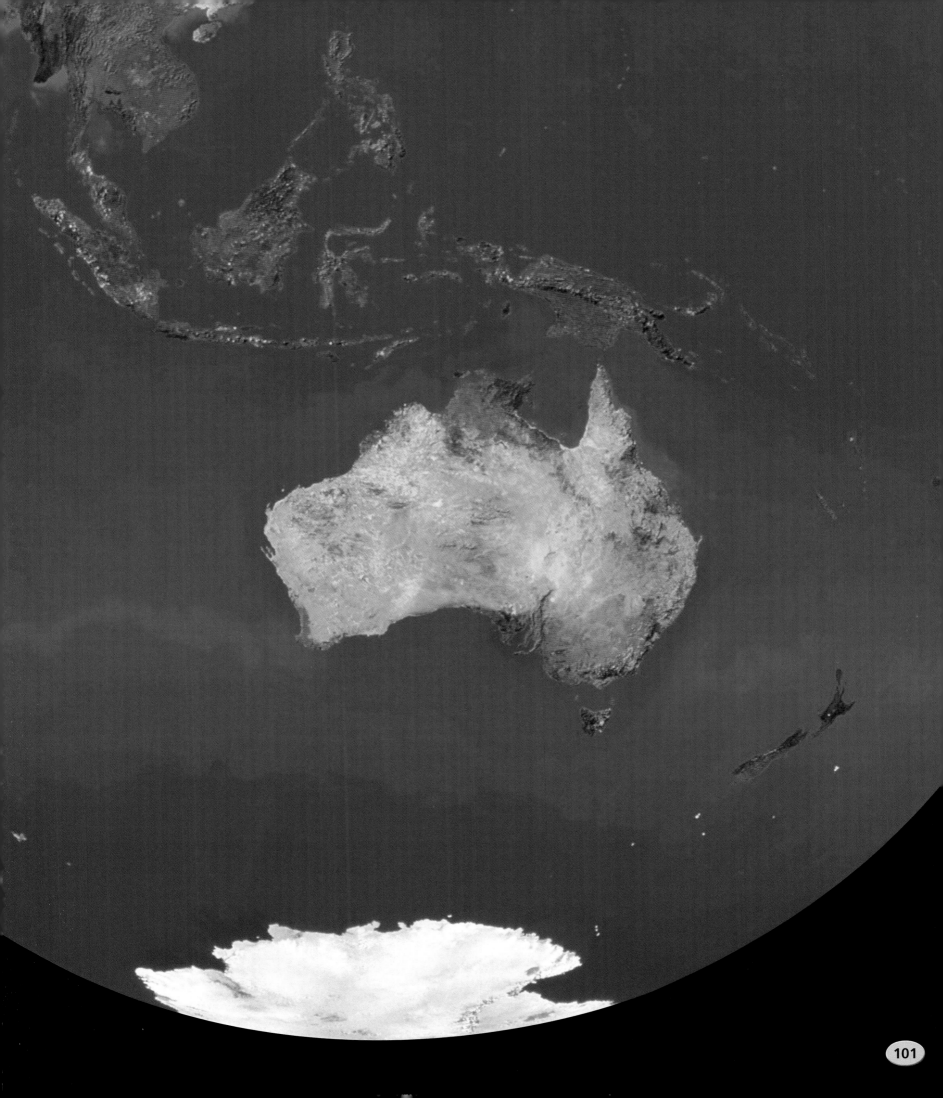

SW Pacific

THE ISLANDS OF THE southwest Pacific are home to people of many different cultures and languages. The islands are divided into three general groups based on their location and the similarities between their peoples. The Polynesian islands to the east include Tonga, Samoa, the Cook Islands, and Tahiti. Melanesia includes Fiji, the Solomon Islands, and Vanuatu. The smallest group, Micronesia, includes the Marshall, Kiribati, and Caroline Islands. The first Europeans came to the southwest Pacific in the 1600s, several thousand years after Melanesians, Micronesians, and Polynesians first settled there.

MEN from Papua New Guinea wearing traditional makeup

ISLAND VACATIONS

White sandy beaches and warm water makes this region ideal for tourists.

LAND OF MANY LANGUAGES

Historically, the mountainous landscape of Papua New Guinea made contact between the villages difficult. As a result of many years of isolation, some villages developed their own individual languages. Nationwide, about 750 different languages evolved.

Did you know?

On some Melanesian Islands, people have overcome the problems caused by having so many languages by learning an additional language—Pidgin English. This language is a mixture of English and some common words from island languages.

Beads, shells, and feathers form part of the decoration.

A MIX OF RELIGIONS

Christianity is the dominant religion on most southwest Pacific islands; however, Islam and Hinduism are also practiced. Many people also retain beliefs from traditional religions that existed before the islands were colonized by people from Europe and Asia.

VANUATU tribespeople dance at a religious ceremony.

Map labels

NORTHERN MARIANA ISLANDS (to US)
Tinian
Saipan
Rota
GUAM (to US) — HAGÅTÑA

MICRONESIA
Yap
Babeldaob
OREOR
PALAU

MARSHALL
Enewetak Atoll
Bikini Atoll
Rongelap Atoll
Ujelang Atoll
Ratak Chain
Ralik Chain
Kwajalein Atoll
Namu Atoll
Ailinglaplap Atoll
Jaluit Atoll
Ebon Atoll
Chuuk Islands
PALIKIR
Pohnpei
Caroline Islands
Kosrae

NAURU
Banab

INDONESIA
Admiralty Islands
St. Matthias Group
Bismarck Archipelago
Bismarck Sea
New Ireland
Madang
Central Range
Mount Wilhelm 14,793ft (4509m)
New Guinea
Lae
Owen Stanley Range
Gulf of Papua
PORT MORESBY
PAPUA NEW GUINEA
Bougainville Island
New Britain
Solomon Sea
Choiseul
Santa Isabel
New Georgia Islands
HONIARA
Malaita
Guadalcanal
San Cristobal
Rennell
D'Entrecasteaux Islands
Louisiade Archipelago
SOLOMON ISLANDS
Santa Cruz Islands

Melanesia

CORAL SEA ISLANDS (to Australia)
Coral Sea

VANUATU
Banks Islands
Espiritu Santo
Maéwo
Pentec
Malekula
Ambry
Epi
PORT-VILA
Efate
Erromango
Tanna
Aneityu
NEW CALEDONIA (to France)
Ouvéa
New Caledonia
Iles Loyauté
Lifou
Maré
NOUMÉA
Tropic of Capricorn

Equator
10°
140°
150°
160°
20°

FOOD CROPS

Most Pacific islanders live in small villages near the sea. Inland areas are often mountainous, making farming difficult. Instead, people grow foods such as sweet potatoes, bananas, and coconuts in lowland areas. As well as providing milk, the coconut meat is used to produce copra, a substance for making soap and cosmetics.

COPRA WORKER in Fiji scooping coconut kernels

THE KINGDOM OF TONGA

Tonga is the only Pacific nation never fully brought under foreign rule. Instead, it is run in the traditional way by its own king. All land is owned by the royal family and is allotted to households for their use. Now, some young, westernized Tongans have started calling for more democracy.

THE ROYAL PALACE IN TONGA

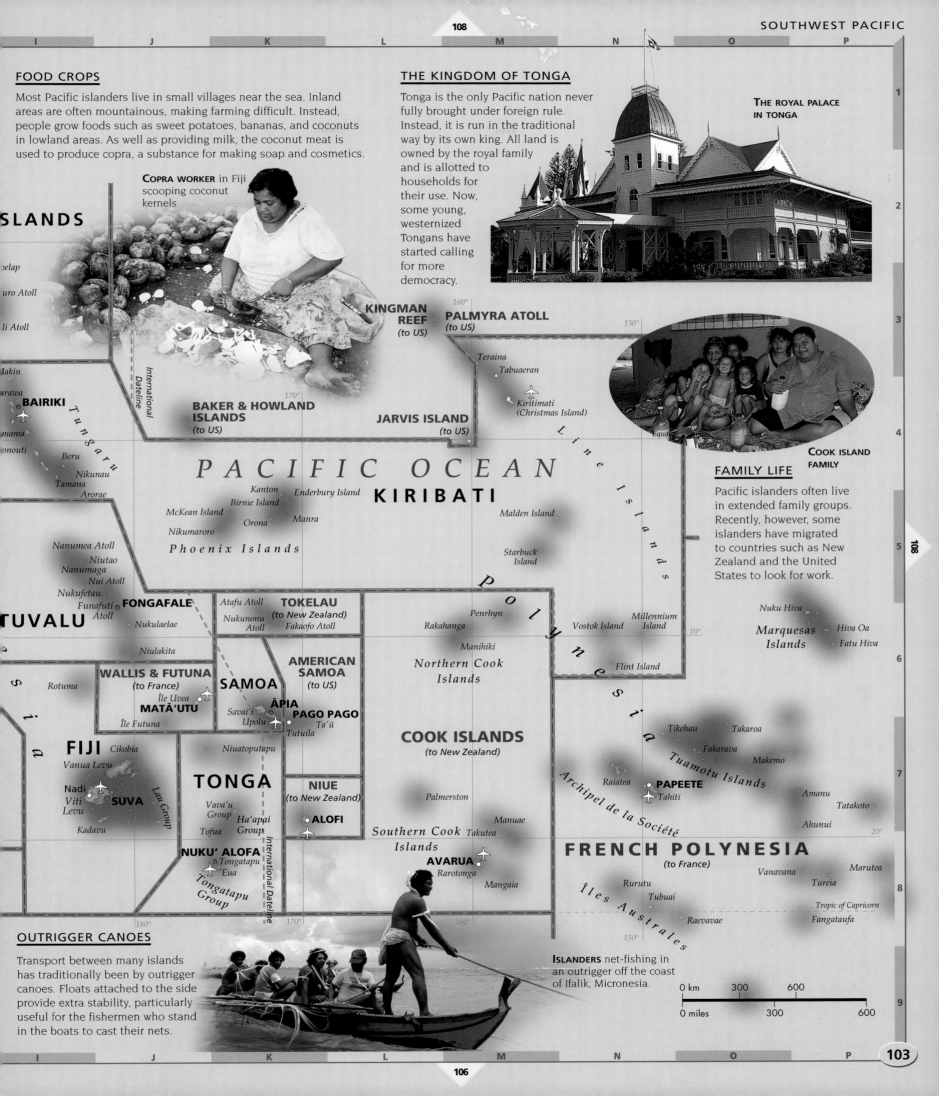

ISLANDS

Kelap

uro Atoll

li Atoll

Makin

arawa

BAIRIKI

mama

onouti

Tungaru

International Dateline

180°

170°

KINGMAN REEF *(to US)*

BAKER & HOWLAND ISLANDS *(to US)*

160°

PALMYRA ATOLL *(to US)*

Teraina

Tabuaeran

Kiritimati (Christmas Island)

150°

JARVIS ISLAND *(to US)*

Equator

Line Islands

COOK ISLAND FAMILY

FAMILY LIFE

Pacific islanders often live in extended family groups. Recently, however, some islanders have migrated to countries such as New Zealand and the United States to look for work.

Beru

Nikunau

Tamana

Arorae

P A C I F I C   O C E A N

KIRIBATI

Kanton

Enderbury Island

Birnie Island

McKean Island

Manra

Malden Island

Nikumaroro

Orona

Phoenix Islands

Starbuck Island

Nanumea Atoll

Niutao

Nanumaga

Nui Atoll

Nukufetau

Funafuti

Atoll

FONGAFALE

TUVALU

Nukulaelae

Atafu Atoll

Nukunonu Atoll

TOKELAU *(to New Zealand)*

Fakaofo Atoll

Penrhyn

Rakahanga

Manihiki

Vostok Island

Millennium Island

10°

Nuku Hiva

Marquesas Islands

Hiva Oa

Fatu Hiva

Flint Island

Niulakita

WALLIS & FUTUNA *(to France)*

Rotuma

Île Uvea

MATĀ'UTU

Île Futuna

SAMOA

ĀPIA

Savai'i

Upolu

PAGO PAGO

Ta'ū

Tutuila

AMERICAN SAMOA *(to US)*

Northern Cook Islands

Manuae

Tikehau

Takaroa

Fakarava

Makemo

Tuamotu Islands

P o l y n e s i a

FIJI

Cikobia

Vanua Levu

Nadi

Viti Levu

SUVA

Kadavu

Lau Group

Niuatoputapu

TONGA

Vava'u Group

Ha'apai Group

Tofua

NIUE *(to New Zealand)*

ALOFI

COOK ISLANDS *(to New Zealand)*

Palmerston

Southern Cook Islands

Takutea

AVARUA

Rarotonga

Mangaia

Raiatea

PAPEETE

Tahiti

Archipel de la Société

Amanu

Tatakoto

Ahunui

20°

FRENCH POLYNESIA *(to France)*

Vanavana

Marutea

Tureia

NUKU' ALOFA

Tongatapu

'Eua

Tongatapu Group

International Dateline

Îles Australes

Rurutu

Tubuai

Raevavae

Fangataufa

Tropic of Capricorn

180°

170°

160°

150°

OUTRIGGER CANOES

Transport between many islands has traditionally been by outrigger canoes. Floats attached to the side provide extra stability, particularly useful for the fishermen who stand in the boats to cast their nets.

ISLANDERS net-fishing in an outrigger off the coast of Ifalik, Micronesia.

0 km   300   600

0 miles   300   600

Australia

A HUGE, GENERALLY FLAT COUNTRY, Australia has relatively few inhabitants. This is mainly because most of the land is hot, semi-arid desert—known as the outback—unsuitable for towns or farms. In places where there is some vegetation, or the land has been irrigated, sheep and cattle are grazed. Wheat is grown in the fertile south. The first people to live here were the Aboriginals, who arrived from Asia at least 50,000 years ago. Today, most Australians are descendants of European immigrants, with a more recent addition of Asians.

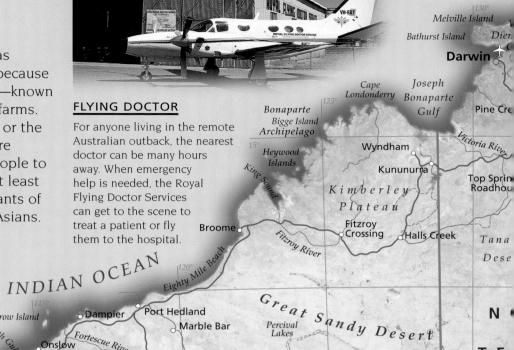

FLYING DOCTOR

For anyone living in the remote Australian outback, the nearest doctor can be many hours away. When emergency help is needed, the Royal Flying Doctor Services can get to the scene to treat a patient or fly them to the hospital.

AUSTRALIAN ABORIGINALS

The original inhabitants of Australia had an intimate understanding of their environment. This connection to the land, and its plants and animals, affects every aspect of their culture. When Europeans started arriving in the late 18th century, only the Aboriginals in remote areas escaped contact with the diseases they brought. Today, Aboriginals rarely live off the land, but work in factories or farms.

MINING

Australia has one of the world's most important mining industries, with resources including gold (left), coal, natural gas, iron ore, copper, and opals. However, damage to the environment, and Aboriginal claims over land used for mining, still need to be faced.

0 km   200   400

0 miles   200   400

AUSTRALIAN FOOTBALL

A popular sport here is Australian Rules Football. One of the rules is that players can kick or punch the ball but they must not throw it. Many Australians either play the game themselves or support their favorite team. As the name implies, the game originated in Australia, but it now has leagues in other countries, such as Great Britain and the US.

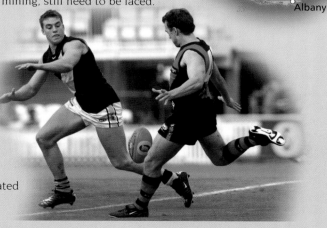

OUTDOOR SPORTS

A warm climate, with easy access to beaches and wilderness areas, has made outdoor activities an important part of modern Australian life. Water sports, such as swimming, sailing, and surfing, are especially popular. Because of the danger of exposure to strong sunlight, people are told to cover up and always use sunscreen.

INDIAN OCEAN

Melville Island
Bathurst Island   Dier
Darwin

Cape Londonderry   Joseph
Bonaparte   Bonaparte   Pine Cre
Bigge Island   Gulf
Archipelago
Heywood   Wyndham
Islands   Kununurra   Top Sprin
King Sound   Kimberley   Roadhou
Plateau
Fitzroy
Broome   Crossing   Halls Creek   Tana
Fitzroy River
Eighty Mile Beach   Dese

Barrow Island   Dampier   Port Hedland   Great Sandy Desert
Exmouth Gulf   Marble Bar   Percival   N
Onslow   Fortescue River   Lakes
Exmouth   Hamersley Range   WESTERN   TE
Ashburton River   Lake Mackay   Macd
Newman   Lake
Tropic of Capricorn   Barlee Range   Disappointment   AUS
Bernier Island   Gascoyne River   Gibson Desert   Lake
Dorre Island   Carnarvon   Amadeus
Shark Bay   Murchison River   Uluru
Dirk Hartog   Denham   Robinson Ranges   Lake Carnegie   (Ayers Rock)
Island   Lake Wells   2844ft (867m)
Meekatharra   AUSTRALIA   Musgrave Ran
Kalbarri   Great Victoria
Mount Magnet   Lake Carey   Desert
Geraldton   Lake Barlee
Lake Moore   Lake Rebecca
Moora   Kalgoorlie   Reid
Southern Cross   Coolgardie   Zanthus   Nullarbor Plain
Gingin   Merredin   Lake Cowan   Eucla
Perth   Northam
Fremantle   Brookton   Norseman   Balladonia
Mandurah   Narrogin
Bunbury   Wagin   Esperance   Great Australian Bigh
Collie   Katanning
Busselton   Manjimup
Augusta
Albany

UNIQUE WILDLIFE

Animal parks and refuges allow "townies" and tourists to get close to Australia's unique wildlife. They can see marsupials, such as koalas and wallabies (left), as well as crocodiles, snakes, and the world's only egg-laying mammals—the platypus and the echidna.

Did you know?

▶ Voting in government elections in Australia is compulsory. Citizens who fail to vote can be fined.

▶ July and August are the coldest months, when some Australians like to go skiing.

▶ The deadly blue-ringed octopus lives in the waters off the Australian coast.

TOURIST ATTRACTIONS

Tourism is important to Australia's economy, and there is plenty to attract visitors. Popular destinations include the tropical waters around the Great Barrier Reef (above), the modern cities of Sydney and Melbourne, and the impressive sight of Uluru (Ayers Rock), a mountainous rock sacred to the Aboriginals.

VINEYARDS

Australia boasts an impressive range of high-quality wine-growing regions, specializing in different grapes. Wines are exported to more than 90 countries.

LIFE IN THE CITIES

Most Australians live in the coastal towns and cities of southeastern Australia where the climate is cooler. Although Canberra is the capital, Sydney is the largest and oldest city, and is beautifully situated around Sydney Harbor. One of the world's most famous landmarks is the Sydney Opera House (below) which has five separate halls for concerts, operas, and plays. The design echoes the sails of a ship.

Map labels

Arafura Sea
Torres Strait
Badu Island
Moa Island
Prince of Wales Island
Cape York
Endeavour Strait
Wessel Islands
Croker Island
South Goulburn Island
Arnhem Land
Katherine
Gulf of Carpentaria
Cape York Peninsula
Princess Charlotte Bay
Great Barrier Reef
Coral Sea
Daly Waters
Groote Eylandt
Sir Edward Pellew Group
Wellesley Islands
Mornington Island
Cooktown
Port Douglas
Cairns
Atherton
Innisfail
Tully
Hinchinbrook Island
Barkly Tableland
Burketown
Normanton
Mitchell River
Gilbert River
Gregory Range
Flinders River
Great Dividing Range
Bowen
Whitsunday Group
NORTHERN TERRITORY
Tennant Creek
Mount Isa
Cloncurry
Selwyn Range
Hughenden
Charters Towers
Townsville
Bloomsbury
Mackay
Alice Springs
Macdonnell Ranges
Winton
QUEENSLAND
Longreach
Barcaldine
Great Dividing Range
Clermont
Emerald
Maryborough
Yeppon
Rockhampton
Tropic of Capricorn
Curtis Island
Gladstone
AUSTRALIA
Springsure
Biloela
Fraser Island
Blackall
Bundaberg
Simpson Desert
Windorah
Augathella
Gayndah
Murgon
Maryborough
Gympie
SOUTH
Charleville
Mitchell
Roma
Miles
Caloundra
Lake Eyre North
-52ft (-16m)
Lake Blanche
Cooper Creek
Dalby
Moonie
Brisbane
Ipswich
Coober Pedy
Lake Eyre South
Grey Range
Cunnamulla
St. George
Toowoomba
Warwick
Surfers Paradise
Murwillumbah
AUSTRALIA
Marree
Lake Callabonna
Bollon
Goondiwindi
Stanthorpe
Lismore
Narcoola
Lake Everard
Lake Frome
Moree
Grafton
Eucla
Lake Torrens
Barrier Range
Warrego River
Barwon River
Walgett
Narrabri
Armidale
Coffs Harbour
Flinders Ranges
Bourke
Wilcannia
Gunnedah
Port Macquarie
Port Augusta
Whyalla
Broken Hill
Cobar
Nyngan
Tamworth
Taree
Elliston
Eyre Peninsula
NEW SOUTH WALES
Dubbo
Muswellbrook
Port Pirie
Peterborough
Ivanhoe
Lachlan River
Parkes
Orange
Newcastle
Port Lincoln
Crystal Brook
Darling River
Mildura
WALES
Bathurst
Gosford
Parramatta
Sydney
Gawler
Elizabeth
Murray River
Hay
Cootamundra
Goulburn
Wollongong
Adelaide
Tailem Bend
Murrumbidgee River
Wagga Wagga
CANBERRA
Kangaroo Island
Ouyen
Deniliquin
Albury
Mount Kosciuszko 7310ft (2228m)
AUSTRALIAN CAPITAL TERRITORY
Keith
Shepparton
Wodonga
Cooma
Investigator Strait
Horsham
Bendigo
Wangaratta
Australian Alps
Bega
Naracoorte
VICTORIA
Ballarat
Sunbury
Melbourne
Tasman Sea
Mount Gambier
Portland
Moe
Sale
Warrnambool
Geelong
Traralgon
South East Point
King Island
Bass Strait
Flinders Island
Hunter Island
Banks Strait
Cape Barren Island
Marrawah
Burnie
Devonport
Launceston
TASMANIA
Hobart
Maria Island

New Zealand

MADE UP OF TWO MAIN ISLANDS and several smaller islands, New Zealand is one of the most isolated countries in the world. Located in the southern Pacific, the country has a mild climate, with warm summers and cool, wet winters. Both islands have mountains, short, swift-flowing rivers, forests, and fertile farmland. Until the Europeans arrived, most of the landscape was covered in dense forest, known as native bush. Today, although forests remain, much has been cleared for farming. Most New Zealanders live on North Island, which is warmer and less mountainous. Although New Zealanders are of mainly British descent, the Maoris—a people of Polynesian origin—were the first to arrive, about 1,000 years ago. Today, non-Maori Polynesians and Asians are adding to the ethnic mix. The country has a liberal, clean, green image and a high standard of living.

AUCKLAND

With its safe harbour and nearby scenic islands, Auckland is known as the City of Sails. It boasts more pleasure boats per person than anywhere else in the world. The water that separates the bigger islands is home to dolphins, families of blue penguins, and the occasional whale.

MAORI CULTURE

Maoris make up almost 16 percent of the population, with most living on North Island. Before the coming of the *Pakeha* (white man), Maori history was passed on orally to succeeding generations. This included many legends and *waiata* (song). Their carvings in wood (left) and stone (right) were another way they recorded and remembered events. In recent years, interest in Maori culture has increased, and schoolchildren are now taught the Maori language.

GREENSTONE (jade) carving is an example of Maori art.

Did you know?

The Maori name for New Zealand is Aotearoa, meaning "land of the long white cloud."

In 1893, New Zealand was the first country to grant women the vote.

There is only one poisonous animal here, the katipo spider.

PACIFIC OCEAN

North Island

Tasman Sea

Bay of Plenty

Three Kings Islands
North Cape
Cape Reinga
Te Kao
Ninety Mile Beach
Great Exhibition Bay
Kaitaia
Okaihau
Kaikohe
Hokianga Harbour
Kerikeri
Paihia
Hikurangi
Whangarei
Waitoa
Dargaville
Ruawai
Wellsford
Helensville
Waikworth
Kaipara Harbour
Takapuna
Waiuku
Auckland
Manurewa
Papakura
Pukekohe
Huntly
Morrinsville
Ngaruawahia
Hamilton
Cambridge
Otorohanga
Te Kuiti
Taumarunui
Ohura
Waitara
New Plymouth
North Taranaki Bight
Cape Egmont
Mount Taranaki (Mount Egmont) 8261ft (2518m)
South Taranaki Bight
Hawera
Patea
Stratford
Raetihi
Waiouru
Mount Ruapehu 9175ft (2797m)
Taihape
Turangi
Waiouru
Marton
Feilding
Wanganui
Palmerston North
Little Barrier Island
Great Barrier Island
Colville Channel
Mayor Island
Hauraki Gulf
Coromandel
Whitianga
Thames
Paeroa
Katikati
Tauranga
Matamata
Kawerau
Whakatane
Opotiki
Te Puke
Rotorua
Lake Rotorua
Tokoroa
Murupara
Lake Taupo
Taupo
Lake Waikaremoana
Wairoa
Mahia Peninsula
Poverty Bay
Gisborne
Ruatoria
East Cape
Raukumara Range
Kaimanawa Range
Napier
Hastings
Havelock North
Waipawa
Waipukurau
Dannevirke
Woodville
Hawke Bay
Cape Farewell

100
50
0 km
100
50
0 miles

AN AGRICULTURAL NATION

Agriculture is of prime importance and accounts for more than half of national export earnings. Orchards produce a vast range of fruit, from apples to kiwi fruit (above and below). Cereal and other crops, such as sunflowers, add color and variety to the landscape. Traditional sheep and cattle farming has expanded to include deer, goats, and even ostriches.

VOLCANIC ACTIVITY

A fault line runs through New Zealand where two major tectonic plates meet. It has caused devastating earthquakes, but has also helped create breathtaking scenery. This includes South Island's Southern Alps, and many smaller volcanic mountains, hot springs, and geysers in North Island.

LADY KNOX geyser, North Island

FLIGHTLESS KIWI BIRD

UNIQUE WILDLIFE

New Zealand has many unique and endangered animal species, especially birds. Because there were no mammal predators before humans introduced them, many species have few means of defense, and some birds, such as the kiwi (above), cannot fly. Conservation programs are now in place to protect these birds.

GREEN ENERGY

Most of the country's electricity comes from hydroelectric power. It is generated by river water gushing through turbines inside dams at power stations (left). New Zealand also has geothermal energy using heat from inside the Earth.

FILM INDUSTRY

New Zealand has a well-established film industry. Today, thanks to the acclaimed Tolkien trilogy, Lord of the Rings (above), the country has become increasingly popular with international studios for location work. The country offers an unusually wide range of scenery as well as technical experts.

ADVENTURE SPORTS PARADISE

New Zealand offers a huge range of adventure sports and outdoor activities, from whitewater rafting (below) to bungee jumping. The latter originated in Queenstown in South Island. The town is billed as the country's top adventure tourism destination because its surrounding lakes, mountains, and rivers, and its mostly dry climate, are ideal for outdoor pursuits.

NEW ZEALAND

WELLINGTON

Masterton
Lower Hutt
Porirua
Cape Palliser
Cape Campbell
Blenheim
Seddon
Clarence
Picton
Nelson
Kaikoura
Motueka
Richmond
Wairau
Richmond Range
Mount Owen
6152ft
(1875m)
Bay
Karamea
Bight
Hanmer Springs
Springs Junction
Waipara
Pegasus Bay
Rangiora
Reefton
Seddonville
Westport
Cape Foulwind
Lake Brunner
Oxford
Kaiapoi
Christchurch
Lyttelton
Banks Peninsula
Runanga
Greymouth
Otira
Arthur's Pass
3031ft (920m)
Rakaia
Darfield
Mayfield
Canterbury Plains
Lake Ellesmere
Canterbury Bight
Hokitika
Ross
Southern Alps
Mt Cook
12,283ft (3744m)
Geraldine
Temuka
Ashburton
Hinds
Fairlie
Timaru
Abut Head
Whataroa
Fox Glacier
Mount Cook
Studholme
Waimate
Oamaru
Haast
Waitaki
South Island
Lake Pukaki
Lake Hawea
Lake Wanaka
Wanaka
Cromwell
Alexandra
Hampden
Dunedin
Otago Peninsula
Mosgiel
Milton
Balclutha
Queenstown
Lake Wakatipu
Taieri
Clutha
Milford Sound
Lumsden
Mataura
Te Anau
Lake Te Anau
Lake Manapouri
Gore
Tokanui
Mataura
Winton
Invercargill
Riverton
Ruapuke Island
Toetoes Bay
Foveaux Strait
Stewart Island
Halfmoon Bay
Codfish Island
South West Cape
Muttonbird Islands
Resolution Island
West Cape
George Sound
Caswell Sound
Fiordland
Eyre Mts
Livingstone Mts
Takitimu Mts
Waiau
Lake Monowai
Lake Hauroko
Te Waewae Bay

Cook Strait

Pacific Ocean

THE LARGEST OCEAN ON EARTH, the Pacific covers one-third of the Earth's surface. The island nations of Japan, Indonesia, Australia, New Zealand, and many others are completely surrounded by this enormous ocean, which stretches from the Arctic in the north to the Antarctic in the south. The Pacific is also the world's deepest ocean—its greatest known depth is in the Mariana Trench, off Guam, which plunges steeply for 36,198 ft (11,033 m). Within the Pacific, there are many smaller seas that lie near land. These include the Tasman Sea, the South China Sea, and the Bering Sea. There are more than 30,000 islands in the Pacific. Most are too small or too barren to be inhabited, but others are home to people of many different cultures and religions. The native island peoples fall into three main groups—Polynesians, Melanesians, and Micronesians. Although the word "pacific" means "peaceful," strong currents, tropical storms, and tsunamis can all make this ocean far from peaceful.

HAWAIIAN conch shells were once blown to sound a warning.

MARINE iguana on the black volcanic rocks of the Galápagos Islands

HAWAII

This chain of eight volcanic islands and 124 islets forms the 50th state of the United States and was admitted to the union in 1959. The dramatic landscape and palm-fringed beaches make Hawaii a popular destination for tourists. Today, native Hawaiians are a minority in their own land.

Tsunami

Earthquakes beneath the sea may cause giant waves called tsunamis. These can travel great distances across the ocean, building into a huge wall of water as they approach the coast. They can leave immense damage in their wake.

SURFING

The Hawaiian sport of surfing ranks as the oldest sport in the US. It was practiced by the nobility as a form of religious ceremony until the 1820s, when missionaries, who thought it immoral, tried to ban it. Today, surfing is one of the most popular watersports and can be seen from Australia and New Zealand to Mexico.

GALÁPAGOS ISLANDS

When British naturalist Charles Darwin (1809–82) went to the Galápagos Islands, he found many unusual animals. He also noticed differences between animals of the same species living elsewhere. This led him to believe that, over time, animals adapt, or evolve, to suit their habitats.

Black smoker chimneys

Large red tube worms

DEEP-SEA VENTS

Underwater exploration has revealed some amazing places deep in the Pacific. Large vents, formed by solidified minerals, act as chimneys for superheated steam and gas that rises from the seabed. These are known as black smokers. Scientists have found a host of new creatures living in this hostile environment.

ASIA

Sea of Japan
Japan
Yellow Sea
East China Sea
Ryukyu Trench
Emperor Seamounts
Shikoku Basin
Taiwan
Philippine Sea
Philippine Basin
NORTHERN MARIANA ISLANDS (to US)
GUAM (to US)
Mariana Trench
South China Basin
Philippines
Challenger Deep 36,201ft (11,034m)
South China Sea
PALAU
Caroline Island
MICRO
Celebes Sea
Borneo
Celebes
Me
East Indies
Java Sea
Banda Sea
New Guinea
Java
Timor
Timor Sea
Arafura Sea
Torres Strait
Co Se
Great Ba
Reef

INDIAN OCEAN

AUSTRALASIA & OCEANIA

Great Australian Bight
South Australian Basin
Bass St
Tasma

Did you know?

▸ The Pacific is larger than Earth's entire land surface.

▸ The Pacific is surrounded by a zone of violent volcanic and earthquake activity, known as the Pacific Ring of Fire.

Sea of
khotsk

Kurile
lands

Northwest Pacific
Basin

Bering Strait

Bering
Sea

Aleutian
Basin

Aleutian Islands

Aleutian Trench

Gulf of
Alaska

Chinook Trough

Cascadia
Basin

Rocky Mountains

NORTH
AMERICA

Mendocino Fracture Zone

MIDWAY
ISLANDS
(to US)

Murray Fracture Zone

Hawaiian Ridge

Molokai Fracture Zone

Gulf of California

Gulf of
Mexico

WAKE ISLAND
(to US)

JOHNSTON ATOLL
(to US)

HAWAII
(US STATE)

Mid-Pacific Mountains

Clarion Fracture Zone

Middle America Trench

Caribbean Sea

MARSHALL
ISLANDS

PACIFIC

Central

Pacific

KINGMAN REEF
(to US)

Clipperton Fracture Zone

CLIPPERTON
ISLAND
(to France)

Guatemala
Basin

SIA

Micronesia

Melanesian
Basin

PALMYRA
ATOLL
(to US)

Basin

JARVIS ISLAND
(to US)

OCEAN

Galapagos Fracture Zone

Cocos Ridge

Galapagos Islands
(to Ecuador)

SOUTH
AMERICA

NAURU

BAKER &
HOWLAND ISLANDS
(to US)

Gallego
Rise

Peru-Chile Trench

nes

TUVALU

TOKELAU
(to NZ)

KIRIBATI

Polynesia

Marquesas
Islands

Marquesas Fracture Zone

Bauer
Basin

LOMON
LANDS

North Fiji
Basin

WALLIS & FUTUNA
(to France)

AMERICAN
SAMOA
(to US)

Tiki
Basin

Galapagos
Rise

VANUATU

SAMOA

Tahiti

Mendaña Fracture Zone

Nazca Ridge

Peru
Basin

EW CALEDONIA
(to France)

FIJI

TONGA

COOK
ISLANDS
(to NZ)

NIUE
(to NZ)

FRENCH
POLYNESIA
(to France)

Austral
Fracture Zone

Andes

South
Fiji
Basin

Íles Gambier

Sala y Gomez
(to Chile)

Isla San Félix
(to Chile)

Isla San Ambrosio
(to Chile)

NORFOLK
ISLAND
(to Australia)

Tonga Trench

▽Horizon Deep
▲ Ozbourn Seamount

Kermadec
Islands
(to NZ)

Íles Australes

PITCAIRN ISLANDS
(to UK)

Easter Island
(to Chile)

Lord Howe Basin

Southwest
Pacific
Basin

East Pacific Rise

Islas Juan Fernández
(to Chile)

Chile Basin

NEW
ZEALAND

North Island

Louisville Ridge

Challenger Fracture Zone

Chile Rise

Tasman
Sea

South
Island

Chatham Rise

Agassiz Fracture Zone

sman
nteau

Tasman Basin

Bounty
Trough

Chatham Islands
(to NZ)

Mornington
Abyssal
Plain

Campbell
Plateau

Eltanin Fracture Zone

Pacific-Antarctic Ridge

Southeast
Pacific Basin

Amundsen Plain

TUNA FISHING needs
to be carefully
monitored.

EASTER ISLAND

Easter Island in the Pacific lies over 2,000 miles
(3,218 km) from the nearest populated land.
It is best known for the gigantic stone figures,
known as M*oai*, which were carved from
volcanic rock and erected facing the sea. It
is thought that the people who built the
statues were of Peruvian descent.

EL NIÑO

Every few years, winds off the
South American coast weaken,
causing an unusually warm ocean
current, known as El Niño. This
kills off plankton that provide
food for fish such as anchovies.
Scientists use heat-sensitive
cameras to map ocean temperatures
and keep track of El Niño. Warm
waters are shown in orange/red (above).

SOUTH PACIFIC FISH

Fish stocks in the South Pacific are an
important food source for the island countries
and a major source of employment. Migratory
tuna are the most important fish. However, it is
becomingly clear that the industry needs to be
effectively managed to avoid the dangers
of overfishing and the
collapse of fish
stocks.

Antarctica

THE FROZEN CONTINENT OF ANTARCTICA is covered by a vast icecap, many thousands of years old, and surrounded by the freezing seas of the Southern Ocean. It is the only continent with no permanent inhabitants—the only people who come here are scientists or tourists. Although the land is rich in oil and minerals, mining is prohibited under the laws of the Antarctic Treaty. This Treaty, signed by 45 countries, made Antarctica a "continent for science" to be used for peaceful purposes only.

DAY-TRIPPERS

Tourists visit Antarctica in summer. There are no resorts, so visitors generally stay on small cruise ships. When they come ashore, people have to wear insulated clothing and goggles to protect their eyes from glare off the ice.

LONG DAYS

Seasons at the poles are extreme. Polar summers are short but there can be sunshine 24 hours a day. This is because Earth rotates at an angle to the Sun.

RESEARCH

The only people who stay in Antarctica are scientists. They come to study the climate, weather, and geology. By taking ice samples, for example, they can learn about changes in the world's climate over the years.

SCIENTISTS check an ice core.

FLOATING ICE

Icebergs are giant chunks of floating ice that break away, or calve, from ice sheets or glaciers. Most of their mass lies hidden below sea level.

Did you know?

▶ Antarctica is actually a desert—a barren region, incapable of supporting people or vegetation.

KRILL

Tiny, shrimp-like creatures, krill are the primary food source for a great number of Antarctic animals. These include whales, seals, penguins, squid, and fish.

EMPEROR PENGUINS huddle for warmth.

PENGUINS

Penguins walk awkwardly on land, but can swim swiftly to catch fish. Waterproof feathers and a thick layer of fat help keep them warm.

SOUTHERN OCEAN

Orcadas (Argentina)
South Orkney Islands
Signy (UK)
South Shetland Islands
Esperanza (Argentina)
Drake Passage
Capitán Arturo Prat (Chile)
Palmer (US)
Antarctic Peninsula
Graham Land
Palmer Land
Rothera (UK)
San Martín (Argentina)
Weddell Sea
Ronne Ice Shelf
Berkner Island
Coats Land
Halley (UK)
Belgrano II (Argentina)
Sanae (South Africa)
Georg von Neumayer (Germany)
Novolazarevskaya (Russian Federation)
Dronning Maud Land
Lützow Holmbukta
Syowa (Japan)
Molodezhnaya (Russian Federation)
Enderby Land
Mawson (Australia)
Cape Darnley
Mackenzie Bay
Prydz Bay
Princess Elizabeth Land
Davis (Australia)
Bellingshausen Sea
PETER I ISLAND (to Norway)
Ellsworth Land
Vinson Massif 16,066ft (4897m)
Lesser Antarctica
Transantarctic Mountains
ANTARCTICA
Amundsen-Scott (US)
South Pole
Greater Antarctica
Mirny (Russ. Fed.)
Vostok (Russian Federation)
Shackleton Ice Shelf
Casey (Australia)
Cape Poinsett
Amundsen Sea
Marie Byrd Land
Mount Sidley 13,717ft (4181m)
Mount Siple 10,171ft (3100m)
Roosevelt Island
Mount Kirkpatrick 14,856ft (4528m)
Mount Markham 14,275ft (4351m)
Ross Ice Shelf
Scott Base (NZ)
McMurdo Base (US)
Mount Erebus 12,448ft (3794m)
Victoria Land
Wilkes Land
Terre Adélie
Dumont d'Urville (France)
SOUTHERN OCEAN
Ross Sea
Cape Adare
George V Land
Leningradskaya (Russian Federation)
South Geomagnetic Pole
Antarctic Circle
Balleny Islands

0 km   500
0 miles   500

Arctic Ocean

THE SMALLEST OF THE world's oceans, the Arctic is almost entirely surrounded by the northern edges of North America, Europe, and Asia. For most of the year, its waters are covered by a thick sheet of ice, although warmer currents from the Pacific and Atlantic melt the ice along the continental coasts for a short time in summer. Despite the harsh conditions, the region is home to a range of wildlife, such as reindeer, muskox, foxes, and wolves. Some people, including the Inuit of Canada and the Sami of northern Scandinavia, have also adapted to this tough environment.

OZONE HOLE

High in the atmosphere, ozone (a gas) forms a natural shield that protects us from the Sun's ultraviolet rays. Scientists (right) at both poles have found holes in the ozone layer, caused by chemicals known as CFCs, once used in aerosols, fridges, and plastic packaging.

SATELLITE image shows hole over the Arctic.

ALASKAN OIL

Reserves of oil and gas in the Beaufort Sea, off the coast of Alaska, have attracted interest. However, the introduction of ships and oil platforms brings problems. In a bid to protect the area, several environmental organizations are actively working to prevent drilling for more oil in this area.

Did you know?

▶ The main Arctic icepack is not stationary—strong winds cause it to rotate very slowly clockwise

▶ The Sami are an indigenous people who form an ethnic minority in Norway, Sweden, Finland, and Russia.

▶ Walruses breed off the Arctic coasts.

0 km 250 500

0 miles 250 500

ARCTIC SURVIVORS

Polar bears live along the Arctic coasts of Canada, Greenland, and Russia. They hunt seals and fish at points where the sea ice melts. The bears have an insulating layer of fat, called blubber, which helps them survive the cold. Their white fur also provides essential camouflage on the ice.

NORTHERN LIGHTS

In midwinter, the north polar skies are sometimes lit up by dramatic curtains of red and green light. Known as the Northern Lights, these special effects are caused by disturbances in the upper atmosphere. The same happens near Antarctica, where the effect is called the Southern Lights.

Map labels

Bering Strait
180°
Arctic Circle
170°
170°
Chukchi Sea
Ostrov Vrangelya
East Siberian Sea
70°
70°
160°
150°
75°
Beaufort Sea
Amundsen Gulf
130°
Novosibirskiye Ostrova
140°
80°
Banks Island
120°
Laptev Sea
120°
110°
70°
Victoria Island
110°
CANADA
North Geomagnetic Pole
85°
ARCTIC
RUSSIAN FEDERATION
Melville Island
Queen Elizabeth Islands
100°
90°
Severnaya Zemlya
75°
100°
North Pole +
OCEAN
80°
Lancaster Sound
Ellesmere Island
Lincoln Sea
Franz Josef Land
Kara Sea
70°
60°
Nares Strait
80°
Knud Rasmussen Land
70°
Kap Morris Jesup
50°
Baffin Bay
60°
Wandel Sea
SVALBARD (to Norway)
40°
Kong Frederik VIII Land
Spitsbergen
75°
LONGYEARBYEN
GREENLAND (to Denmark)
Greenland Sea
30°
Bjørnøya (to Norway)
Barents Sea
20°
NUUK 65°
Kong Christian IX Land
JAN MAYEN (to Norway)
10°
Norwegian Sea
10°
20°
50°
40°
65°
30°
Denmark Strait
ICELAND
REYKJAVÍK

Gazetteer

HOW TO USE THE GAZETTEER

This gazetteer is a selection of the names in *Children's World Atlas*, and can be used to help you find places on the maps. For example, to find the city of Lisbon in Portugal, look up its name in the gazetteer. The entry reads:

Lisbon *Capital* Portugal 58 E6

The first number, 58, tells you that Lisbon appears on the map on page 58. The second number, E6, shows that it is in square E6. Turn to page 58. Trace down from the letter E along the top of the grid (or up from the letter E on the bottom of the grid), and then across from the number 6 on the side of the grid. You will find Lisbon in the area where the letter and number meet.

A

Aachen *Town* Germany 56 B7
Aalborg *Town* Denmark 49 B11
Aalen *Town* Germany 57 E9
Aalst *Town* Belgium 53 D11
Aalter *Town* Belgium 53 C10
Äänekoski *Town* Finland 48 G8
Aba *Town* Nigeria 41 L8
Aba *Town* Democratic Republic of Congo 42 I8
Ābādān *Town* Iran 82 E7
Abakan *Town* Russian Federation 78 H7
Abbeville *Town* France 54 E5
Abéché *Town* Chad 42 F6
Abengourou *Town* Côte d'Ivoire 41 I8
Aberdeen *Town* South Dakota, US 12 G4
Aberdeen *Town* Maryland, US 9 H8
Aberdeen *Town* Scotland, UK 50 F5
Aberystwyth *Town* Wales, UK 51 E10
Abhā *Town* Saudi Arabia 83 C11
Abidjan *Town* Côte d'Ivoire 40 H8
Abilene *Town* Texas, US 17 K5
Åbo *see* Turku
Abomey *Town* Benin 41 J7
Abrantes *Town* Portugal 58 F6
Abu Dhabi *Capital* United Arab Emirates 83 F9
Abu Hamed *Town* Sudan 38 E6
Abuja *Capital* Nigeria 41 L7
Abū Kamāl *Town* Syria 80 I7
Abū Ẓaby *see* Abu Dhabi
Acapulco *Town* Mexico 19 J9
Acarigua *Town* Venezuela 26 D5
Accra *Capital* Ghana 41 I8
Aconcagua, Cerro *Mountain* Argentina 30 D7
A Coruña *Town* Spain 58 E2
Açu *Town* Brazil 29 M3
Adamawa Highlands *Mountain range* Cameroon 42 D8
'Adan *see* Aden
Adana *Town* Turkey 76 G6
Adapazari *Town* Turkey 76 E4
Ad Dahnā' *Desert* Saudi Arabia 83 E9
Ad Dakhla *Town* Western Sahara 36 C7
Ad Dammām *Town* Saudi Arabia 83 E9
Ad Dawḩah *see* Doha
Addis Ababa *Capital* Ethiopia 39 F9
Adelaide *Town* South Australia, Australia 105 J7
Aden *Town* Yemen 83 D13

Aden, Gulf of *Indian Ocean* 83 E13
Adirondack Mountains New York, US 8 H4
Ādīs Ābeba *see* Addis Ababa
Adiyaman *Town* Turkey 76 H6
Adrar *Town* Algeria 36 G6
Aegean Sea *Greece* 67 F9
Afghanistan *Country* 84 H7
Afmadow *Town* Somalia 39 G11
Afyon *Town* Turkey 76 E5
Agadez *Town* Niger 41 L4
Agadir *Town* Morocco 36 E5
Agen *Town* France 55 D10
Agialoúsa *Town* Cyprus 80 B7
Āgra *Town* India 87 I3
Ağri *Town* Turkey 77 K4
Agrigento *Town* Sicily, Italy 61 E13
Agropoli *Town* Italy 61 F10
Aguachica *Town* Colombia 26 C5
Agua Prieta *Town* Mexico 18 F3
Aguascalientes *Town* Mexico 19 I7
Aguaytía *Town* Peru 27 B10
Aguilas *Town* Spain 59 J8
Aguililla *Town* Mexico 19 I8
Ahaggar *Mountain range* Algeria 37 I7
Ahlen *Town* Germany 56 C7
Ahmadābād *Town* India 86 G4
Ahuachapán *Town* El Salvador 22 E5
Ahvāz *Town* Iran 82 E7
Aiken *Town* South Carolina, US 11 J4
Ailigandí *Town* Panama 23 N7
'Aïn Ben Tili *Town* Mauritania 40 G2
Aiquile *Town* Bolivia 27 E12
Aïr, Massif de l' *Mountain range* Niger 41 L4
Aix-en-Provence *Town* France 55 G11
Aizu *Town* Japan 93 G9
Ajaccio *Town* France 55 I13
Ajo *Town* Arizona, US 16 E5
Akchâr *Desert* Mauritania 40 E3
Akhalts'ikhe *Town* Georgia 77 K3
Akhisar *Town* Turkey 76 C5
Akhtubinsk *Town* Russian Federation 73 D11
Akita *Town* Japan 92 F8
Akjoujt *Town* Mauritania 40 E3
Akkeshi *Town* Japan 92 H5
Akron *Town* Ohio, US 13 M6
Akrotírion *Town* Cyprus 80 A8
Aksai Chin *Administrative region* China 88 D6
Aksaray *Town* Turkey 76 F5
Akşehir *Town* Turkey 76 E5
Aktau *Town* Kazakhstan 78 D6
Aktobe *Town* Kazakhstan 78 E6
Aktsyabrski *Town* Belarus 71 F11
Akula *Town* Democratic Republic of Congo 43 F9
Akune *Town* Japan 93 B14
Alabama *State* US 10 G5
Alabama River Alabama, US 10 G6
Al 'Amārah *Town* Iraq 82 D7
Alamo *Town* Nevada, US 14 H7
Alamogordo *Town* New Mexico, US 16 H5
Åland *Island group* Finland 49 F9
Alanya *Town* Turkey 76 E7
Al 'Aqabah *Town* Jordan 81 D14
Alaşehir *Town* Turkey 76 D5
Alaska *Province* Canada 4 E5
Alaska, Gulf of Alaska, US 4 E6
Alaska Range *Mountain Range* Alaska, US 4 E5
Albacete *Town* Spain 59 J6
Alba Iulia *Town* Romania 68 E6
Albania *Country* 65 F12
Albany *River* Ontario, Canada 6 F5
Albany *Town* Western Australia, Australia 104 E7
Albany *Town* Georgia, US 10 H6
Albany *Town* New York, US 9 I5
Al Bāridah *Town* Syria 80 F8
Al Baṣrah *Town* Iraq 82 D7
Alberta *Province* Canada 4 H7
Albert, Lake Democratic Republic of Congo 43 I9
Albuquerque *Town* New Mexico, US 16 H4
Alcañiz *Town* Spain 59 K5
Alcoy *Town* Spain 59 K7
Alderney *Island* Channel Islands, UK 51 G13
Aleksin *Town* Russian Federation 73 C9
Alençon *Town* France 54 D7
Alenquer *Town* Brazil 29 I2

Aleppo *Town* Syria 80 E6
Alessandria *Town* Italy 60 C5
Aleutian Islands *Island Group* Alaska, US 4 B5
Alexander Archipelago *Island* British Colombia, Canada 4 E7
Alexandria *Town* Louisiana, US 10 E6
Alexandria *Town* Egypt 38 D4
Alexandria *Town* Romania 68 F7
Alexandroúpoli *Town* Greece 66 G8
Alga *Town* Kazakhstan 78 E6
Algarve *Region* Spain 58 E8
Algeciras *Town* Spain 58 G9
Alger *see* Algiers
Algeria *Country* 36 H5
Al Ghābah *Town* Oman 83 G10
Algiers *Capital* Algeria 36 H3
Algona *Town* Iowa, US 12 H5
Al Ḩasakah *Town* Syria 80 H5
Al Ḩillah *Town* Iraq 82 D7
Al Hudaydah *see* Hodeida
Al Hufūf *Town* Saudi Arabia 83 E9
Alíartos *Town* Greece 67 E11
Alicante *Town* Spain 59 L7
Alice Springs *Town* Northern Territory, Australia 105 H4
Aliquippa *Town* Pennsylvania, US 8 E7
Al Jafr *Town* Jordan 81 E13
Al Jaghbūb *Town* Libya 37 N5
Al Jahrā' *Town* Kuwait 82 D8
Al Jawf *Town* Saudi Arabia 82 B8
Al Jazīrah *Physical region* Syria/Iraq 80 I5
Al Karak *Town* Jordan 81 E12
Al Khufrah *Town* Libya 37 N7
Al Khums *Town* Libya 37 K4
Alkmaar *Town* Netherlands 52 E7
Al Kūt *Town* Iraq 82 D7
Al Kuwayt *see* Kuwait
Al Lādhiqīyah *Town* Syria 80 D7
Allahābād *Town* India 87 I4
Allegheny Plateau Pennsylvania/New York, US 8 F6
Allentown *Town* Pennsylvania, US 9 H7
Al Līth *Town* Saudi Arabia 83 B11
Alma-Ata *see* Almaty
Al Madīnah *see* Medina
Al Mafraq *Town* Jordan 81 E10
Al Majma'ah *Town* Saudi Arabia 83 D9
Al Mālikīyah *Town* Syria 80 I4
Al Manāmah *see* Manama
Almansa *Town* Spain 59 K7
Al Marj *Town* Libya 37 M4
Almaty *Town* Kazakhstan 78 G8
Al Mawşil *Town* Iraq 82 C6
Al Mayādīn *Town* Syria 80 H6
Almelo *Town* Netherlands 52 G8
Almere *Town* Netherlands 52 F8
Almería *Town* Spain 59 J8
Al'met'yevsk *Town* Russian Federation 73 F9
Almirante *Town* Panama 23 K8
Al Mukallā *Town* Yemen 83 E13
Alofi *Capital* Niue 103 K7
Alotip *Town* Indonesia 97 N8
Alpena *Town* Michigan, US 13 L4
Alpine *Town* Texas, US 17 I7
Alps *Mountain range* Central Europe 57 D12
Al Qāmishlī *Town* Syria 80 I4
Al Qunayţirah *Town* Syria 81 D9
Altai Mountains *Mountain range* Mongolia/Russian Federation 88 F4
Altamaha River Georgia, US 11 I5
Altamira *Town* Brazil 29 J2
Altamura *Town* Italy 61 H10
Altar, Desierto de *Desert* Mexico 18 D2
Altay *Town* China 88 F3
Altay *Town* Mongolia 88 H3
Altin Köprü *Town* Iraq 82 C6
Altiplano *Physical region* Bolivia 27 E13
Altoona *Town* Pennsylvania, US 9 F7
Altun Ha *Ancient site* Belize 22 F2
Altun Shan *Mountain range* China 88 G5
Al 'Umarī *Town* Jordan 81 F11
Al 'Uwaynāt *Town* Libya 37 J6
Alupka *Town* Ukraine 69 K7
Alva *Town* Oklahoma, US 17 L3

Al Wajh *Town* Saudi Arabia 83 A9
Alwar *Town* India 86 H3
Al Wari'ah *Town* Saudi Arabia 82 D8
Alytus *Town* Lithuania 70 D8
Amamapare *Town* Indonesia 97 N7
Amantea *Town* Italy 61 G12
Amarapura *Town* Myanmar 94 B6
Amarillo *Town* Texas, US 17 J4
Amazon *River* Brazil 29 J2
Amazon Basin Brazil 28 G3
Ambanja *Town* Madagascar 45 M4
Ambarchik *Town* Russian Federation 78 L3
Ambato *Town* Ecuador 26 A8
Amboasary *Town* Madagascar 45 L6
Ambon *Town* Indonesia 97 K7
American Samoa *Dependent territory* US, Pacific Ocean 103 K6
Amersfoort *Town* Netherlands 52 F8
Amfilochía *Town* Greece 67 C10
Amherst *Town* Nova Scotia, Canada 7 K7
Amiens *Town* France 54 E6
Amman *Capital* Jordan 81 E11
'Ammān *see* Amman
Ammóchostos *Town* Cyprus 80 B8
Āmol *Town* Iran 82 F5
Amos *Town* Quebec, Canada 6 H6
Amritsar *Town* India 86 H2
Amstelveen *Town* Netherlands 52 F8
Amsterdam *Capital* Netherlands 52 E8
Am Timan *Town* Chad 42 F6
Amu Darya *River* Uzbekistan 84 G4
Amundsen Gulf Canada 4 H4
Amundsen-Scott *Research station* Antarctica 110 E6
Amundsen Sea Southern Ocean 110 B7
Amuntai *Town* Indonesia 96 H7
Amur *River* China 89 L2
Anadyr' *Town* Russian Federation 78 M2
Anamur *Town* Turkey 76 F7
Anápolis *Town* Brazil 29 K5
Anatolia *Plateau* Turkey 76 E6
Anchorage *Town* Alaska, Canada 4 E5
Ancona *Town* Italy 60 F7
Andalucía *Region* Spain 58 H8
Andaman Islands *Island group* India 87 M8
Andaman Sea Indian Ocean 87 M8
Anderson *Town* Indiana, US 13 K6
Andes *Mountain range* South America 26–27, 30–31
Andijon *Town* Uzbekistan 85 K4
Andkhvoy *Town* Afghanistan 84 H5
Andorra *Country* 55 D12
Andorra la Vella *Capital* Andorra 55 D12
Andreanof Islands *Island Group* Alaska, US 4 A4
Andrews *Town* Texas, US 17 J5
Andria *Town* Italy 61 H10
Andros Island Bahamas 24 F2
Andros Town *Town* Bahamas 24 F2
Angarsk *Town* Russian Federation 79 I7
Angeles *Town* Philippines 97 I2
Angel Falls *Waterfall* Venezuela 26 F6
Ångermanälven *River* Sweden 48 E7
Angers *Town* France 54 C7
Angkor Wat *Ancient site* Cambodia 95 F10
Anglesey *Island* Wales, UK 51 E9
Angola *Country* 44 E3
Angola Basin *Undersea feature* Atlantic Ocean 33 M6
Angoulême *Town* France 55 D9
Angren *Town* Uzbekistan 85 J3
Anguilla *Dependent territory* UK, Atlantic Ocean 25 N5
Anhui *Administrative region* China 91 J5
Ankara *Capital* Turkey 76 F4
Annaba *Town* Algeria 37 I3
An Nafūd *Desert* Saudi Arabia 82 B8
'Annah *Town* Iraq 82 C6
An Najaf *Town* Iraq 82 C7
Annamitique, Chaîne *Mountain range* Laos 94 F8
Annapolis *Town* Maryland, US 8 G8
Ann Arbor *Town* Michigan, US 13 L5
An Nāşirīyah *Town* Iraq 82 D7
Annecy *Town* France 55 G9

H

Linares *Town* Spain 59 I7
Linares *Town* Chile 31 C9
Linares *Town* Mexico 19 J5
Linchuan *Town* China 91 J7
Lincoln *Town* England, UK 51 H9
Lincoln *Town* Maine, US 9 L2
Lincoln *Town* Nebraska, US 12 G6
Lincoln Sea Arctic Ocean 111 M6
Linden *Town* Guyana 26 G6
Lindi *Town* Tanzania 39 G13
Line Islands *Island group* Kiribati 103 N5
Lingen *Town* Germany 56 C6
Linköping *Town* Sweden 49 D10
Linz *Town* Austria 57 G10
Lipetsk *Town* Russian Federation 73 C9
Lipu *Town* China 91 I8
Lira *Town* Uganda 39 E11
Lisala *Town* Democratic Republic of Congo 43 F9
Lisboa *see* Lisbon
Lisbon *Capital* Portugal 58 E6
Liski *Town* Russian Federation 73 C10
Litang *Town* China 90 F6
Lithuania *Country* 70 D7
Little Cayman *Island* West Indies 24 E5
Littlefield *Town* Texas, US 17 J5
Little Rock *Town* Arkansas, US 10 E4
Liuzhou *Town* China 90 H8
Liverpool *Town* England, UK 51 E9
Livingstone *Town* Zambia 44 H4
Livonia *Town* Michigan, US 13 L5
Livorno *Town* Italy 60 D7
Ljubljana *Capital* Slovenia 57 G12
Ljungby *Town* Sweden 49 D11
Lleida *Town* Spain 59 K4
Löbau *Town* Germany 56 G7
Lobito *Town* Angola 44 D3
Lockport *Town* New York, US 8 F5
Lodwar *Town* Kenya 39 F10
Łódź *Town* Poland 62 F7
Logan *Town* Utah, US 15 I5
Logroño *Town* Spain 59 J3
Loi-Kaw *Town* Myanmar 94 C7
Loire *River* France 54 C8
Loja *Town* Ecuador 26 A8
Lomami *River* Democratic Republic of Congo 43 G10
Lomas *Town* Peru 27 C11
Lomas de Zamora *Town* Argentina 30 G8
Lombardia *see* Lombardy
Lombardy *Region* Italy 60 D4
Lomé *Capital* Togo 41 J8
Lomela *Town* Democratic Republic of Congo 43 G10
Lommel *Town* Belgium 53 E10
Lomond, Loch *Lake* Scotland, UK 50 E6
Lom Sak *Town* Thailand 95 D9
Łomża *Town* Poland 62 G6
Loncoche *Town* Chile 31 C10
London *Town* Ontario, Canada 6 G8
London *Capital* United Kingdom 51 H11
Londonderry *Town* Northern Ireland, UK 50 C7
Londrina *Town* Brazil 29 J7
Long Beach *Town* California, US 14 G8
Longford *Town* Ireland 50 C8
Long Island Bahamas 24 H3
Long Island New York, US 9 J7
Longlac *Town* Ontario, Canada 6 F6
Longreach *Town* Queensland, Australia 105 L4
Longview *Town* Texas, US 17 N5
Long Xuyên *Town* Vietnam 95 G11
Longyan *Town* China 91 J7
Longyearbyen *Capital* Svalbard 111 F7
Lop Buri *Town* Thailand 95 D9
Lorca *Town* Spain 59 J8
Loreto *Town* Mexico 18 F5
Lorient *Town* France 54 B7
Los Angeles *Town* California, US 14 G8
Los Ángeles *Town* Chile 31 C9
Los Mochis *Town* Mexico 18 F5
Louangnamtha *Town* Laos 94 D7
Louangphabang *Town* Laos 94 E7
Loudéac *Town* France 54 B7
Loudi *Town* China 91 I7
Loughrea *Town* Ireland 51 B9

Louisiade Archipelago *Island chain* Papua New Guinea 102 F6
Louisiana *State* US 10 E5
Louisville *Town* Kentucky, US 10 H2
Louth *Town* England, UK 51 H9
Lowell *Town* Massachusetts, US 9 J5
Lower Hutt *Town* New Zealand 107 F9
Lowestoft *Town* England, UK 51 I10
Loyauté, Iles *Island group* New Caledonia 102 H8
Loznica *Town* Serbia & Montenegro 64 F8
Lualaba *River* Democratic Republic of Congo 43 G10
Luanda *Capital* Angola 44 D2
Luanshya *Town* Zambia 44 H3
Luarca *Town* Spain 58 G2
Lubań *Town* Poland 62 C7
Lubango *Town* Angola 44 D4
Lubao *Town* Democratic Republic of Congo 43 G11
Lubbock *Town* Texas, US 17 J5
Lübeck *Town* Germany 56 E5
Lubin *Town* Poland 62 D7
Lubumbashi *Town* Democratic Republic of Congo 43 H13
Lubutu *Town* Democratic Republic of Congo 43 H10
Lucan *Town* Ireland 51 D9
Lucca *Town* Italy 60 D6
Lucena *Town* Philippines 97 J2
Lucena *Town* Spain 58 H8
Lučenec *Town* Slovakia 63 F10
Lucknow *Town* India 87 J3
Lüderitz *Town* Namibia 44 E7
Ludhiāna *Town* India 86 H2
Ludwigsburg *Town* Germany 57 D9
Ludwigsfelde *Town* Germany 56 F6
Ludwigshafen *Town* Germany 57 D9
Luebo *Town* Democratic Republic of Congo 43 F11
Luena *Town* Angola 44 F3
Lufkin *Town* Texas, US 17 N6
Luga *Town* Russian Federation 72 B7
Lugano *Town* Switzerland 57 D12
Lugo *Town* Spain 58 F3
Lugoj *Town* Romania 68 D6
Luhans'k *Town* Ukraine 69 M4
Luhuo *Town* China 90 F5
Lukovit *Town* Bulgaria 66 E6
Luleå *Town* Sweden 48 F6
Lund *Town* Sweden 49 D12
Lüneburg *Town* Germany 56 E5
Luoyang *Town* China 91 I4
Lusaka *Capital* Zambia 44 H4
Luton *Town* England, UK 51 G10
Luts'k *Town* Ukraine 68 F2
Luxembourg *Country* 53 F13
Luxembourg *Capital* Luxembourg 53 G13
Luxor *Town* Egypt 38 E5
Luza *Town* Russian Federation 72 F7
Luzern *Town* Switzerland 57 C11
Luzon *Island* Philippines 97 J2
L'viv *Town* Ukraine 68 F3
Lynchburg *Town* Virginia, US 11 K2
Lyon *Town* France 55 F9
Lysychans'k *Town* Ukraine 69 M4

M

Ma'arrat an Nu'mān *Town* Syria 80 E6
Maastricht *Town* Netherlands 53 F11
Macao *Town* China 91 I8
Macapá *Town* Brazil 29 J2
Macdonnell Ranges *Mountain range* Northern territory, Australia 104 H4
Macedonia *Country* 65 G12
Maceió *Town* Brazil 29 N4
Machala *Town* Ecuador 26 A8
Machanga *Town* Mozambique 45 J5
Machias *Town* Maine, US 9 L3
Machu Picchu *Ancient site* Peru 27 C11
Mackay *Town* Queensland, Australia 105 M4

Macon *Town* Georgia, US 11 I5
Ma'dabā *Town* Jordan 81 E11
Madagascar *Country* 45 L5
Madang *Town* Papua New Guinea 102 E5
Madawaska *Town* Maine, US 9 K1
Madeira, Rio *River* Brazil 28 H3
Madīnat ath Thawrah *Town* Syria 80 F6
Madison *Town* Wisconsin, US 13 J5
Madiun *Town* Indonesia 96 G8
Madras *see* Chennai
Madrid *Capital* Spain 59 I5
Madurai *Town* India 87 I8
Maebashi *Town* Japan 93 F10
Magadan *Town* Russian Federation 79 L4
Magdalena *Town* Mexico 18 E3
Magdalena *Town* Bolivia 27 E11
Magdeburg *Town* Germany 56 E6
Magelang *Town* Indonesia 96 G8
Magellan, Strait of Chile 31 E14
Maggiore, Lake Italy 60 C4
Magnitogorsk *Town* Russian Federation 78 F6
Magţa' Laijar *Town* Mauritania 40 F4
Mahajanga *Town* Madagascar 45 M4
Mahalapye *Town* Botswana 44 H6
Mahdia *Town* Tunisia 37 J4
Mahilyow *Town* Belarus 71 G10
Maidstone *Town* England, UK 51 H11
Maiduguri *Town* Nigeria 41 M6
Main *River* Germany 56 D8
Maine *State* US 9 K3
Maine, Gulf of *Coastal feature* US 9 L5
Maingkwan *Town* Myanmar 94 C4
Mainz *Town* Germany 56 C8
Majorca *Island* Balearic Islands, Spain 59 N6
Makarska *Town* Croatia 65 D9
Makassar Strait Indonesia 97 I6
Makay *Mountain range* Madagascar 45 L5
Makeni *Town* Sierra Leone 40 F7
Makhachkala *Town* Russian Federation 73 D14
Makiyivka *Town* Ukraine 69 M5
Makkah *see* Mecca
Makkovik *Town* Newfoundland & Labrador, Canada 7 L3
Makoua *Town* Congo 43 E10
Makrany *Town* Belarus 71 C10
Mākū *Town* Iran 82 D5
Makurdi *Town* Nigeria 41 L7
Malabo *Capital* Equatorial Guinea 42 B8
Malacca, Strait of Malaysia 96 D5
Maladzyechna *Town* Belarus 71 E9
Málaga *Town* Spain 58 H8
Malakal *Town* Sudan 39 E9
Malang *Town* Indonesia 96 G8
Mälaren *Lake* Sweden 49 E10
Malatya *Town* Turkey 76 H5
Malawi *Country* 45 J3
Malaysia *Country* 96 E5
Maldives *Country* 99 J4
Malekula *Island* Vanuatu 102 H7
Male' *Capital* Maldives 99 J4
Mali *Country* 41 I4
Mallawi *Town* Egypt 38 D5
Mallorca *see* Majorca
Malmberget *Town* Sweden 48 F5
Malmédy *Town* Belgium 53 F12
Malmö *Town* Sweden 49 C12
Malta *Country* 61 F14
Malta *Town* Montana, US 15 K2
Malta Channel Mediterranean Sea 61 F14
Maluku *see* Moluccas
Malung *Town* Sweden 49 D9
Mamou *Town* Guinea 40 F6
Mamoudzou *Capital* Mayotte 45 L3
Manado *Town* Indonesia 97 K6
Managua *Capital* Nicaragua 22 H6
Managua, Lago de *Lake* Nicaragua 22 H6
Manama *Capital* Bahrain 83 E9
Mananjary *Town* Madagascar 45 M6
Manaus *Town* Brazil 28 H3
Manavgat *Town* Turkey 76 E6
Manbij *Town* Syria 80 F5
Manchester *Town* England, UK 51 F9
Manchester *Town* New Hampshire, US 9 J5
Manchuria *Cultural region* China 89 L3

Mandalay *Town* Myanmar 94 B6
Manduria *Town* Italy 61 H11
Manfredonia *Town* Italy 61 G9
Mangai *Town* Democratic Republic of Congo 43 F11
Mangalmé *Town* Chad 42 F6
Mangalore *Town* India 86 G7
Manila *Capital* Philippines 97 I2
Manisa *Town* Turkey 76 C5
Manitoba *Province* Canada 5 J8
Manitoba, Lake Manitoba, Canada 5 J8
Manitoulin Island Quebec, Canada 6 F7
Maniwori *Town* Indonesia 97 M7
Manizales *Town* Colombia 26 B6
Mankato *Town* Minnesota, US 12 H4
Manmād *Town* India 86 H5
Mannar, Gulf of Indian Ocean 87 I9
Mannheim *Town* Germany 57 D9
Manokwari *Town* Indonesia 97 M6
Manono *Town* Democratic Republic of Congo 43 H12
Manosque *Town* France 55 G11
Mansfield *Town* Ohio, US 13 L6
Mansfield *Town* Pennsylvania, US 8 G6
Manta *Town* Ecuador 26 A8
Mantova *Town* Italy 60 D5
Manurewa *Town* New Zealand 106 G5
Manzanares *Town* Spain 59 I6
Manzanillo *Town* Cuba 24 G4
Manzanillo *Town* Mexico 18 H8
Manzhouli *Town* China 89 K2
Maoke, Pegunungan *Mountain range* Indonesia 97 N7
Maoming *Town* China 91 I8
Maputo *Capital* Mozambique 45 I6
Maquinchao *Town* Argentina 31 D10
Marabá *Town* Brazil 29 K3
Maracaibo *Town* Venezuela 26 C4
Maracay *Town* Venezuela 26 E5
Marādah *Town* Libya 37 M5
Maradi *Town* Niger 41 L5
Marāgheh *Town* Iran 82 D5
Marajó, Ilha de *Island* Brazil 29 K2
Marañón, Río *River* Peru 27 B9
Marbella *Town* Spain 58 H9
Marburg an der Lahn *Town* Germany 56 D7
Marche-en-Famenne *Town* Belgium 53 F12
Mardān *Town* Pakistan 86 G1
Mar del Plata *Town* Argentina 31 G9
Mardin *Town* Turkey 77 J6
Margarita, Isla de *Island* Venezuela 26 E4
Margate *Town* England, UK 51 I11
Mariana Trench *Undersea feature* Pacific Ocean 108 H4
Maribor *Town* Slovenia 57 H11
Marie Byrd Land *Region* Antarctica 110 C6
Marie-Galante *Island* Guadeloupe 25 O6
Marijampolé *Town* Lithuania 70 C7
Marília *Town* Brazil 29 J7
Marín *Town* Spain 58 E3
Maringá *Town* Brazil 29 J7
Mariupol' *Town* Ukraine 69 M5
Marka *Town* Somalia 39 H11
Marmara Denizi *see* Marmara, Sea of
Marmara, Sea of Turkey 76 D4
Maroantsetra *Town* Madagascar 45 M4
Maroua *Town* Cameroon 42 D6
Marquesas Islands *Island group* French Polynesia 103 O6
Marquette *Town* Michigan, US 13 J3
Marrakech *Town* Morocco 36 E4
Marrawah *Town* Tasmania, Australia 105 K9
Marsā al Burayqah *Town* Libya 37 M5
Marsala *Town* Sicily, Italy 61 D12
Marsberg *Town* Germany 56 D7
Marseille *Town* France 55 G12
Marshall Islands *Country* 102 G2
Marsh Harbour *Town* Bahamas 24 G1
Mars Hill *Town* Maine, US 9 L1
Martha's Vineyard *Island* Massachusetts, US 9 K6
Martin *Town* Slovakia 63 E10
Martinique *Dependent territory* France, Atlantic Ocean 25 O7

Salta *Town* Argentina 30 E5
Saltillo *Town* Mexico 19 J5
Salt Lake City *Town* Utah, US 15 I5
Salto *Town* Uruguay 30 G7
Salvador *Town* Brazil 29 M5
Salween *River* Myanmar 94 C7
Salyan *Town* Nepal 87 J3
Salzburg *Town* Austria 57 F10
Salzgitter *Town* Germany 56 E6
Samalayuca *Town* Mexico 18 G3
Samar *Island* Philippines 97 K3
Samara *Town* Russian Federation 73 E10
Samarinda *Town* Indonesia 97 I6
Samarqand *Town* Uzbekistan 85 I4
Şamaxi *Town* Azerbaijan 77 N3
Sambalpur *Town* India 87 J5
Samoa *Country* 103 K6
Sampit *Town* Indonesia 96 G7
Samsun *Town* Turkey 76 H3
Samtredia *Town* Georgia 77 K3
Samui, Ko *Island* Thailand 95 D12
Samut Prakan *Town* Thailand 95 E10
San *Town* Mali 40 H6
Şan'ā' *see* Sana
Sana *Capital* Yemen 83 C12
Sanae *Research station* Antarctica 110 D3
Sanandaj *Town* Iran 82 D6
San Andrés Tuxtla *Town* Mexico 19 L8
San Angelo *Town* Texas, US 17 K6
San Antonio *Town* Chile 30 C8
San Antonio *Town* Texas, US 17 L7
San Antonio Oeste *Town* Argentina 31 E10
Sanāw *Town* Yemen 83 E11
San Bernardino *Town* California, US 14 G8
San Carlos de Bariloche *Town* Argentina 31 D10
San Cristóbal *Town* Venezuela 26 C5
San Cristóbal *Town* Venezuela 26 C5
San Cristóbal de Las Casas *Town* Mexico 19 N8
Sancti Spíritus *Town* Cuba 24 F3
Sandakan *Town* Malaysia 97 I4
Sand Hills *Mountain range* Nebraska, US 12 E5
San Diego *Town* California, US 14 G9
Sandoway *Town* Myanmar 94 B8
Sandpoint *Town* Idaho, US 14 H2
Sandvika *Norway* 49 B9
Sandy City *Town* Utah, US 15 I5
San Fernando *Town* Venezuela 26 E5
San Fernando *Town* Spain 58 G9
San Fernando *Town* Trinidad & Tobago 25 O9
San Fernando del Valle de Catamarca *Town* Argentina 30 E6
San Francisco *Town* California, US 14 F6
San Francisco del Oro *Town* Mexico 18 H5
San Francisco de Macorís *Town* Dominican Republic 25 J5
San Ignacio *Town* Guatemala 22 E2
San Ignacio *Town* Mexico 18 E5
San Joaquin Valley *California*, US 14 F7
San Jorge, Golfo *Gulf* Argentina 31 E12
San José *Town* Bolivia 27 F12
San José *Capital* Costa Rica 23 J7
San José *Town* Guatemala 22 D5
San Jose *Town* California, US 14 F6
San Juan *Capital* Puerto Rico 25 L5
San Juan *Town* Argentina 30 D7
San Juan del Norte *Town* Nicaragua 23 J6
San Juan Mountains *New Mexico/Colorado*, US 16 H3
Sankt Gallen *Town* Switzerland 57 E11
Sankt-Peterburg *see* Saint Petersburg
Sankt Pölten *Town* Austria 57 H10
Sankuru *River* Democratic Republic of Congo 43 G11
Şanliurfa *Town* Turkey 77 I6
San Luis *Town* Guatemala 22 E3
San Luis *Town* Argentina 30 E8
San Luis *Town* Mexico 18 D2
San Luis Potosí *Town* Mexico 19 J6
San Marcos *Town* Guatemala 22 D4
San Marino *Country* 60 E7
San Marino *Capital* San Marino 60 E7
San Martín *Research station* Antarctica 110 B5
San Matías *Town* Bolivia 27 G12
San Matías, Golfo *Gulf* Argentina 31 F10

Sanmenxia *Town* China 91 I4
San Miguel *Town* El Salvador 22 F5
San Miguel *Town* Mexico 19 I4
San Miguel de Tucumán *Town* Argentina 30 E6
San Miguelito *Town* Panama 23 M8
Sanming *Town* China 91 K7
San Pedro *Town* Belize 22 F2
San Pedro de la Cueva *Town* Mexico 18 F4
San Pedro de Lloc *Town* Peru 27 A9
San Pedro Mártir, Sierra *Mountain range* Mexico 18 D3
San Pedro Sula *Town* Honduras 22 F3
San Rafael *Town* Argentina 30 D8
San Remo *Town* Italy 60 B6
San Salvador *Capital* El Salvador 22 F5
San Salvador de Jujuy *Town* Argentina 30 E5
Sansanné-Mango *Town* Togo 41 J6
Sansepolcro *Town* Italy 60 E7
San Severo *Town* Italy 61 G9
Santa Ana *Town* California, US 14 G8
Santa Ana *Town* El Salvador 22 E4
Santa Barbara *Town* California, US 14 G8
Santa Clara *Town* Cuba 24 E3
Santa Cruz *Town* Bolivia 27 F12
Santa Fe *Town* New Mexico, US 16 H3
Santa Fe *Town* Argentina 30 F7
Santa Maria *Town* Brazil 29 J8
Santa Marta *Town* Colombia 26 C4
Santander *Town* Spain 59 I2
Santarém *Town* Brazil 29 I2
Santa Rosa *Town* Argentina 31 E9
Santa Rosa *Town* California, US 14 F6
Santa Rosa de Copán *Town* Honduras 22 F4
Santiago *Capital* Chile 30 D8
Santiago *Town* Dominican Republic 25 J5
Santiago *Town* Spain 58 F3
Santiago de Cuba *Town* Cuba 24 G5
Santiago del Estero *Town* Argentina 30 E6
Santo Domingo *Capital* Dominican Republic 25 J5
Santo Domingo de los Colorados *Town* Ecuador 26 A7
Santos *Town* Brazil 29 K7
Santo Tomé *Town* Argentina 30 H6
San Vicente *Town* El Salvador 22 F5
São Fransisco, Rio *River* Brazil 29 L4
Sao Hill *Town* Tanzania 39 F13
São José do Rio Preto *Town* Brazil 29 K6
São Luís *Town* Brazil 29 L2
São Paulo *Town* Brazil 29 K7
São Roque, Cabo de *Coastal feature* Brazil 29 N3
São Tomé *Capital* São Tomé & Príncipe 43 B10
Sao Tome & Principe *Country* 43 B9
Sapele *Town* Nigeria 41 K8
Sapporo *Town* Japan 92 F5
Saqqez *Town* Iran 82 D6
Sarajevo *Capital* Bosnia & Herzegovina 64 E8
Sarakhs *Town* Iran 82 H5
Saraktash *Town* Russian Federation 73 G11
Saran' *Town* Kazakhstan 78 F7
Saransk *Town* Russian Federation 73 E9
Saratov *Town* Russian Federation 73 D10
Sarawak *Cultural region* Malaysia 96 G6
Sardegna *see* Sardinia
Sardinia *Island* Italy 61 A9
Sargasso Sea *Atlantic Ocean* 33 I3
Sargodha *Town* Pakistan 86 G2
Sarh *Town* Chad 42 E7
Sārī *Town* Iran 82 F5
Sariwŏn *Town* North Korea 91 L3
Sark *Island* Channel Islands, UK 51 G13
Sarmiento *Town* Argentina 31 D12
Sarnia *Town* Ontario, Canada 6 F8
Sarny *Town* Ukraine 68 G2
Sasebo *Town* Japan 93 B13
Saskatchewan *River* Saskatchewan, Canada 5 I8
Saskatchewan *Province* Canada 5 I8
Saskatoon *Town* Saskatchewan, Canada 5 I8
Sasovo *Town* Russian Federation 73 D9
Sassari *Town* Sardinia, Italy 61 B9
Sātpura Range *Mountain range* India 86 H5
Sattanen *Town* Finland 48 G5
Satu Mare *Town* Romania 68 E4
Saudi Arabia *Country* 83 D10
Sault Ste. Marie *Town* Ontario, Canada 6 F7

Sava *River* Serbia & Montenegro 64 F8
Savá *Town* Honduras 22 H3
Savannah *Town* Georgia, US 11 J5
Savannah River *Georgia/South Carolina*, US 11 I5
Saverne *Town* France 54 H7
Savona *Town* Italy 60 C6
Savu Sea *Indonesia* 97 J8
Saxony *Region* Germany 56 G7
Sayat *Town* Turkmenistan 84 H4
Sayhūt *Town* Yemen 83 F12
Saynshand *Town* Mongolia 89 J4
Say'ūn *Town* Yemen 83 E12
Scarborough *Town* England, UK 50 H8
Schaerbeek *Town* Belgium 53 D11
Schagen *Town* Netherlands 52 E7
Schefferville *Town* Newfoundland & Labrador, Canada 7 J4
Scheldt *River* Belgium 53 D10
Schenectady *Town* New York, US 8 I5
Schwandorf *Town* Germany 57 F9
Schwaz *Town* Austria 57 F11
Schweinfurt *Town* Germany 56 E8
Schwerin *Town* Germany 56 E5
Schwyz *Town* Switzerland 57 D11
Scilly, Isles of *Island group* England, UK 51 D13
Scotland *Political region* UK 50 E5
Scott Base *Research station* Antarctica 110 E7
Scottsbluff *Town* Nebraska, US 12 E5
Scottsdale *Town* Arizona, US 16 E5
Scranton *Town* Pennsylvania, US 8 H6
Seattle *Town* Washington, US 14 G2
Sébaco *Town* Nicaragua 22 H5
Sedan *Town* France 54 G6
Sedona *Town* Arizona, US 16 E4
Seesen *Town* Germany 56 E6
Segezha *Town* Russian Federation 72 D6
Ségou *Town* Mali 40 H5
Segovia *Town* Spain 58 H5
Séguédine *Town* Niger 41 M3
Seine *River* France 54 E6
Sekondi-Takoradi *Town* Ghana 41 I8
Selby *Town* South Dakota, US 12 F4
Selwyn Range *Mountain range* Queensland, Australia 105 K4
Semarang *Town* Indonesia 96 G8
Semipalatinsk *Town* Kazakhstan 78 G7
Semnān *Town* Iran 82 F6
Sendai *Town* Japan 93 B14
Sendai *Town* Japan 92 G8
Sendai-wan *Bay* Japan 92 G8
Senegal *Country* 40 E5
Senegal *River* Senegal 40 E4
Senj *Town* Croatia 64 B6
Senlis *Town* France 54 E6
Sennar *Town* Sudan 38 E8
Sens *Town* France 54 F7
Seoul *Capital* South Korea 91 M3
Sept-Îles *Town* Quebec, Canada 7 J5
Seraing *Town* Belgium 53 F11
Serang *Town* Indonesia 96 F7
Serbia *Administrative region* Serbia & Montenegro 64 F8
Serbia & Montenegro *Country* 64 G8
Seremban *Town* Malaysia 96 E5
Serov *Town* Russian Federation 78 F5
Serpukhov *Town* Russian Federation 73 C9
Sérres *Town* Greece 66 E8
Sesto San Giovanni *Town* Italy 60 C5
Setana *Town* Japan 92 F6
Sète *Town* France 55 F11
Sétif *Town* Algeria 37 I3
Setté Cama *Town* Gabon 43 C10
Setúbal *Town* Portugal 58 E7
Sevan *Town* Armenia 77 L4
Sevastopol' *Town* Ukraine 69 J7
Severn *River* England, UK 51 F11
Severnaya Zemlya *Island group* Russian Federation 79 I3
Severnyy *Town* Russian Federation 72 H5
Severodvinsk *Town* Russian Federation 72 E6
Severomorsk *Town* Russian Federation 72 E4
Sevilla *see* Seville
Seville *Town* Spain 58 G8

Sevlievo *Town* Bulgaria 66 F6
Seychelles *Country* 99 I5
Sfákia *Town* Greece 67 E14
Sfântu Gheorghe *Town* Romania 68 F6
Sfax *Town* Tunisia 37 J4
's-Gravenhage *see* Hague, The
Shaanxi *Administrative region* China 90 H5
Shanxi *Administrative region* China 91 I4
Shackleton Ice Shelf *Ice feature* Antarctica 110 G6
Shāhrūd *Town* Iran 82 F5
Shandong *Administrative region* China 91 J4
Shanghai *Town* China 91 L5
Shangrao *Town* China 91 K6
Shannon *River* Ireland 51 C9
Shan Plateau *Myanmar* 94 C6
Shantou *Town* China 91 J8
Shaoguan *Town* China 91 J7
Shar *Town* Kazakhstan 78 G7
Shari *Town* Japan 92 H4
Shchuchinsk *Town* Kazakhstan 78 F6
Sheberghān *Town* Afghanistan 85 I6
Sheboygan *Town* Wisconsin, US 13 J5
Shebshi Mountains *Mountain range* Nigeria 41 M7
Sheffield *Town* England, UK 51 G9
Shelby *Town* Montana, US 15 I2
Shenyang *Town* China 91 L2
Shepparton *Town* Victoria, Australia 105 K8
Sherbrooke *Town* Quebec, Canada 7 I7
's-Hertogenbosch *Town* Netherlands 53 F9
Shetland Islands *Island group* Scotland, UK 50 F2
Shihezi *Town* China 88 F4
Shijiazhuang *Town* China 91 J3
Shikārpur *Town* Pakistan 86 F3
Shikoku *Island* Japan 93 E13
Shiliguri *Town* India 87 K3
Shimoga *Town* India 86 H7
Shimonoseki *Town* Japan 93 B13
Shīndand *Town* Afghanistan 84 G7
Shingū *Town* Japan 93 E12
Shintoku *Town* Japan 92 G5
Shinyanga *Town* Tanzania 39 E12
Shiprock *Town* New Mexico, US 16 G3
Shirataki *Town* Japan 92 G4
Shīrāz *Town* Iran 82 F8
Shivpuri *Town* India 86 H4
Shizugawa *Town* Japan 92 G8
Shizuoka *Town* Japan 93 F11
Shkodër *Town* Albania 65 E11
Shouzhou *Town* China 91 I3
Shreveport *Town* Louisiana, US 10 D5
Shrewsbury *Town* England, UK 51 F9
Shu *Town* Kazakhstan 78 F8
Shumen *Town* Bulgaria 66 F6
Shuqrah *Town* Yemen 83 D13
Shwebo *Town* Myanmar 94 B6
Shymkent *Town* Kazakhstan 78 F8
Šiauliai *Town* Lithuania 70 D6
Šibenik *Town* Croatia 64 C8
Siberia *Region* Russian Federation 79 J5
Sibi *Town* Pakistan 86 F2
Sibir *see* Siberia
Sibiu *Town* Romania 68 F6
Sibolga *Town* Indonesia 96 D5
Sibut *Town* Central African Republic 42 E8
Sibuyan Sea *Philippines* 97 J3
Sichuan *Administrative region* China 90 F5
Sichuan Pendi *Depression* China 90 G6
Sicilia *see* Sicily
Sicily *Island* Italy 61 E13
Sicily, Strait of *Mediterranean Sea* 61 E14
Sidas *Town* Indonesia 96 G6
Sidi Barrâni *Town* Egypt 38 C4
Sidi Bel Abbès *Town* Algeria 36 G4
Sidney *Town* Nebraska, US 12 E6
Sidney *Town* Montana, US 15 L2
Siedlce *Town* Poland 62 G7
Siegen *Town* Germany 56 C7
Siena *Town* Italy 60 D7
Sieradz *Town* Poland 62 E7
Sierra Leone *Country* 40 F7
Sierra Madre *Mountain range* Guatemala 22 D4

Sierra Madre Occidental *Mountain range* Mexico 18 G5
Sierra Madre Oriental *Mountain range* Mexico 19 J6
Sierra Nevada *Mountain range* Spain 59 I8
Sierra Nevada *Mountain Range* California, US 14 G6
Sierra Vieja *Mountain Range* Texas, US 17 I7
Sigli *Town* Indonesia 96 C4
Signy *Research station* Antarctica 110 B3
Siguiri *Town* Guinea 40 G6
Siirt *Town* Turkey 77 K6
Sikhote-Alin', Khrebet *Mountain range* Russian Federation 79 M6
Silchar *Town* India 87 L4
Silesia *Region* Poland 62 C7
Silifke *Town* Turkey 76 F7
Silistra *Town* Bulgaria 66 H5
Sillamäe *Town* Estonia 70 H4
Silvan *Town* Turkey 77 J5
Silverek *Town* Turkey 76 H6
Simferopol' *Town* Ukraine 69 K7
Simpson Desert *Northern Territory/ Queensland/South Australia*, Australia 105 J5
Sinai *Desert* Egypt 38 E4
Sincelejo *Town* Colombia 26 B5
Singapore *Country* 96 E6
Singida *Town* Tanzania 39 E12
Singkang *Town* Indonesia 97 I7
Singkawang *Town* Indonesia 96 F6
Siniscola *Town* Sardinia, Italy 61 C9
Sinnamary *Town* French Guiana 26 I6
Sinsheim *Town* Germany 57 D9
Sint Maarten *Island* Caribbean Sea 25 N5
Sint-Niklaas *Town* Belgium 53 D10
Sinŭiju *Town* North Korea 91 L3
Sioux City *Town* Iowa, US 12 G5
Sioux Falls *Town* South Dakota, US 12 G5
Siping *Town* China 89 M3
Siquirres *Town* Costa Rica 23 J7
Siracusa *Town* Sicily, Italy 61 F13
Sīrjan *Town* Iran 82 G8
Şırnak *Town* Turkey 77 K6
Sirte, Gulf of *Libya* 37 L4
Sittang *River* Myanmar 94 C8
Sittwe *Town* Myanmar 94 A7
Siuna *Town* Nicaragua 23 I4
Sivas *Town* Turkey 76 H4
Sjælland *Island* Denmark 49 C12
Skagerrak *Sea* Norway 49 B11
Skaudvilė *Town* Lithuania 70 D6
Skegness *Town* England, UK 51 H9
Skellefteå *Town* Sweden 48 F7
Skopje *Capital* Macedonia 65 G11
Skovorodino *Town* Russian Federation 78 K6
Slagelse *Town* Denmark 49 C12
Slatina *Town* Romania 68 E7
Slavonski Brod *Town* Croatia 64 E7
Sligo *Town* Ireland 50 B8
Sliven *Town* Bulgaria 66 G6
Slonim *Town* Belarus 71 D9
Slovakia *Country* 63 E10
Slovenia *Country* 57 G12
Slov"yans'k *Town* Ukraine 69 M4
Słupsk *Town* Poland 62 D5
Slutsk *Town* Belarus 71 E10
Smallwood Reservoir *Nova Scotia*, Canada 7 K4
Smara *Town* Western Sahara 36 D6
Smederevo *Town* Serbia & Montenegro 64 G8
Smolensk *Town* Russian Federation 72 B8
Snake River *Idaho/Oregon*, US 14 H3
Snowdonia *Physical region* Wales, UK 51 F9
Sochi *Town* Russian Federation 73 B12
Société, Archipel de la *Island chain* French Polynesia 103 N7
Socotra *Island* Yemen 83 F13
Soc Trăng *Town* Vietnam 95 G12
Söderhamn *Town* Sweden 49 E9
Södertälje *Town* Sweden 49 E10
Sofia *Capital* Bulgaria 66 E6
Sofiya *see* Sofia
Sogamoso *Town* Colombia 26 C6
Sohâg *Town* Egypt 38 E5
Sokal' *Town* Ukraine 68 F2

Sokhumi *Town* Georgia 77 J2
Sokodé *Town* Togo 41 J7
Sokone *Town* Senegal 40 E5
Sokoto *Town* Nigeria 41 K6
Solāpur *Town* Pakistan 86 H6
Sol, Costa del *Coastal region* Spain 58 H9
Soledad *Town* Colombia 26 B4
Solikamsk *Town* Russian Federation 72 G8
Solingen *Town* Germany 56 C7
Sollentuna *Town* Sweden 49 E10
Solok *Town* Indonesia 96 D6
Solomon Islands *Country* 102 H5
Solomon Islands *Island group* Papua New Guinea/Solomon Islands 102 F5
Solomon Sea *Pacific Ocean* 102 F5
Solwezi *Town* Zambia 44 H3
Sōma *Town* Japan 93 G9
Somalia *Country* 39 H9
Somerset *Town* Kentucky, US 10 H3
Somme *River* France 54 E5
Somotillo *Town* Nicaragua 22 G5
Somoto *Town* Nicaragua 22 H5
Songea *Town* Tanzania 39 F14
Songkhla *Town* Thailand 95 D13
Sonoran Desert *Arizona*, US 16 D5
Sonsonate *Town* El Salvador 22 E5
Sop Hao *Town* Laos 94 F7
Sopron *Town* Hungary 63 D11
Sorgun *Town* Turkey 76 G4
Soria *Town* Spain 59 J4
Sorong *Town* Indonesia 97 L6
Sortavala *Town* Russian Federation 72 C6
Sŏul *see* Seoul
Sousse *Town* Tunisia 37 J3
South Africa *Country* 44 G7
Southampton *Town* England, UK 51 F12
Southampton Island *Nunavut*, Canada 5 K5
South Australia *State* Australia 105 J6
South Bend *Town* Indiana, US 13 K6
South Carolina *State* US 11 J4
South China Sea *Pacific Ocean* 91 L8
South Dakota *State* US 12 F4
Southeast Indian Ridge *Undersea feature* Indian Ocean 99 K7
Southend-on-Sea *Town* England, UK 51 H11
Southern Alps *Mountain range* New Zealand 107 C11
Southern Cook Islands *Island group* Cook Islands 103 L8
Southern Cross *Town* Western Australia, Australia 104 E6
Southern Ocean 110 G3
Southern Uplands *Mountain range* Scotland, UK 50 E7
South Georgia & The Sandwich Islands *Dependent Territory* UK, Atlantic Ocean 33 J8
South Island *New Zealand* 107 D11
South Korea *Country* 91 M4
South Orkney Islands *Island group* Antarctica 110 B3
South Shetland Islands *Island group* Antarctica 110 B4
South Shields *Town* England, UK 50 G7
Southwest Indian Ridge *Undersea feature* Indian Ocean 99 I6
Southwest Pacific Basin *Undersea feature* Pacific Ocean 109 K7
Soweto *Town* South Africa 44 H6
Spain *Country* 58 H5
Spanish Town *Town* Jamaica 24 G5
Spartanburg *Town* South Carolina, US 11 I4
Spijkenisse *Town* Netherlands 53 D9
Spīn Būldak *Town* Afghanistan 85 I8
Spitsbergen *Island* Arctic Ocean 111 M7
Split *Town* Croatia 64 C8
Spokane *Town* Washington, US 14 H2
Springfield *Town* Massachusetts, US 8 J6
Springfield *Town* Illinois, US 13 J7
Springfield *Town* Ohio, US 13 L6
Springfield *Town* Missouri, US 12 H8
Spring Hill *Town* Florida, US 11 I7
Srbobran *Town* Serbia & Montenegro 64 F7
Srebrenica *Town* Bosnia & Herzegovina 64 F8
Sri Lanka *Country* 87 J9

Stafford *Town* England, UK 51 F9
Stakhanov *Town* Ukraine 69 M4
Stalowa Wola *Town* Poland 62 G8
Stamford *Town* Connecticut, US 8 I6
Starachowice *Town* Poland 62 F8
Stara Zagora *Town* Bulgaria 66 G6
Stargard Szczeciński *Town* Poland 62 C5
Starobil's'k *Town* Ukraine 69 M4
Staryy Oskol *Town* Russian Federation 73 C10
State College *Town* Pennsylvania, US 8 F7
Statesboro *Town* Georgia, US 11 I5
Staunton *Town* Virginia, US 11 K2
Stavanger *Town* Norway 49 A10
Stavropol' *Town* Russian Federation 73 C11
Steamboat Springs *Town* Colorado, US 15 K5
Steinkjer *Town* Norway 48 C7
Sterling *Town* Illinois, US 13 J6
Sterlitamak *Town* Russian Federation 73 G10
Stevenage *Town* England, UK 51 H10
Stevens Point *Town* Wisconsin, US 13 J4
Stewart Island *New Zealand* 107 B14
Stillwater *Town* Okahoma, US 17 L3
Stockholm *Capital* Sweden 49 E10
Stockton *Town* California, US 14 F6
Stockton Plateau *Texas*, US 17 J7
Stěng Trěng *Town* Cambodia 95 G10
Stoke-on-Trent *Town* England, UK 51 F9
Stonehenge *Ancient site* England, UK 51 G11
Stornoway *Town* Scotland, UK 50 D4
Storuman *Town* Sweden 48 E6
Stralsund *Town* Germany 56 F4
Strasbourg *Town* France 54 H7
Strelka *Town* Russian Federation 78 H6
Strumica *Town* Macedonia 65 H12
Stryy *Town* Ukraine 68 F3
Stuttgart *Town* Germany 57 D9
Subotica *Town* Serbia & Montenegro 64 F6
Suceava *Town* Romania 68 G5
Sucre *Capital* Bolivia 27 E12
Sudan *Country* 38 D8
Sudbury *Town* Ontario, Canada 6 G7
Sudd *Region* Sudan 39 D9
Sudeten *Region* Poland 62 C8
Suez *Town* Egypt 38 E4
Suez, Gulf of *Egypt* 38 E4
Sühbaatar *Town* Mongolia 89 I2
Suhl *Town* Germany 56 E8
Sujāwal *Town* Pakistan 86 F4
Sukabumi *Town* Indonesia 96 F8
Sukagawa *Town* Japan 93 G9
Sukkur *Town* Pakistan 86 F3
Sukumo *Town* Japan 93 D13
Sulawesi *see* Celebes
Sullana *Town* Peru 27 A9
Sulu Archipelago *Island chain* Philippines 97 I5
Sulu Sea *Pacific Ocean* 97 J4
Sumatera *see* Sumatra
Sumatra *Island* Indonesia 96 E7
Sumbawanga *Town* Tanzania 39 E13
Sumbe *Town* Angola 44 D3
Sumqayit *Town* Azerbaijan 77 N3
Sumy *Town* Ukraine 69 K2
Sunderland *Town* England, UK 50 F7
Sundsvall *Town* Sweden 48 E8
Sungaipenuh *Town* Indonesia 96 D7
Sunnyvale *Town* California, US 14 F6
Suŏng *Town* Cambodia 95 G11
Superior *Town* Wisconsin, US 13 I3
Superior, Lake *Canada/US*, 13 I3
Suqutrā *see* Socotra
Şūr *Town* Oman 83 H10
Surabaya *Town* Indonesia 96 G8
Surakarta *Town* Indonesia 96 G8
Sūrat *Town* India 86 G5
Surat Thani *Town* Thailand 95 D12
Surdulica *Town* Serbia & Montenegro 65 H10
Surfers Paradise *Town* Queensland, Australia 105 N6
Surgut *Town* Russian Federation 78 G5
Suriname *Country* 26 G6
Surt *Town* Libya 37 L5
Surt, Khalīj *see* Sirte, Gulf of
Susa *Town* Italy 60 B5
Susteren *Town* Netherlands 53 F10

Susuman *Town* Russian Federation 78 L4
Suva *Capital* Fiji 103 J7
Suwałki *Town* Poland 62 G5
Suzhou *Town* China 91 K5
Svalbard *Dependent Territory* Norway, Arctic Ocean 111 F7
Svartisen *Glacier* Norway 48 D5
Svenstavik *Town* Sweden 48 D8
Svilengrad *Town* Bulgaria 66 G7
Svobodnyy *Town* Russian Federation 79 L6
Svyetlahorsk *Town* Belarus 71 F11
Swansea *Town* Wales, UK 51 E11
Swaziland *Country* 45 I7
Sweden *Country* 48 D7
Świdnica *Town* Poland 62 D8
Świebodzin *Town* Poland 62 C7
Swindon *Town* England, UK 51 G11
Świnoujście *Town* Poland 62 B5
Switzerland *Country* 57 C11
Sydney *Town* New South Wales, Australia 105 M7
Syeverodonets'k *Town* Ukraine 69 M4
Syktyvkar *Town* Russian Federation 72 F7
Sylhet *Town* Bangladesh 87 L4
Syowa *Research station* Antarctica 110 F4
Syracuse *Town* New York, US 8 G5
Syria *Country* 80 F7
Syrian Desert *Jordan* 81 G10
Syzran' *Town* Russian Federation 73 E10
Szczecin *Town* Poland 62 C5
Szeged *Town* Hungary 63 F12
Székesfehérvár *Town* Hungary 63 E11
Szolnok *Town* Hungary 63 F11
Szombathely *Town* Hungary 63 D11

T

Tabora *Town* Tanzania 39 E12
Tabrīz *Town* Iran 82 D5
Tabūk *Town* Saudi Arabia 82 A8
Täby *Town* Sweden 49 E10
Tacloban *Town* Philippines 97 K3
Tacoma *Town* Washington, US 14 F2
Tacuarembó *Town* Uruguay 30 H7
Tademaït, Plateau du *Algeria* 36 H6
Tādpatri *Town* Bhutan 87 I7
Taegu *Town* South Korea 91 M4
Taejŏn *Town* South Korea 91 M4
Taganrog *Town* Russian Federation 73 B11
Taguatinga *Town* Brazil 29 K5
Tagus *River* Spain/Portugal 58 F6
Tahoua *Town* Niger 41 K5
T'aichung *Town* Taiwan 91 L8
T'ainan *Town* Taiwan 91 K8
Taipei *Capital* Taiwan 91 L7
Taiping *Town* Malaysia 96 D5
Taiwan *Country* 91 L8
Taiwan Strait *China/Taiwan* 91 L8
Taiyuan *Town* China 91 I4
Ta'izz *Town* Yemen 83 C13
Tajikistan *Country* 85 K5
Takaoka *Town* Japan 93 E10
Takapuna *Town* New Zealand 106 F5
Takasaki *Town* Japan 93 F10
Takhiatosh *Town* Uzbekistan 84 F2
Takikawa *Town* Japan 92 F5
Takla Makan Desert *China* 88 E5
Talamanca, Cordillera de *Mountain range* Costa Rica 23 J8
Talas *Town* Kyrgyzstan 85 K3
Talavera de la Reina *Town* Spain 58 H5
Talca *Town* Chile 30 C8
Talcahuano *Town* Chile 31 C9
Taldykorgan *Town* Kazakhstan 78 G8
Tallahassee *Town* Florida, US 10 H6
Tallinn *Capital* Estonia 70 G3
Talnakh *Town* Russian Federation 78 H4
Talsi *Town* Latvia 70 E5
Talvik *Town* Norway 48 F3
Tamale *Town* Ghana 41 I7
Tamanrasset *Town* Algeria 37 I7
Tamazunchale *Town* Mexico 19 K7
Tambacounda *Town* Senegal 40 E5

Tambov *Town* Russian Federation 73 D10
Tampa *Town* Florida, US 11 I7
Tampa Bay Florida, US 11 I8
Tampere *Town* Finland 48 G8
Tampico *Town* Mexico 19 K6
Tamworth *Town* New South Wales, Australia 105 M6
Tana *Town* Norway 48 G3
Tanabe *Town* Japan 93 E12
Tanami Desert Northern Territory, Australia 104 H3
Tandil *Town* Argentina 31 G9
Tane Range *Mountain range* Thailand 94 D8
Tanezrouft *Desert* Algeria 36 H7
Tanga *Town* Tanzania 39 G12
Tanganyika, Lake Democratic Republic of Congo 43 I12
Tanggula Shan *Mountain range* China 88 G7
Tangier *Town* Morocco 36 F3
Tangshan *Town* China 91 K3
Tan-Tan *Town* Morocco 36 D5
Tanzania *Country* 39 E12
Taoudenni *Town* Mali 40 H3
Tapa *Town* Estonia 70 G4
Tapachula *Town* Mexico 19 N9
Tapajós, Rio *River* Brazil 29 I3
Ţarābulus *see* Tripoli
Tarancón *Town* Spain 59 I6
Taranto *Town* Italy 61 H10
Taranto, Gulf Italy 61 H11
Tarapoto *Town* Peru 27 B9
Taraz *Town* Kazakhstan 78 F8
Tarbes *Town* France 55 D11
Târgoviște *Town* Romania 68 F7
Târgu Jiu *Town* Romania 68 E7
Târgu Mureș *Town* Romania 68 F5
Tarija *Town* Bolivia 27 E13
Tarim Basin China 88 F5
Tarnobrzeg *Town* Poland 62 G8
Tarnów *Town* Poland 63 F9
Tarragona *Town* Spain 59 L4
Tarsus *Town* Turkey 76 G6
Tartu *Town* Estonia 70 G5
Ţarţūs *Town* Syria 80 D7
Tarvisio *Town* Italy 60 F4
Tashkent *Capital* Uzbekistan 85 J3
Tash-Kumyr *Town* Kyrgyzstan 85 K3
Tasikmalaya *Town* Indonesia 96 F8
Tasmania *State* Australia 105 K9
Tasman Sea Pacific Ocean 105 M8
Tassili-n-Ajjer *Plateau* Algeria 37 I6
Tatabánya *Town* Hungary 63 E11
Tathlīth *Town* Saudi Arabia 83 C11
Tatra Mountains Slovakia 63 F9
Tatvan *Town* Turkey 77 K5
Taungdwingyi *Town* Myanmar 94 B7
Taunggyi *Town* Myanmar 94 C7
Taunton *Town* England, UK 51 F11
Taupo *Town* New Zealand 106 G7
Taupo, Lake New Zealand 106 G7
Tauranga *Town* New Zealand 106 G6
Taurus Mountains *Mountain range* Turkey 76 E6
Tavoy *Town* Myanmar 95 C10
Tawau *Town* Malaysia 97 I5
Taxco *Town* Mexico 19 K8
Taymā' *Town* Saudi Arabia 82 B8
Taymyr Peninsula Russian Federation 79 I3
T'bilisi *Capital* Georgia 77 L3
Tczew *Town* Poland 62 E5
Te Anau *Town* New Zealand 107 B13
Teapa *Town* Mexico 19 N8
Tebingtinggi *Town* Indonesia 96 D5
Tecomán *Town* Mexico 19 I8
Tecpan *Town* Mexico 19 J9
Tecuci *Town* Romania 68 G6
Tedzhen *Town* Turkmenistan 84 F5
Tegal *Town* Indonesia 96 F7
Tegucigalpa *Capital* Honduras 22 G4
Tehrān *Capital* Iran 82 E6
Tehuacán *Town* Mexico 19 L8
Tehuantepec *Town* Mexico 19 M9
Tehuantepec, Gulf of Mexico 19 M9
Tehuantepec, Istmo de *Isthmus* Mexico 19 M8
Te Kao *Town* New Zealand 106 E3

Tekeli *Town* Kazakhstan 78 G8
Tekirdağ *Town* Turkey 76 C3
Tel Aviv-Yafo *Town* Israel 81 C11
Temirtau *Town* Kazakhstan 78 F7
Temple *Town* Texas, US 17 M6
Temuco *Town* Chile 31 C10
Ténéré *Physical region* Niger 41 M4
Tennessee *State* US 10 G3
Tennessee River Alabama/Tennessee, US 10 G4
Tepic *Town* Mexico 19 I7
Teplice *Town* Czech Republic 62 B8
Tequila *Town* Mexico 19 I7
Teramo *Town* Italy 60 F8
Teresina *Town* Brazil 29 M3
Termiz *Town* Uzbekistan 85 I5
Ternate *Town* Indonesia 97 K6
Terni *Town* Italy 60 E8
Ternopil' *Town* Ukraine 68 G3
Terrassa *Town* Spain 59 M4
Terre Haute *Town* Indiana, US 13 K7
Teruel *Town* Spain 59 K5
Teseney *Town* Eritrea 38 F8
Tessalit *Town* Mali 41 J3
Tete *Town* Mozambique 45 I4
Tetouan *Town* Morocco 36 F3
Tevere *River* Italy 60 E8
Texarkana *Town* Texas, US 17 N5
Texas *State* US 17 L6
Teziutlán *Town* Mexico 19 K7
Thai Binh *Town* Vietnam 94 G7
Thailand *Country* 95 D9
Thailand, Gulf of Pacific Ocean 95 E11
Thai Nguyên *Town* Vietnam 94 G6
Thakhèk *Town* Laos 94 F8
Thamarit *Town* Oman 83 G11
Thames *River* England, UK 51 G11
Thanh Hoa *Town* Vietnam 94 F7
Thar Desert Pakistan/India 86 F3
Thaton *Town* Myanmar 94 C8
Thayetmyo *Town* Myanmar 94 B7
The Fens *Physical region* England, UK 51 H9
The Gulf Asia 82 E8
Thessaloníki *see* Salonica
The Valley *Capital* Anguilla 25 N5
Thimphu *Capital* Bhutan 87 L3
Thíra *Town* Greece 67 G13
Thracian Sea Greece 66 F8
Thun *Town* Switzerland 57 C11
Thunder Bay *Town* Ontario, Canada 6 E6
Thurso *Town* Scotland,UK 50 E3
Tianjin *Town* China 91 J3
Tianjin Shu *Administrative region* China 91 J3
Tianshui *Town* China 89 J6
Tiberias, Lake Israel 81 D10
Tibesti *Mountain range* Chad 42 E3
Tibet *Administrative region* China 88 F7
Tibet, Plateau of China 88 F6
Tichît *Town* Mauritania/China 40 G4
Ticul *Town* Mexico 19 O6
Tien Shan *Mountain range* Kyrgyzstan 85 L3
Tierra del Fuego *Region* Argentina/Chile 31 D14
Tifu *Town* Indonesia 97 K7
Tighina *Town* Moldova 68 H6
Tigris *River* Iraq 82 C6
Tiguentourine *Town* Algeria 37 J6
Tijuana *Town* Mexico 18 C2
Tikal *Ancient site* Guatemala 22 E2
Tikhoretsk *Town* Russian Federation 73 C12
Tikhvin *Town* Russian Federation 72 C7
Tiksi *Town* Russian Federation 78 J4
Tilburg *Town* Netherlands 53 E10
Timaru *Town* New Zealand 107 D12
Timbedgha *Town* Mauritania 40 G5
Timbuktu *Town* Mali 41 I4
Timișoara *Town* Romania 68 D6
Timor Sea Asia/Australasia 97 J9
Tindouf *Town* Algeria 36 E6
Tirana *Capital* Albania 65 F11
Tiranë *see* Tirana
Tiraspol *Town* Moldova 68 H6
Tirol *Region* Austria 57 F11
Tiruchchirāppalli *Town* India 87 I8
Tisza *River* Hungary 63 F11
Titicaca, Lake *Lake* Peru 27 D12

Tivoli *Town* Italy 61 E9
Tizi Ouzou *Town* Algeria 36 H3
Tiznit *Town* Morocco 36 E5
Tlaquepaque *Town* Mexico 19 I7
Tlaxcala *Town* Mexico 19 K8
Tlemcen *Town* Algeria 36 G4
Toamasina *Town* Madagascar 45 M5
Tobago *Island* Trinidad & Tobago 25 O8
Tobol'sk *Town* Russian Federation 78 G5
Tocantins, Rio *River* Brazil 29 K4
Tocopilla *Town* Chile 30 D4
Todi *Town* Italy 60 E8
Togo *Country* 41 J7
Tokar *Town* Sudan 38 F7
Tokat *Town* Turkey 76 H4
Tokelau *Dependent territory* New Zealand, Pacific Ocean 103 K6
Tokmak *Town* Kyrgyzstan 85 L3
Tokmak *Town* Ukraine 69 L5
Tokoroa *Town* New Zealand 106 G6
Tokushima *Town* Japan 93 D12
Tōkyō *Capital* Japan 93 G10
Toledo *Town* Spain 59 I6
Toledo *Town* Ohio, US 13 L6
Toliara *Town* Madagascar 45 L6
Tolitoli *Town* Indonesia 97 J6
Tolmin *Town* Slovenia 57 G12
Toluca *Town* Mexico 19 J8
Tol'yatti *Town* Russian Federation 73 E10
Tomakomai *Town* Japan 92 F5
Tomaszów Mazowiecki *Town* Poland 62 F7
Tombouctou *see* Timbuktu
Tomini, Gulf of Indonesia 97 J6
Tomsk *Town* Russian Federation 78 H6
Tonga *Country* 103 K7
Tongatapu Group *Island group* Tonga 103 J8
Tongchuan *Town* China 90 H4
Tonghe *Town* China 89 M2
Tongzi *Town* China 90 H6
Tongking, Gulf of South China Sea 90 H9
Tongliao *Town* China 89 L3
Tongxin *Town* China 89 J6
Tongzi *Town* China 90 H6
Tônlé Sap *Lake* Cambodia 95 F10
Tonopah *Town* Nevada, US 14 H6
Tooele *Town* Utah, US 15 I5
Toowoomba *Town* Queensland, Australia 105 M6
Topeka *Town* Kansas, US 12 G7
Torez *Town* Ukraine 69 M5
Torgau *Town* Germany 56 F7
Torino *see* Turin
Torkestan Mountains *Mountain range* Afghanistan 84 H6
Toro *Town* Spain 58 H4
Toronto *Town* Ontario, Canada 6 G8
Toros Dağlari *see* Taurus Mountains
Torquay *Town* England, UK 51 F12
Torre del Greco *Town* Italy 61 F10
Torrejón de Ardoz *Town* Spain 59 I5
Torrelavega *Town* Spain 59 I2
Torrente *Town* Spain 59 K6
Torreón *Town* Mexico 19 I5
Torres Strait Australia/Papua New Guinea 105 K1
Torres Vedras *Town* Portugal 58 E6
Torrington *Town* Wyoming, US 15 L5
Toruń *Town* Poland 62 E6
Torzhok *Town* Russian Federation 72 C8
Toscana *see* Tuscany
Toscano, Archipelago *Coastal feature* Italy 60 D8
Toshkent *see* Tashkent
Totness *Town* Suriname 26 H6
Tottori *Town* Japan 93 D11
Touggourt *Town* Algeria 37 I4
Toukoto *Town* Mali 40 G5
Toul *Town* France 54 G7
Toulon *Town* France 55 G12
Toulouse *Town* France 55 D11
Tourcoing *Town* France 54 F5
Tournai *Town* Belgium 53 C11
Tours *Town* France 54 F4
Tovarkovskiy *Town* Russian Federation 73 C9
Towada *Town* Japan 92 G7
Townsville *Town* Queensland, Australia 105 L3
Towson *Town* Maryland, US 8 G8

Toyama *Town* Japan 93 F10
Toyota *Town* Japan 93 F11
Tozeur *Town* Tunisia 37 I4
Trabzon *Town* Turkey 76 H3
Trang *Town* Thailand 95 D13
Transantarctic Mountains *Mountain range* Antarctica 110 D6
Transylvania *Cultural region* Romania 68 E5
Transylvanian Alps *Mountain range* Romania 68 E6
Trapani *Town* Sicily, Italy 61 D12
Trâpeăng Vêng *Town* Cambodia 95 F10
Trasimeno, Lago *Lake* Italy 60 E7
Tra Vinh *Town* Vietnam 95 G12
Tremelo *Town* Belgium 53 E11
Trenčín *Town* Slovakia 63 E10
Trenque Lauquen *Town* Argentina 31 F9
Trent *River* England, UK 51 G9
Trento *Town* Italy 60 E4
Trenton *Town* Pennsylvania, US 8 G7
Tres Arroyos *Town* Argentina 31 F9
Treviso *Town* Italy 60 E5
Trier *Town* Germany 56 B8
Trieste *Town* Italy 60 F5
Trincomalee *Town* Sri Lanka 87 I9
Trinidad *Island* Trinidad & Tobago 25 O9
Trinidad *Town* Uruguay 30 G8
Trinidad *Town* Bolivia 27 E11
Trinidad & Tobago *Country* 25 O9
Tripoli *Town* Lebanon 80 D8
Tripoli *Capital* Libya 37 K4
Tristan de Cunha *Dependent Territory* St. Helena, Atlantic Ocean 33 L7
Trivandrum *Town* India 86 H9
Trnava *Town* Slovakia 63 D10
Trois-Rivières *Town* Quebec, Canada 7 I7
Trollhättan *Town* Sweden 49 C10
Tromsø *Town* Norway 48 E4
Trondheim *Town* Norway 48 C7
Troy *Town* New York, US 8 I5
Troyes *Town* France 54 F7
Trujillo *Town* Spain 58 G6
Trujillo *Town* Peru 27 A10
Trzcianka *Town* Poland 62 D6
Tshela *Town* Democratic Republic of Congo 43 D11
Tshikapa *Town* Democratic Republic of Congo 43 F12
Tsu *Town* Japan 93 E11
Tsugaru-kaikyō *Strait* Japan 92 F7
Tsuruga *Town* Japan 93 E11
Tsuruoka *Town* Japan 92 F8
Tuamotu Islands *Island group* French Polynesia 103 O7
Tuapse *Town* Russian Federation 73 B12
Tuba City *Town* Arizona, US 16 E3
Tubmanburg *Town* Liberia 40 F7
Ţubruq *Town* Libya 37 N4
Tucson *Town* Arizona, US 16 E5
Tucumcari *Town* New Mexico, US 17 I4
Tudmur *Town* Syria 80 F7
Tuguegarao *Town* Philippines 97 J1
Tukums *Town* Latvia 70 E5
Tula *Town* Russian Federation 73 C9
Tulancingo *Town* Mexico 19 K7
Tulcán *Town* Ecuador 26 B7
Tulcea *Town* Romania 68 H7
Tulsa *Town* Oklahoma, US 17 M3
Tuluá *Town* Colombia 26 B6
Tumbes *Town* Peru 26 A8
Tumuc Humac Mountains *Mountain range* Brazil 29 I1
Tungaru *Island chain* Kiribati 103 I4
Tungsten *Town* Northwest Territories, Canada 4 G6
Tunis *Capital* Tunisia 37 J3
Tunisia *Country* 37 J4
Tunja *Town* Colombia 26 C6
Tương Đương *Town* Vietnam 94 G7
Tupelo *Town* Mississippi, US 10 G4
Turan Lowland *Plain* Central Asia 84 F2
Ţurayf *Town* Saudi Arabia 82 B7
Turbat *Town* Pakistan 86 E3
Turda *Town* Romania 68 F5

Index

Credits

The publisher would like to thank the following for their kind permission to reproduce their photographs:

Abbreviations key: a=above, c=center; b=below; l=left; r=right; t=top

Agence France Presse: 59tr; 84c; 91cra.

Alaska Stock: 4clb.

American Museum of Natural History: 12cl.

Art Directors & TRIP: 61car, T. Bognar 87tr, D. Iusupov 73c, P. Mercea 68br, D. Mossienko 69tr, T. Noorits 70tl, N & J Wiseman 69cr.

British Antarctic Survey: R. Mulvaney 110clb.

British Library: 82c.

British Museum: 27br, 37tc.

Cephas Picture Library: Fred R Palmer 6tr.

Bruce Coleman Ltd.: Astrophoto iv t.

Corbis: 94cl; 96cl, Theo Allofs 99cra, Jean Pierre Amet/Corbis Sygma 49tl, Tony Arruza 11br; 30br, William A. Bake 7br, Anthony Bannister 44cl, Paul Barton 9cr, Dave Bartruff 49tr; 53bc, Morton Beebe 58bl, Niall Benvie 71cr, Yann Arthus Bertrand 28cr, Georgina Bowater 54cb, Tom Brakefield 96tr, B.S.P.I. i tr; 16br; 20br; 102tr, Dean Conger 15c; 73br; 97br, Keith Dannemiller 18tr, Tim Davis 100cla; 111bc, Carlos Dominguez 32ccr, Terry W. Eggers vii clb; 3cla, Jim Erickson vi bl, Robert Estall vii car, Macduff Everton 19tr, Owen Franken 10cbr; 52br; 53tl; 53cr, Stephen Frink ii crb; 22cl, Arvino Garg 23tcl, Bill Gentile 24cl, Philip Gould 13br, Farrell Grehan 9c, Julie Habel 13tl, John Heseltine 65cb, Ralf-Finn Hestoft/Corbis Saba 9tl, Arne Hodalic 77bl, Robert Holmes 92tl, Dave G. Houser 76br, Robbie Jack 72bc, Ray Juno vii cal; 53br; 57br, Wolfgang Kaehler vii cla; 25bc; 32br; 79bl; 100cbr; 103bc; 109tr, Bob Krist vii cra; 100car; 105cra, Frank Leather/Eye Ubiquitous viii clb, Lester Lefkowitz 15br, Danny Lehman 18br, Charles & Josette Lenars 41bl; 48tcl, George D. Lepp vii tr; 33br, Barry Lewis 69bl, Steve Liss/Corbis Sygma 108tc, Lawrence Manning 76cl, Gunter Marx Photography 4bl, Stephanie Maze 29cra; 49cla; 109br, NASA iv bc, Richard J. Nowitz 7cra, Charles O'Rear 4tcr, Christine Osborne 81crb, Douglas Peebles v br; 90car, Caroline Penn viii tl, Clay Perry 67tl, Ledru Philippe/Corbis Sygma 37bc, Perrin Pierre/Corbis Sygma 55bl, Sergio Pitamitz iii br; 22br; 105br, Richard Ransier 16tr, Steve Rayner ibr; 72tr, Roger Ressmeyer 54tl, Benjamin Rondel 6bl, Bill Ross viii b, Galen Rowell v cla; 110cal, Saba/Shepard Sherbell 111tr, Michael St. Maur Sheil 50br, Kim Sayer 55bc, Alan Schein Photography 3cra; 9br, Gregor Schmid 79crb, Flip Schulke 11c, Attal Serge/Corbis Sygma 71bl, Alex Steedman 51tr, Hans Strand 33br, Vince Streano 11cla, Keren Su 86br, Torleif Svensson 111cr, TempSport 71tc, Tim Thompson 19tc, David Turnley 77tr; 80cal; 83tr; 85cr, Peter Turnley 25bl; 45bl; 78bc, Penny Tweedie 100clb; 104cla, Pablo Corral Vega 26cl, Francesco Venturi 19cr, Patrick Ward 59br, Nevada Wier 74cla; 85cra; 85tr; 85cb, Nik Wheeler 71tl; 77br, Staffan Widstrand 5tc; 71bc, Peter M. Wilson 3crb; 5bcr, Wildcountry 50tr, Adam Woolfitt 76tc, Michael S. Yamashita 91bc; 93bcl.

Empics Ltd.: Tony Marshall 3bl; 6bc; 64bc, Phil Walter104bc.

Getty Images: Samuel Ashfield 47crb, Paul Chesley 92cl, Jim Cummins ii cra; 13cr, Frans Lemmens iii tl, Photodisc/Jeremy Woodhouse 108car, Martin Puddy 86c, Andy Sacks 10cl, Bruce Stoddard 19tl.

Getty Images News Service: Scott Harrison 60cl, Mike Powell 55ca, Matthew Stockman 11tc.

Robert Harding Picture Library: vii crb; 12ccl; 28cl; 31tr; 32tr; 62tc; 66tr; 79br; 83tc; 87tl; 95bl, Max Alexander 10br, Paul Allen 34bl; 45br, Mohamed Amin 83bcl, Bildagentur Schuster GMBH 108bl, Bildagentur Schuster/Gluske 30cl, Jeremy Bright 107c, Martyn F. Chillmaid 45ccr, Neale Clark 105crb, Victor Englebert 31bl, Alain Evrard 95tr, Explorer/D. Riffet 43cra, Warren Finlay/International Stock 109cr, Nigel Francis 8bl, Robert Francis 14tc, Robert Frerck iii cl; 27cr; 31tl; 59bc, Robert Frerck/Odyssey/Chicago 18cl, Lee Frost vii cbr, Kim Hart 48tl, Gavin Hellier 89br; 3ca, D. Jacobs 104tr, Maurice Joseph 70bc, Paolo Koch 88-89; 107tl, J. Lightfoot 40cla, David Lomax 74cca; 84bl, John Miller 25tr, MPH 56bc, Louise Murray vii cbl, Nakamura 23crbl; 38ca; 110br, Mike Newton 58cla, J. Nov. iii cra; 87clb, Photrl1LC.056.XXXX 15tc, Roy Rainford 9tr; 32ca, Geoff Renner 110tr, G. R. Richardson 65tr, R. Richardson 60br, Phil Robinson 65bl, Peter Scholey 66tl, Schuster 30tl; 44bc, Michael Short 81br, Johnny Stockshooter 67cbr, J. C. Thoret 42tr, Doug Traverso 89cr, Hardie Truesdale 12bl, Upperhall Ltd 103cal, Tony Waltham 85br, Nik Wheeler 14bl, T.D. Winter 37tl, Keith Wood/International Stock 17bl; 50tc, Adam Woolfitt 32cl; 52tl.

Hopi Learning Center: 16bc.

Hutchison Library: 39tr; 43c; 64ca; 78bl; 81bc; 82tc; 91br; 94tl, Jon Burbank 93tl, Sarah Errington 39bc; 42bcr; 45tl; 86bl, Robert Francis 22cb; 23cbl; 104–105bc, Melanie Friend 66cb; 66br; 89bl; 90cbl, Norman Froggatt 95cr, John Fuller 25tc, Bernard Gerard 82bc, Andrew Hill 45tr, John Halt 96br, Nick Haslam 68clb; 93clb; 103cra, J. Henderson 81tr, Jeremy Horner 39bl; 56tc; 87bc; 90bl; 91tl; 97c, Crispin Hughes 41cr; 41bc; 45tc, Mary Jelliffee 27tr; 36bc, Eric Lawrie 27ca, R. Ian Lloyd 96bl, Michael Macintyre 102bc; 103tr, N. Durrell McKenna 104clb, Sarah Murray 88bc, John Nowell 83cr, Trevor Page 43br; 61bc, Stephen Pem 88cla, PERN 89tr, Dr Nigel Smith 28br; 97cr, Liba Taylor 63cb; 69br; 73tl; 73bl, Isabella Tree 98tr; 110bl, David Watson 65br, Philip Wolmoth 51br, Andrey Zvoznikov vi cl; vi cla; vi clb; vi tr; 73tr; 79tl; 79tr.

Impact Photos: Rupert Connant 62tr.

Barnabas Kindersley: 40bcl; 83bcr.

Masterfile UK: Didier Dorval 56tr.

NASA: 17tr.

Natural History Museum: 43ca.

N.H.P.A.: B & C Alexander 32bl, T. Kitchin and V. Hurst 5cbr, Stephen Oliver 15bcl, Andy Rouse 5br.

Panos Pictures: David Constantine 59cr; 62cl, Neil Cooper 38tcr, Clive Shirley 41tl, Teun Voeten 40bcr.

Pictorial Press Ltd.: 87crb.

Pictures Color Library: 8ca; 16tc; 50bc; 51cr; 61cl; 68cla; 79cra; 92tc, © FMGB Guggenheim Bilbao Museoa. Photo by Charles Bowman. All rights reserved. Total or partial reproduction is prohibited. 59tl.

Pitt Rivers Museum: 73tc.

Popperfoto: 51bc, Ho/Reuters 108ccl.

Powell Cotton Museum: 42bcl.

Redferns: 10bc.

Rex Features: Stuart Clarke 82tl, Simon Runting 107bl, Enrica Scalfari 60tr, Sipa Press 12bc; 15bc; 97tr, Tim Rooke 96cr, Wilhemsen 99br.

Floyd Sayers: 39br; 45bcr.

Science Photo Library: George Bernard 15bl, Laboratory for Atmospheres, NASA/ Goddard Space Flight Center 111car, Nasa vi br, Tom Van Sant, Geosphere Project/Planetary Visions 34–35; 46–47; 74–75, 1995 Worldsat International and J. Knighton 2–3; 20–21; 100–101.

South American Pictures: 26tl; 28bl; 31br.

Still Pictures: Julio Etchart 18bl, Roland Seitre 98cb, Annelies Van Brink viii tr; 74crb.

Marie Tharp: v tr.

Topham Picturepoint: Francis Dean/Imageworks 49crb.

V. Tunnicliffe: 108cbr.

World Pictures: i bl; i tl; 4bc; 7tl; 7tr; 20clb; 20crb; 22bl; 23tr; 24bl; 25ca; 26cr; 27bl; 29cr; 29br; 30bc; 31ca; 34car; 36tr; 36cl; 37tr; 38bc; 42tc; 44bl; 47tr; 47cla; 47clb; 48bc; 52bc; 54tc; 55tc; 57tr; 57cr; 61r; 63cr; 63tr; 63br; 64tl; 67tr; 67br; 67bcl; 68bl; 71br; 72cl; 74bl; 76bl; 80cla; 80cb; 80bcr; 81tc; 89c; 90cl; 91cb; 92br; 93tr; 94tc; 94tr; 95br; 98bl; 98ccl; 98ccr; 99tr; 104cal; 106tl; 106crb; 106br; 107tr.

Jacket images

Front: Corbis: Owen Franken cra, Richard Ransier crb, Stephen Frink br, Getty Images: Keren Su ca, Robert Harding Picture Library: Lee Frost bcl, Masterfile UK: Hans Blohm cb.

Front Inside Flap: Corbis: Richard Ransier br, Owen Franken tr, Masterfile UK: Hans Blohm bl, Getty Images: Keren Su tl.

Back: Corbis: Dave Bartruff cb, B.S.P.I. cbr, Stephen Frink br, Alan Schein Photography crb, Tim Davis cbl, Robert Harding Picture Library: Lee Frost bcl, Getty Images: Kevin Morris clb.

Spine: Corbis: Owen Franken t, Richard Ransier b.

All other images © Dorling Kindersley

For further information see: **www.dkimages.com**

Dorling Kindersley would also like to thank:

Clare Shedden, Philip Letsu, Kate Bradshaw, and Neal Cobourne for the jacket design, and Chris Bernstein for the index.

NORTH AMERICA

CANADA
Pages 4–7

UNITED STATES OF AMERICA
Pages 8–17

MEXICO
Pages 18–19

CENTRAL & SOUTH AMERICA

BELIZE
Pages 22–23

COSTA RICA
Pages 22–23

EL SALVADOR
Pages 22–23

GUATEMALA
Pages 22–23

HONDURAS
Pages 22–23

GRENADA
Pages 24–25

HAITI
Pages 24–25

JAMAICA
Pages 24–25

ST. KITTS & NEVIS
Pages 24–25

ST. LUCIA
Pages 24–25

ST. VINCENT & THE GRENADINES
Pages 24–25

TRINIDAD & TOBAGO
Pages 24–25

BOLIVIA
Pages 26–27

CHILE
Pages 30–31

PARAGUAY
Pages 30–31

URUGUAY
Pages 30–31

AFRICA

ALGERIA
Pages 36–37

LIBYA
Pages 36–37

MOROCCO
Pages 36–37

TUNISIA
Pages 36–37

BURUNDI
Pages 38–39

TANZANIA
Pages 38–39

UGANDA
Pages 38–39

BENIN
Pages 40–41

BURKINA FASO
Pages 40–41

CAPE VERDE
Pages 40–41

CÔTE D'IVOIRE (IVORY COAST)
Pages 40–41

GAMBIA
Pages 40–41

GHANA
Pages 40–41

SIERRA LEONE
Pages 40–41

TOGO
Pages 40–41

CAMEROON
Pages 42–43

CENTRAL AFRICAN REPUBLIC
Pages 42–43

CHAD
Pages 42–43

CONGO
Pages 42–43

DEM. REP. CONGO
Pages 42–43

EQUATORIAL GUINEA
Pages 42–43

MAURITIUS
Pages 44–45

MOZAMBIQUE
Pages 44–45

NAMIBIA
Pages 44–45

SOUTH AFRICA
Pages 44–45

SWAZILAND
Pages 44–45

ZAMBIA
Pages 44–45

ZIMBABWE
Pages 44–45

EUROPE

DENMARK
Pages 48–49

NETHERLANDS
Pages 52–53

ANDORRA
Pages 54–55

FRANCE
Pages 54–55

MONACO
Pages 54–55

AUSTRIA
Pages 56–57

GERMANY
Pages 56–57

LIECHTENSTEIN
Pages 56–57

SLOVENIA
Pages 56–57

HUNGARY
Pages 62–63

POLAND
Pages 62–63

SLOVAKIA
Pages 62–63

ALBANIA
Pages 64–65

BOSNIA & HERZEGOVINA
Pages 64–65

CROATIA
Pages 64–65

MACEDONIA
Pages 64–65

SERBIA & MONTENEGRO (YUGOSLAVIA)
Pages 64–65

ASIA

LITHUANIA
Pages 70–71

RUSSIAN FEDERATION
Pages 78–79

CYPRUS
Pages 80–81

ARMENIA
Pages 76–77

AZERBAIJAN
Pages 76–77

GEORGIA
Pages 76–77

TURKEY
Pages 76–77

ISRAEL
Pages 80–81

QATAR
Pages 82–83

SAUDI ARABIA
Pages 82–83

UNITED ARAB EMIRATES
Pages 82–83

YEMEN
Pages 82–83

KAZAKHSTAN
Pages 78–79

AFGHANISTAN
Pages 84–85

KYRGYZSTAN
Pages 84–85

TAJIKISTAN
Pages 84–85

MONGOLIA
Pages 88–89

NORTH KOREA
Pages 90–91

SOUTH KOREA
Pages 90–91

TAIWAN
Pages 90–91

JAPAN
Pages 92–93

CAMBODIA
Pages 94–95

LAOS
Pages 94–95

MYANMAR (BURMA)
Pages 94–95

AUSTRALASIA & OCEANIA

MALDIVES
Pages 98–99

SEYCHELLES
Pages 98–99

FIJI
Pages 102–103

KIRIBATI
Pages 102–103

MARSHALL ISLANDS
Pages 102–103

MICRONESIA
Pages 102–103

NAURU
Pages 102–103

PALAU
Pages 102–103